DOGOPOLIS

ANIMAL LIVES

Jane C. Desmond, Series Editor; Barbara J. King, Associate Editor for Science; Kim Marra, Associate Editor

BOOKS IN THE SERIES

Displaying Death and Animating Life: Human-Animal Relations in Art, Science, and Everyday Life
by Jane C. Desmond

Voracious Science and Vulnerable Animals: A Primate Scientist's Ethical Journey
by John P. Gluck

The Great Cat and Dog Massacre: The Real Story of World War Two's Unknown Tragedy
by Hilda Kean

Animal Intimacies: Interspecies Relatedness in India's Central Himalayas
by Radhika Govindrajan

Minor Creatures: Persons, Animals, and the Victorian Novel
by Ivan Kreilkamp

Equestrian Cultures: Horses, Human Society, and the Discourse of Modernity
by Kristen Guest and Monica Mattfeld

Precarious Partners: Horses and Their Humans in Nineteenth-Century France
by Kari Weil

Dogopolis

HOW DOGS AND HUMANS MADE MODERN NEW YORK, LONDON, AND PARIS

CHRIS PEARSON

The University of Chicago Press
Chicago and London

The University of Chicago Press, Chicago 60637
The University of Chicago Press, Ltd., London

Published 2021
Printed in the United States of America

30 29 28 27 26 25 24 23 22 21 1 2 3 4 5

ISBN-13: 978-0-226-79699-4 (cloth)
ISBN-13: 978-0-226-79816-5 (paper)
ISBN-13: 978-0-226-79704-5 (e-book)
DOI: https://doi.org/10.7208/chicago/9780226797045.001.0001

Library of Congress Cataloging-in-Publication Data

Names: Pearson, Chris (Environmental historian), author.
Title: Dogopolis : how dogs and humans made modern New York, London, and Paris / Chris Pearson.
Other titles: Animal lives (University of Chicago Press)
Description: Chicago : University of Chicago, 2021. | Series: Animal lives | Includes bibliographical references and index.
Identifiers: LCCN 2020056576 | ISBN 9780226796994 (cloth) | ISBN 9780226798165 (paperback) | ISBN 9780226797045 (ebook)
Subjects: LCSH: Dogs—Behavior. | Human-animal relationships. | City and town life.
Classification: LCC SF422.5 .P437 2021 | DDC 636.7—dc23
LC record available at https://lccn.loc.gov/2020056576

CONTENTS

Introduction

The belief that humans and dogs share an ancient and unshakable bond is popular and pervasive. Dogs have lived and worked with humans since they were first domesticated thousands of years ago. This timeless and universal relationship, so the story goes, is marked by love and loyalty. Dogs are "man's best friend." An important—if now often overlooked—step in the creation of this narrative was taken in rural Missouri. In 1870 lawyer George Vest praised the faithfulness of dogs during a lawsuit brought by a farmer who suspected a neighbor of shooting Old Drum, his favorite hunting dog. In arguing the farmer's case, Vest declared that "the one absolutely unselfish friend that a man can have in this selfish world, the one that never deserts him, the one that never proves ungrateful or treacherous, is the dog." Vest's eulogy of Old Drum helped win the case, and the speech was reprinted as an ode to human-canine friendship and fidelity.[1]

For nineteenth-century dog lovers, canine affection for humans was redemptive. As London-based writer, feminist, and antivivisectionist Frances Power Cobbe asked, "How many lonely, deceived and embittered hearts have been saved from breaking or turning to stone by the humble sympathy of a dog[?]." Dogs kept humans emotionally healthy in the glow of their unconditional love. Such rhetoric was not restricted to Anglophone cultures. In a subtle subversion of seventeenth-century philosopher René Descartes's famous depiction of animals as machines, dogs were "love machines," according to French animal protectionist Baron de Vaux, and felt an "extreme devotion" to humans.[2]

Scientists now conduct various experiments, including taking MRI scans of canine brains, to prove what many dog owners know instinctively: dogs and humans love each other. Animal history scholars complicate this rosy picture, however. They show that not only does the relationship between dogs and humans vary from place to place and across time, it is a relationship shaped by class, race, and gender.[3] Seen in this light, Vest's praise of Old Drum glorified white rural masculinity, rooted in farming and hunting in the wake of the Civil War, during which Vest had served as a Confederacy congressman.

I embrace the historical approach to human-dog relations. I argue that what many Europeans and North Americans now consider to be the universal and natural relationship between dogs and humans is deeply rooted in the distinct emotional histories of urbanization in the West. The three cities discussed here—London, New York, and Paris—were key sites of this transformation of human-canine relations. Innovations could be found in other European and North American cities, such as early experiments with police dogs in Ghent, Belgium. But as globally significant metropolises, developments in London, New York, and Paris were central to the transformation, influencing human-canine relations in other cities as well as in rural areas.

A model of Western human-canine relations eventually emerged, which I call dogopolis. This was the somewhat shaky agreement that slowly, and sometimes agonizingly, arose between the middle classes of London, New York, and Paris on how urban dogs should cohabit with urban humans in a civilized, healthy, and safe way. Dogs and humans were thrown together in these rapidly expanding and developing municipalities, generating a host of feelings: love, compassion, disgust, fear. Eventually, dogs were integrated into city life in line with middle-class emotional values that centered on revulsion to dirt, fears of vagabondage, anxieties about crime, and the promotion of humanitarian sentiments. By the late 1930s, fears of biting and straying dogs had diminished; canine death had been rendered mostly acceptable through the management of canine suffering; dogs had fulfilled emotionally satisfying roles as pets and as police dogs (who in theory soothed worries about criminality); and the first steps had been taken to reduce the disgust provoked by canine defecation. Dogs' straying and defecating were tamed, their suffering reduced, and their thinking harnessed. Underscoring this transformation was dogs' actual and perceived ability to bond emotionally with humans.[4]

Dogopolis was not an inevitable end state. It emerged through choice, contingency, and conflict. Its complicated creation was also part of a wider reworking of urban human-animal relations in the nineteenth and early twentieth centuries that often focused on the management of animals in urban public spaces. By the mid-1870s, for instance, New York's Sanitary Code included regulations addressing horse diseases, animal slaughter, and tanning and rendering processes as well as restrictions on stray dogs.[5] In New York and elsewhere, cows, pigs, and other livestock were incrementally being pushed from city centers, and the number of horses rose and then fell as trains, trams, and cars came to dominate urban transportation. Animal protectionists rallied against cruelty to urban animals, decrying the condition of working animals and campaigning against animal sports. So, too, did urban authorities launch campaigns against various pests in cities in the metropole and the colonies. Public health measures against rats, flies, and other unwanted creatures met with varying degrees of success and came and went. But one constant was the blame directed at the colonized, the poor, people of color, and immigrants for allegedly creating the environments in which vermin thrived, while the authorities and elites overlooked deep social, racial, and economic inequalities.[6]

Dogopolis did not obliterate earlier aspects of human-dog relations. Some dogs kept on straying and biting, police canine units did not work out straightaway, and dog mess remained an unresolved problem. Nor is it a fixed state, having evolved since the 1930s. Notable developments include the introduction of widespread neutering, the firm establishment of police canine units after World War II, and the "pooper-scooper revolution" of the late 1970s. Dog hating has also continued: see calls in the 1970s and 1980s to ban dogs from Paris because of dog mess. But the place of dogs within the Western city was assured and a model of urban human-dog cohabitation established, within which Western urbanites still reside.

Moreover, the creation of dogopolis contained an exclusionary edge. This echoed, but did not equate to, the layers of exclusion and marginalization along lines of class, race, gender, and sexuality that have marked modern urban life. As pet keeping became a central feature of dogopolis, municipal authorities and animal protectionists increasingly rounded up and slaughtered countless stray dogs. Meanwhile, the supposedly degenerate state of dogs that did not conform to middle-class standards was used to further condemn the poor. Police dogs were deployed to reinforce boundaries between the poor and the rich as well as, in the case of New York, to maintain racial divisions. This history illustrates that interspecies intimacy encompassed violent exclusion of certain humans and animals, not simply feelings and declarations of love and compassion.[7]

This reworking of human-canine relations to dogopolis was informed by assumptions of racial superiority. Cobbe boasted that "the devotion and trustfulness of the dog toward man in every land peopled by an Aryan Race seem to prove that, with all our faults, he has not found us such bad masters after all."[8] Alongside reinforcing notions of white supremacy and overlooking the slaughter of stray dogs, Cobbe's remarks pointed to the peculiar ways of human-canine cohabitation that emerged in the West. For dogopolis struck non-Western observers as unusual. In 1897 G. Paramaswaran Pillai, an Indian lawyer and founder of the *Madras Standard*, visited the French capital and confessed that

> the first time I saw a lady's dog, in Paris, I was puzzled. It was a dog, surely: but I had never seen such a dog before. One-half of its body was hairy and I found clusters of hair at the end of its fore-feet and at the tip of its tail. It was a wonder to me when I first saw it and it was not after I had stared at it steadfastly for about five minutes that I realised that the razor was responsible for the dog's appearance.

Pillai then met many of the dog barbers responsible for the canine haircuts that exposed the city's dogs to its "piercingly cold winds."[9] He may have played up his bemusement to make a humorous anecdote for his readers in southern India, and his account aligns itself with others that mocked the fashionable excesses of Parisian women toward their dogs. But his observations nonetheless reveal the peculiarity of French fin-de-siècle dog-keeping fashions in comparison with the lives of Indian street dogs.

It is worth stressing that the loathing and repression of strays, along with other facets of dogopolis, were not and are not universal. Only a minority of the global population of dogs lived—and live—in the ways promoted and practiced in the West, where dogs' breeding and mobility are largely restricted. The world's far more numerous street dogs, according to biologists Raymond and Lorna Coppinger, are the "real dogs" and "part of a continuous worldwide and ancient population of dogs." To varying extents, street dogs are still accepted as part of urban communities. In Chennai, India, for instance, dogs are seen as *paavam* and as *jeevan*. These Tamil terms convey that dogs are "vulnerable living beings who are susceptible to various harms and suffering, and who are a part of society." That is not to say that dog breeding and pet keeping were absent in non-Western countries, since Asian breeds, such as the Pekingese, were imported to Britain through colonialism. But these practices were not so fetishized, codified, and extensive in societies beyond Europe and North America. Dogopolis is peculiarly Western. It is a provincial rather than a universal manifestation of human-canine relatedness.[10]

Making Middle-Class Dogs

The rise of dog breeds and the veneration of domesticity that fetishized pet dogs informed the making of dogopolis. But the middle-class emotional experiences of urbanization were central to these developments. The middle classes of London, New York, and Paris were far from unified. Most notably for the purposes of this book, they were split over what geographer Philip Howell has termed the "dog question," which related to the place and acceptability of dogs within society. But despite such disputes, there was enough coherence among the middle classes of all three cities, formed through intricate cultural, political, and economic transnational networks, to foster a realignment of human-dog relations to reflect their values, fears, and desires.[11]

Although the middle classes prospered in London, New York, and Paris, they often experienced these cities as disorienting and destabilizing. Rapid and seemingly chaotic urban growth fueled fears of social unrest and disintegration, exacerbated by disease outbreaks, riots, foul smells, slums, and strikes. From anxieties about criminal gangs to worries that bodies and minds would decline in the febrile sensory urban environment, city life was often experienced as profoundly troubling.[12]

Accordingly, the emotional ties between dogs and humans morphed in dialogue with evolving middle-class responses to urban life. Many of these reactions developed in the eighteenth century but took firm hold in the nineteenth, crystallizing into emotional norms. Historians of emotions have stressed the importance of changing emotional norms in framing how individuals feel and express their emotions, and in determining what is acceptable and desirable. These norms unite and divide communities, are repeatedly challenged, and cause anguish to those who do not conform.[13] To insulate themselves from the turbulence of modernizing cities, the middle classes promoted domesticity, kindness, efficiency, self-improvement, respectability, restraint, and cleanliness. They recoiled at pain, cruelty, dirt, violence, vagabondage, disease, and disorder. Questions then arose about how to reshape cities in line with these evolving emotional norms. The solutions were many and challenging: combating cruelty, removing filth, cleaning bodies, refining and controlling emotions, creating parks, bringing light to homes and streets, and investigating and reforming slums. Dogs were caught up in these middle-class efforts to order, cleanse, and rehabilitate London, New York, and Paris between 1800 and the 1930s.[14]

Middle-class anxieties about urban life merged with physical and emotional encounters with ever-multiplying urban dogs. Just how many dogs is hard to gauge accurately, especially as estimates tend to include only licensed ones and so exclude ownerless street dogs and those belonging to the many owners who wanted to avoid paying the license fee. France's canine population grew steadily from 1 million before the 1789 revolution to 3 million in 1914. In Britain, the number of licensed dogs rose from 830,000 in 1867 to over 1.3 million by 1878, and it continued to increase thereafter. By the late 1930s, New York had 500,000 dogs, according to an official estimate.[15] All these figures likely underestimate actual numbers; it is safe to say that the population of dogs boomed alongside that of humans as canines carved out niches in London, New York, and Paris, whether ensconced in the homes of the growing ranks of dog owners or scavenging the carrion and waste strewn over the streets.

As abundant and intimate companions to urbanites, dogs became enmeshed in the formation of middle-class emotional standards. They were readily available to soak up the emotional intensity of urban life. Middle-class apprehensions about the "dangerous classes" and vagabondage clung to stray dogs. Fears of disease cleaved to biting dogs. The humanitarian desire to alleviate cruelty fixated on canine suffering. Anxieties about crime adhered to the thinking capabilities of police dogs trained to tackle criminals. And revulsion to dirt stuck to defecating dogs. Evolving middle-class sensibilities shaped canine lives. Many dogs had their movements restricted, their mouths muzzled, and their lives ended. A select few became trained police dogs, and in the 1930s those with conscientious owners began to defecate in gutters. Dogs also shaped the emotional experiences of everyday urban life. Pet dogs might foster love, police dogs might spark gratitude, strays might provoke annoyance, biting dogs might trigger anxiety, defecating dogs might generate disgust, and suffering dogs might stir compassion.[16]

Dogs caused a range of emotions, intensifying middle-class disagreements over their desirable place within the cityscape. Dogopolis arose through these ongoing tussles. Faced with the vicissitudes of urban life, some middle-class city dwellers drew dogs near to soothe themselves. Pet dogs provided comfort in the home, and police dogs had the potential to assuage fears of crime. Emboldened by Darwinism, dog lovers stressed the emotional continuities between dogs and humans, and they blended narratives of loving and devoted dogs with the experienced intimacies of human-canine companionship, whether in the home or on the police dog training ground. However, to ease worries about dirt, disorder, danger, and disease, other urbanites strove to avoid straying, biting, and defecating dogs. They dismissed as sentimental nonsense the claims that dogs were emotionally similar to humans. Instead, they regarded dogs as dangerous nuisances who needed curtailing to ensure public safety and well-being. These feelings were rooted in the wider emotional landscape of urban life and embodied encounters with dogs. They were informed by, and helped support, middle-class emotional standards. For instance, antifouling campaigns arose from and reinforced attempts to ban dirt from the modernizing city. Competing feelings and associated actions toward canine straying, biting, suffering, thinking, and defecating changed how humans and dogs shared urban space. They were the impetus for the creation of dogopolis. In turn, the building of dogopolis gives credence to feminist scholar Sara Ahmed's pithy insight that "emotions *do* things."[17]

Dogs between Cities

Urbanites' emotional responses to dogs were sometimes specific to London, New York, or Paris. But these responses were often formed through transnational or shared characteristics involving regular exchanges between the three cities. This convergence stemmed from similar social and economic conditions in each city, such as rapidly expanding human and canine populations, the existence of a transnational middle-class culture and emotional norms, and the mobility of key individuals. Similarities were further strengthened by the transnational dissemination of public health policies, Darwinism, germ theory, and dog care expertise through the circulation and translation of books, scholarly articles, and other publications. Dog breeders may have confidently assigned breeds to specific countries at the end of the nineteenth century. But the making of the modern Western urban dog was embedded within the period of globalization that intensified in the fin de siècle. Cultural exchanges and improvements in transportation and communication, alongside multiplying international congresses on such topics as public health, strengthened cities' political, economic, and cultural connections. They also heightened the movement of animals across the globe and the deliberations on their use and management. The pages that follow address the flows between London, New York, and Paris as well as the similarities and differences between these cities.[18]

Also during the nineteenth and early twentieth centuries, British and American dog bite victims traveled to Paris for the Pasteur treatment; managers of pounds and refuges exchanged methods of killing strays; pedigree and police dogs crossed the Channel and the Atlantic; and animal protectionists met at international congresses. Certain individuals were particularly mobile: American animal protectionist Henry Bergh traveled to London to learn about the organization of animal protection societies, and French veterinarians such as Alexandre Liautard settled in the United States, helping familiarize their American counterparts with both germ theory and Pasteur's methods. Theories about rabies and canine health circulated across London, New York, and Paris as key medical and veterinary books were translated and republished. Physicians, veterinarians, police officials, and journalists all paid close attention to developments in the other urban areas, often using the evidence they gathered to bemoan the lack of action in their own city. Consequently, dogopolis emerged through multiple connections and exchanges between the three cities.[19]

Not everyone welcomed canine cosmopolitanism, however. Some British commentators lamented the harmful impact of foreign breeds on homegrown ones. Frank Pearce, writing in the London *Daily Mail*, adopted colonialist and nativist language when he declared—in reference to Chow Chows, "weird" Alsatians, and "French Police Dogs"—that Britain "could well do without the[se] aliens . . . and many other freaks imported from Tibet, Afghanistan, and the dark places of the earth." Such canine xenophobia was echoed by certain French breeders who unfavorably compared British breeds with French ones, albeit in less colonialist language and while begrudgingly admiring the British flair for dog breeding. To be sure, Pearce's lament serves as a reminder that canine transnationalism entailed disagreements as well as connections. And there were important differences between the cities. Most notably, London was the most successful of the three in stamping out rabies, and the British authorities' use of quarantine was a striking example of a nation-state obstructing canine mobility.[20] But on the whole, the similarities between the cities are more striking than the dissimilarities.

Dogs and Western Urban Modernity

As large metropolises that symbolized Western urban modernity, London, New York, and Paris were key sites in the reworking of human-canine relations. At a time of colonial expansion, they were nationally and internationally significant centers of economic, cultural, political, architectural, social, and technological innovation that became models for urban life. Often sharing more with each other than with provincial cities in their respective countries, they became exemplar cities for the rest of the world. Other cities, including Chicago, Dakar, Delhi, Manchester, and Vienna, were also sites of urban innovation. But London, New York, and Paris were the particularly important ones in terms of their global reach. They were also significant sites in the emergence of dogopolis. London was home to the first kennel club as well as the Battersea Dogs' Home and the Society for the Prevention of Cruelty to Animals. Paris was the site of the first Pasteur Institute. Along with New York, it was one of the first cities to experiment with police dogs (inspired by developments in Belgium and Germany). New York also played host to perhaps the first public anti–dog mess campaign, and alongside London it was one of the first cities to introduce antifouling laws.[21]

In sum, Western urban modernity both helped create and was created by dogopolis. The emotionally charged transnational attempts to harness, constrain, or eliminate canine straying, biting, suffering, thinking, and defecating became part of the making of modern cities in the West that took place on many levels, from the creation of sewers to the founding of department stores. The histories of the growth of mass consumerism, the emergence of public health, and the construction of dazzling forms of architecture, such as the New York skyscraper, are relatively well known. But the fashioning of modern London, New York, and Paris was also partly founded on the confinement and impoundment of stray dogs, the taming of canine biting, the "humane" killing of millions of unwanted dogs, the training of police dogs, and the launching of campaigns against defecation.

Dogs were tightly bound to the emerging urban modernity in many ways. They became victims of modern technology in the lethal chamber, were fed on modern consumerism though Spratt's dog food, and became the targets of modern public health projects. Deeply felt ambivalences about modern urban life informed the varied and ambivalent feelings about dogs caught within the struggle between progress and tradition in the modernizing cityscape. Pet and police dogs were glossed as modern, and stray dogs were branded as unwelcome remnants of past urban forms. At the same time, the lively presence of dogs deepened tensions between the desire for order and the messy reality of urban life, heightening urbanites' contradictory emotions about the city: despair, hope, fear, and pride.[22]

Dogs were a recurrent presence in the headlines of burgeoning newspaper accounts marking public life in modern London, New York, and Paris. The papers covering dog-related topics sought to foster a sense of "civic responsibility" among the predominantly white and middle-class audience targeted by their publishers, editors, and advertisers. Dogs thus became part of a "civic dialogue" as readers looked to newspapers to help them steer their way through the unpredictable contours of everyday urban life. Newspapers allowed dog lovers and dog loathers of various stripes to debate how dogs (and their owners) ought to behave in the modern city in accordance with middle-class emotional norms and values. They also provided outlets for popularizing scientific knowledge about rabies, parasites, and comparative psychology, as well as for stoking fears of these health issues. Whatever the angle, dog stories made for engaging copy, and editors and journalists fed their readers a constant diet of human-canine interest stories. Moreover, the articles contained traces of actual human-canine interactions, just as they sought to mold them.[23] Adherents of competing emotional values frequently sparred in newspapers, making print media an important site in the building of dogopolis.

At the heart of these debates lay the question of whether dogs could—or even should—become aligned with evolving middle-class visions of modern city life. Even some dog lovers agreed with dog loathers' claims that the animals were ill suited to modern Western cities. A "Harlem flat is just about the worst place in the world for an Airedale," noted William Haynes, an American aficionado of the breed. The "city at best is no place for any dog," he added. Other dog lovers defended the right of dogs to live in the metropolis. James R. Kinney, chief veterinarian of the Ellin Prince Speyer Hospital, and his collaborator Ann Honeycutt stated that dogs could "thrive" in New York and other large cities because they had lived with humans for thousands of years in villages, towns, and cities: "The dog loves cities because he loves to be with people. . . . Intimate association with human beings is what he wants, it's what he has had for centuries, and that's what he gets in cities." From riding in taxis to eating in restaurants, dogs were in their element. The fact that urban pet keepers were "genuine dog lovers" and cared for their dogs better than their rural counterparts made the metropolis a veritable paradise for dogs.[24]

As these differences of opinion suggest, building dogopolis was no easy accomplishment. The chapters that follow explore the clash and convergence of middle-class emotional responses to five central canine actions: straying, biting, suffering, thinking, and defecating. These conflicts reshaped human-dog relations in line with middle-class sensibilities. Chapter 1 discusses how straying became increasingly problematic while pet and pedigree dogs were being held up as the epitome of respectable dogs who could bond most fully with humans. Fear of and revulsion to straying became a foundation of dogopolis. Fear is also a focus of chapter 2. Canine biting stoked anxieties through the spreading of rabies until its partial taming through Pasteurism and muzzling, among other measures, at the end of the nineteenth century. Middle-class humanitarian concerns over canine suffering are considered in chapter 3. The minimization of suffering at the moment of death through "humane" killing legitimated the ongoing slaughter of strays. The destruction of strays and the transformation of nondomesticated dogs into useful creatures became hallmarks of dogopolis. In this vein, chapter 4 tracks the introduction of police dogs, whose thinking was harnessed to dampen middle-class fears of crime. With straying and biting diminished, canine defecation became a source of disgust and a health issue in the 1930s. As chapter 5 outlines, turning dogs into discreet defecators was the final component of building dogopolis. Throughout this process, sparks flew as the relationship between dogs and humans underwent a fundamental transformation within the ever-changing and emotionally charged modernizing city.

CHAPTER 1

Straying

In the nineteenth century, dogs roamed the streets of London, New York, and Paris. Owned or ownerless, they foraged, wandered, mated, and barked their way through the rapidly changing cityscapes. Urbanites had complained about and killed roving dogs well before that time. But after 1800, strays raised increasingly troubling questions about urban life. Were they acceptable creatures within modern cities who deserved toleration and compassion? Or should they be closely managed, even removed? Were they residues of backward urban cultures, or products of modern urbanization? For some, the answer was clear: strays were anathema to the modern and civilized European and North American city. A *New York Daily Times* article noted that "after we have got the west end of Long Island fairly fortified, and a grand free university established, on a firm basis, and the Central Park duly ornamented, we hope our City authorities will turn their attention to the dog-law."[1]

Fears of rabies intensified the calls to contain strays, but they do not fully explain the growing condemnation of straying. In 1872 veterinarian and noted British rabies authority George Fleming regretted that "even without their tendency to become rabid, these parasites are a nuisance, and a source of waste and insalubrity." For Fleming and many others, strays were potentially rabid and irritating pests. The clamor for their capture sprang from feelings of loathing and disgust triggered by the dogs themselves, along with metropolitan authorities' desire to make cities cleaner and safer in the name of public hygiene. Anti-stray attitudes notably dripped with class prejudice, as upper- and middle-class commentators repeatedly blamed the poor for the dogs' proliferation.[2]

Anti-stray campaigns constituted part of the histories of public health in London, New York, and Paris that marked these cities' emergence as models of urban modernity. Public hygienists' desire to sanitize the city, create social order, and promote health by distancing human bodies from harmful biological entities, such as rotting matter, waste, and corpses, both informed and legitimated anti-stray measures. These campaigns shared similarities with better-studied public hygiene crusades against dirt and diseases, including a class-based moralistic tone, disgust at the city's filth, and very often disputed and incomplete outcomes. And alongside rats and other unwelcome creatures, strays became nuisance animals targeted for containment and culling.[3]

A growing number of middle-class commentators viewed strays with disgust and fear. Their feelings arose from their encounters with stray dogs and their wider anxieties about urban life. These observers sought to reject strays and their interventions were characterized by actual and rhetorical violence. Sympathetic Londoners, New Yorkers, and Parisians, meanwhile, defended stray dogs and argued that they deserved protection against cruelty. They depicted strays as emotional creatures who had lost their way in the metropolis and could be redeemed through enlightened care and attention. Stray dogs could—perhaps—be brought within these sympathizers' attempt to build a compassionate city in which cruelty might be banished. On the twentieth anniversary of the creation of the American Society for the Prevention of Cruelty to Animals (ASPCA), its president, Henry Bergh, declared that its work had changed attitudes toward animals through practical measures: "what once seemed to be an abstract sentimental idea, has crystallized into the practice of that most engaging of the human virtues—mercy."[4] But animal protectionists and other sympathetic observers became ever more troubled by roaming dogs, particularly ownerless ones. Middle-class citizens' love and care for dogs were increasingly directed toward pedigree and pet dogs, whom they treasured to shore up notions of civilization, domesticity, and purity within the apparently degenerate cityscape. Intensifying hostility toward straying and the associated practice of impoundment became the bedrock of dogopolis.

"Dangerous Classes" and Dangerous Dogs

Dog loathing intensified in the early nineteenth century when middle-class commentators connected strays with all that they disliked about rapidly expanding cities—disease, dirt, and disorder. They argued that these canines shared a close affinity with the human "dangerous classes," the supposedly uprooted, filthy, and immoral underclass that undermined public security, health, and morality. Similar social conditions and concerns turned strays into canine members of the "dangerous classes" in London, New York, and Paris. Straying affronted middle-class sensibilities, provoking revulsion and fear.

Elite observers blamed the poor for producing a mass of unruly and dangerous dogs whose straying threatened public safety, order, and decency. In 1813 army officer Alexandre Roger bemoaned the more than eighty thousand "useless dogs and cats" infesting Paris. The problem apparently lay with the city's human underclass—the *canaille* (a term meaning "rabble" or "riffraff" that has its roots in the Italian word for "a pack of dogs," *canaglia*)—who thoughtlessly allowed the animals to breed. Dogs offended Roger especially because they spread rabies, a disease that indiscriminately affected rich and poor. It had claimed the lives of four people he knew, including one of his closest friends. The sheer number of stray dogs teeming through the capital's "poorest areas" constituted a threat to "public and private security." The indecent mixing of poor humans and their animals was "a disgusting spectacle." Recognizing that it was unfeasible to eradicate dogs from Paris, let alone France, Roger suggested that police approval be a condition of pet ownership and that public charity be denied to anyone who kept animals. The urban poor and stray dogs formed a mobile, ever-expanding, and uncontrollable human-canine underclass, and Roger subsumed a whole host of social problems—disease, overcrowding, poverty, and social breakdown—into the *canaille*.[5] The slippage between undesirable dogs and undesirable humans was laid bare. The former were imbued with the dubious moral qualities of the urban poor, while the latter were animalized.

In London, strays similarly represented danger, dirt, and disorder. Rabies again fueled middle-class condemnations of working-class dog-keeping habits. In a letter to the *Times* of London, M.R. of Burton Crescent, Bloomsbury, reported "witnessing the terror of a whole neighborhood, produced by one of these animals running foaming down the street." Lamenting the lack of an effective means to prevent the spread of rabies, M.R. called on the government to pay more attention to the "preservation of general safety, by ridding our streets of these numberless dogs which are become a perfect terror to man, and nine-tenths of which are kept by those who have a difficulty in keeping themselves." S.M., another letter writer to the *Times,* complained in 1825 about the "filthy vermin of cur" dogs who populated the "poor neighbourhoods" of London. The correspondent was struck by how poor Londoners' "ignorance of breed has filled our streets with hosts of ugly and useless curs . . . propagating, to the great scandal of the 'Society for the Suppression of Vice,' their filthy species in the most indecent and unbounded manner in all our highways." The dogs' lewdness served to further cement their status as members of the city's "dangerous classes," whose supposed sexual immorality and depravity both fascinated and alarmed the middle classes. As a self-declared pedigree dog breeder, S.M. had presumably encountered multiple mating dogs. But without human control, and conducted on the street, the sight and sounds of canine reproduction became immoral and unacceptable. Strays, S.M. demanded, should be rounded up and their skins turned into shoes ("it is the most soft and pleasant leather imaginable").[6] This was perhaps not a wholly serious suggestion, but it hinted at the potential deadliness of anti-stray sentiments. S.M.'s letter underscores how affection for pet and pedigree dogs often accompanied a dislike of strays.

Like Londoners, wealthy New Yorkers lamented the apparent chaos spread by stray dogs. Clearly unaware of Roger's and the *Times* correspondents' concerns, they fretted that strays sullied their city's reputation and prevented it from attaining the stature of London and Paris. They blamed immigrants and the poor for allowing their animals to disrupt orderly street life, overlooking how the pets of rich New Yorkers also swelled the ranks of dogs who roamed the streets. The links made between strays and poverty reflected and fueled fascination with New York's immigrant populations. A *New York Daily Times* journalist reported on the ramshackle slums between Thirty-Seventh and Fifty-Fifth Streets alongside the Hudson River. These dwellings resembled "an Indian settlement," whose dogs circulated among the huts of Irish and German "squatters." The dogs were friendly to the residents, "barking gaily" upon children's return home. But the "snarling" dogs represented potential threats to respectable New Yorkers, and the reporter was wary of "some villainous-looking dogs at the [huts'] entrance."[7] Despite its condescension toward immigrants, the reportage hints at the shared lives of dogs and humans as well as the bond that grew between them beyond the confines of middle-class pet keeping.

The scavenging, snarling, and potentially rabid stray stood in stark contrast to the feted middle-class mobility of *flânerie* (strolling) and promenading. These ambulatory rituals publicly displayed refinement, respectability, and creativity. They reinforced class distinctions and hierarchies in the starkly unequal societies of nineteenth-century London, New York, and Paris. Although poet and *flâneur* Charles Baudelaire may have celebrated the freedom-loving stray, dominant middle-class attitudes toward canine straying were disparaging. With bourgeois wealth and success rooted in the free movement of individuals and commodities, stray dogs joined prostitutes, manual laborers, beggars, and hawkers as unwelcome and physical obstacles to wealthy metropolitan lifestyles. Cast as mobile, diseased, and disruptive creatures, they had become dislocated from civilized human society.[8] Campaigns to cast them from the city became early building blocks of dogopolis.

Combating Strays

Public hostility toward strays prodded politicians into action. After receiving a petition signed by 1,347 New Yorkers, the Common Council passed the Law concerning Dogs in June 1811. This legislation established the post of Dog Register and Collector, whose task was to round up and kill stray dogs. Police marshal Abner Curtis was the first to hold the post, and he was entitled to fifty cents for every dog he and his men killed. The law also encouraged the citizens of New York to play a role in ridding the streets of dogs by permitting anyone to kill a stray outside the downtown Lamp District.[9]

Parisians' fears about strays bled into their worries about bulldogs. In 1840 Police Prefect Delessert ordered his men to destroy all bulldogs and related breeds because of their alleged aggression toward humans and protection of criminals. An ordinance of May 27, 1845, brought together measures against stray dogs and bulldogs, codifying the links between strays, danger, and criminality. It extended the ban on bulldogs on the public highway and stipulated that all other dogs on the street, leashed or not, must wear a muzzle and collar or risk impoundment and death. But the ordinance's impact was muted, and the police themselves admitted that dog owners openly flouted it.[10]

Nonetheless, from the perspective of London, Parisian police regulations seemed firm and effective. British anxieties about strays and rabies climaxed in 1830—the "era of canine madness," according to home secretary Robert Peel—when journalists reported how "thousands and tens of thousands of dogs kept by the Poor" wandered the streets of London, biting and harassing passersby.[11] We cannot be certain that stray dogs were this abundant or mainly owned by poor Londoners. But the image of uncontainable and potentially rabid strays carried an emotional impact, and calls for violence against them came from municipal authorities. The lord mayor of London stated that "if you have the least suspicion that a dog is mad, kill it. I shall be answerable for the consequences. I wish it to be known as publicly as possible, and do not care a pin who is the owner." Commentators denounced the national government's lame attempts to combat "these pests to the human race." Stung by the criticism, in June 1830 the government proposed a Bill to Prevent the Spreading of Canine Madness that would empower justices of the peace to order that all dogs within a designated area be confined indoors for a defined period. Noncompliant owners would be liable to fines, and police officers, beadles, and other guardians of public order would be instructed to impound stray dogs and kill unclaimed ones. But the bill failed to pass, and the efforts of alderman Mathew Wood to introduce similar ones throughout the 1830s came to nothing. Some attributed the lack of legislation to the influence of liberalism on British politics. The rights of dog owners had trumped public safety, unlike in France, where the "active hand of the law" was believed to be better at stamping out canine nuisances.[12] Aggression toward strays did not lead to effective action on the British side of the Channel.

Financial measures represented a potential solution. Following on from the establishment of a British dog tax in 1796, which after much debate had targeted the luxury dogs of the rich and spared the dogs of the poor, leading veterinarian William Youatt demanded in 1830 that financial obstacles be placed in the way of poor people keeping dogs. In an echo of Roger, he argued that "all relief, in every shape, be denied where a dog is kept." Every "useless" dog should be taxed, with owners forced to pay a "double penalty" if they let their dog roam. But such calls for a stricter dog tax went unheeded. In New York, meanwhile, the dog register and collector was charged with levying a three-dollar tax on dogs but claiming 20 percent of the receipts for himself.[13] The French dog tax came later. In 1855 legislators revived eighteenth-century proposals for a dog tax to discourage the poor from keeping dogs. They envisaged the tax decreasing the number of dogs from 3 million to 1.5 million. Dog owners now had to declare their dog annually at the local town hall and pay tax according to whether they owned a luxury or a working dog. But dog taxes failed to consider that many owners saw their pet as an emotional necessity and a valuable protector of their home. Pet dogs were not frivolous luxuries but instead essential to happy domestic life.[14]

Taxes were ineffectual in reducing the number of strays, as they were all too easy to evade. Public opposition similarly sapped the strength of other measures, because municipal authorities were caught between addressing the demands of urbanites who loathed strays and the demands of those who tolerated and sympathized with them.

Concern about strays had middle- and working-class roots in New York, where resistance to anti-stray measures was at its most confrontational.

Abner Curtis's zeal in enforcing the dog law led to the slaughter of 2,610 dogs in the summer of 1811. Some of his opponents complained about the cruel attacks on the city's dogs, and they defended the canines as loyal companions and servants of humanity. Others took matters into their own hands, confronting, insulting, and manhandling the dogcatchers. When a crowd caught up with dogcatcher Thomas Carlock, they destroyed his cart and released fifty-three dogs.[15] Thereafter, Curtis lessened his assault on the city's dogs, but New Yorkers continued to confront his capturing of dogs with violence. Finding himself caught between dog lovers and dog haters, Curtis resigned in 1818. His replacement, Benjamin Watson, increased the seizure of dogs, resulting in more confrontations between dogcatchers and dog defenders. The Common Council consequently increased the fine for obstructing dogcatchers from thirty to one hundred dollars. But the disturbances continued.[16] The streets had become tougher for dogs, but their catchers also felt the heat.

The confrontations besmirched the dogcatchers' reputation. A report read at an 1838 session of the Common Council noted that they were so unpopular that they had to "despatch their victims in the night time, which was a very bungling business." The aldermen were divided on the level of repression needed against strays. Alderman Willis "would rather see all the dogs in Christendom destroyed than that one individual should be bitten by them."[17] Canine mobility divided politicians and the members of the public, as aggressive and concerned emotional stances clashed. Conflict made it harder for authorities in New York as well as in London and Paris to diminish the number of strays, let alone eradicate them from the streets. Impoundment offered a solution.

Impoundment in Paris

Of the three cities, Paris had the longest-running officially organized dog pound. With French authorities seeking to eradicate public violence against animals through the Grammont Law of 1850, confinement and slaughter within the relatively secluded precincts of the municipal dog pound became the chief means of eliminating strays from Paris. The holding and culling of strays took place in the municipal pound (*fourrière*), which was located initially at 55 quai de la Vallée before moving in 1813 to 31 rue Guénégaud on the Left Bank. Identified in a law of October 6, 1791, as the place for animals "found on the public highway," the pound was where the police received, detained, and killed stray dogs and other wayward animals. They placed a monetary value on the impounded dogs, who could be sold if unclaimed within eight days.[18] In addition to attempting to reduce police expenditure, these regulations were designed to facilitate the efficient processing of dogs by returning pets to their well-heeled owners and killing unclaimed or ownerless dogs. Visible proof of their affectionate bond with humans, such as a hint of pedigree breeding or signs of grooming, offered straying pets a degree of protection.

Impoundment was, however, far from seamless. Policemen showed a marked reluctance to take strays to the pound. They were unwilling to approach possibly rabid dogs or risk confrontation with dog-loving members of the public.[19] With their sense of duty seemingly insufficient to motivate his men, Delessert introduced a financial incentive in 1842: they would receive 1.50 francs for each dog taken to the pound or renderer and 2 francs for two dogs. But this scheme experienced problems. Policemen working in areas teeming with stray dogs seized the opportunity to augment their meager salaries, thereby considerably straining local police budgets. The payment was then reduced in those neighborhoods, and eventually throughout Paris, to 50 cents per dog or 1 franc total for multiple ones, with 1.50 francs given for bulldogs.[20] But whatever their rate, the bounties placed on stray dogs failed to make much headway in reducing their number.

Impoundment in New York

Like its Parisian counterpart, the New York dog pound was plagued with flaws in the impoundment process. The prominent role of dogcatchers, as opposed to policemen, contributed to the pound's insalubrious reputation. Its origins dated to July 1647, when municipal authorities created a pound to detain wayward animals. It underwent various mutations, but the city did not establish a regular and dedicated dog pound until 1851. With the pound opening for the summer months each year upon the order of the mayor, city authorities maintained the policy of paying official and unofficial dogcatchers to capture strays. Given the pound's poor reputation, the authorities struggled to secure a permanent location for the facility. It consequently moved up and down Manhattan's East River shoreline each year.[21]

The pound became a public spectacle as many journalists reported on its unappealing scenes, noises, and odors. Their visits and accounts represented the extension of slumming—the middle-class urge to visit destitute places for the purposes of charity and thrill-seeking—to dogs. A journalist for *Forest and Stream* magazine dubbed the pound the "dog Golgotha":

"The place is not a savory one. It is disgusting, as to odors, enough to make one sick." Nonetheless, heartwarming scenes were also evident as German immigrants were joyfully reunited with their beloved if scruffy pets. One dog gave "his mistress a thankful look with his hazel eyes." Other German New Yorkers were less lucky, and their tears flowed when their pet was not found in the pound. But the dog pound master was unmoved by such displays of emotion.[22] The staff's callous indifference to the plight of dogs and owners confirmed the pound's unwholesome atmosphere. And more so than its secretive Parisian counterpart, New York's pound was a place for the public display of emotions: disgust, sadness, and joy. Love for stray dogs, whom others considered unlovable, was also apparent.

Other journalists described the pound as a seedy and un-American site that required emotional fortitude to visit. A *Harper's Weekly* journalist observed that the "approach to the pound is not altogether inviting. You go through a street bordered with fruit markets . . . where the venders are jabbering in what sounds like Choctaw, but probably is a species of garbled Italian."[23]

In language that broke down the distinction between vagrant dogs and apparently vagrant humans, the *New York Times* reported on fights between the "young roughs" of Italian and other immigrant backgrounds attempting to sell their dogs to the pound: "one human cur had three young miserable dogs . . . roped together, and, because they would not stand quietly, cruelly kicked one of them." Violence reportedly characterized life inside the pound as well. Dogs deemed worthless were "under the care of a stalwart negro, named 'Bill,' who enforce[d] obedience with a whip" and was prone to killing noisy ones. Such reports foregrounded the pound's brutal atmosphere, along with its status as a site where the hatred of dogs was transformed into everyday brutality. They also tapped into stereotypes of southern European immigrants and African Americans as uncivilized and vicious (in contrast to German immigrants, who were accorded a degree of unrefined emotional sensitivity).[24]

The pound contained the subversive movement of thousands of strays. Between 1851 and 1856, more than twenty-two thousand dogs passed through its doors, with numbers increasing each of those years. For some observers, this represented progress. The *Brooklyn Daily Eagle* called for a pound to be established in the New York City borough of Brooklyn to rid it of the "'dangerous classes' of the canine race." A reader welcomed this campaign after counting thirty-four unattended dogs between Nostrand Avenue and Fulton Ferry: "Having been snapped by a canine monster, I am next door to being mad on the subject. But where are the boys and the clubs?" The *New York Daily Times* similarly identified Brooklyn as being infested with strays: "they swarm in all the streets, obstruct the pavements, [and] make night hideous with their howls."[25] Together, stray-chasing street boys and a pound might rid Brooklyn of its noxious strays.

Yet the brutality directed toward dogs during impoundment sparked disapproval and worry. Some commentators fretted about its corrupting effect on New York's street boys. The *New York Daily Times* pointed out that the system gave "employment to ragged boys" skilled in tempting dogs off their owners' property. Many dogs released from the pound were "generally re-stolen and re-sold, and so the good work goes on." And money could be made. By August 2, 1854, the city had paid two thousand dollars to unofficial dogcatchers (or guttersnipes, as they were known).[26] At this time, journalists and social reformers worried about the seemingly uprooted street gangs whose nomadic young members posed a threat to the sanctity of family life and were a source of crime. These worries stuck to juvenile dogcatchers, and it seemed that the pound encouraged the propagation of vice, greed, dishonesty, and emotional desensitization in these young boys. The *New York Observer and Chronicle* lamented the pound's reinforcement of the unsavory system of dog catching:

> The whole effect of this business is hardening upon the hearts of the young. . . . Many a boy will leave honest industry, with its slow gains, to catch a dog, and inhumanely drag him by the neck to the pound, that he may gain the poor reward. The necessity of this summer check upon dogs is most obvious, but its effect upon the morals of the young, and that familiarity with inhumanity it inculcates, is greatly to be deplored.[27]

While it might have dampened fears of rabies in the hot summer months, the pound and the dog-catching system deepened anxieties about emotional hardening and moral corruption among the city's youth. One New Yorker decried the operation as "a disgrace to a civilized and Christian community" and a "blot upon our city" that needed to be opposed.[28]

Certainly, contradiction marked the making of dogopolis. Municipal authorities were under pressure to make New York a functioning and respectable modern metropolis by reducing straying. But impoundment created its own problems and opened these officials up to accusations that they encouraged violence and cruelty. To counter such criticisms, and yielding to the demands of animal protectionists, the City Council reduced the amount paid for each captured dog to twenty-five cents. From 1860 onward, the pound no longer accepted dogs from boys who had reportedly come to regard the animals as "walking capital."[29] This interdiction further lined the pockets of stray dog brokers, who now collected dogs from street children and then presented them to the pound. When in the 1870s the city appointed new dogcatchers, the charges of corruption continued as they became enmeshed in the Tammany Hall patronage machine that dominated New York politics from the 1850s to the 1930s. Unsurprisingly, Pound Master Captain Marriott defended his men against corruption slurs by praising their productivity and bravery. He reported that one among their number, John Hurlick, had single-handedly captured twenty-five hundred dogs and received many bites in the process.[30]

Dogcatchers' disreputable image endured throughout the nineteenth century. In an echo of the 1811 and 1818 confrontations between dogcatchers and dog owners, fights erupted. In 1887 Karl Meyer, a butcher from the Lower East Side, accused dogcatchers Albert Nagel and William Gregory of trying to seize his muzzled and licensed dog, and of striking him when he resisted. Nagel and Gregory denied the charges, claiming that "Meyer come [*sic*] out with a big knife and a mob got around us."[31] The capture of strays stirred emotions again in 1889. Margaretha Fuller was so incensed by the behavior of Brooklyn dogcatchers that she sued the City of Brooklyn for $10,500. She accused the authorities of employing "unsuitable and improper persons" who lacked "fitness, skill and virtuosity in the science of dog catching." Severing the bond between dog and owner, the "violent and brutal" James Scanlon and George W. Weeks had wrenched Fuller's "true and faithful canine" from her arms, injuring and shocking her in the process. The dogcatchers denied the charges, but the case was yet another instance of tussles between dogcatchers and dog-loving New Yorkers.[32] In coming between dogs and their owners, the unscrupulous dogcatchers were human-canine bond breakers and perpetrators of emotional distress.

As in Paris, the pound in New York City had become a site of conflict between dog lovers and dog loathers. Wealthy resident Henry Bergh resolved to oppose cruelty to dogs and other animals. Inspired by the Royal Society for the Prevention of Cruelty to Animals (RSPCA) during a trip to London and driven by his religious beliefs, he founded the American Society for the Prevention of Cruelty to Animals (ASPCA) in 1866. Along with proposing an innovative New York state law against cruelty to animals, the ASPCA launched repeated attacks against the Manhattan pound. Impoundment, which occasioned "cruel and demoralizing scenes in the streets," was an outrage to public sensibilities and an affront to the ASPCA's humanitarian values. Despite mockery by some members of the press, Bergh and his organization succeeded in persuading the State of New York to pass a law on April 12, 1867, that allowed ASCPA agents to check that sufficient food and drink were being provided to impounded dogs and, if necessary, intervene within the pound's confines.[33]

Once more echoing descriptions of the Paris pound, journalists sympathetic to ASPCA's cause joined the organization in depicting the New York pound as a pitiless site of incarceration where dogs faced forty-eight hours of "imprisonment" while "chained to hooks." In this "dog prison," noted one reporter, the "captives [are] inconsolable in their captivity," with some "making frantic endeavors to escape." The thin cords used to restrain the dogs "cut into the necks of the poor beasts until they [were] rendered raw and sore." Despite such concerns, the pound became "one of the 'institutions' of Gotham."[34]

A Home for Lost Dogs in London

The dog pounds of New York and Paris faced a barrage of criticism from dog lovers, who labeled them harsh and cruel places. In midcentury London, devotees of the animal set up an institution they claimed would compassionately remove strays from the streets. In October 1860, RSPCA supporter and animal welfare stalwart Mary Tealby opened the Temporary Home for Lost and Starving Dogs on Hollingsworth Street in Holloway, North London, as a refuge for strays. The press mocked Tealby and her facility. A *Times* editorial wondered whether she and her supporters had "taken leave of their sober senses." Criticism stretched across the Atlantic. New York–based *Harper's Weekly* noted that "it seems a mockery of Christian charity that when the streets of London are full of starving people . . . there should be an extensive asylum . . . for the reception and protection of destitute dogs!" To counter such criticism, Charles Dickens argued that the dogs' home did not compete with charities for homeless humans. He further declared that it provided "evidence of that hidden feeling which survives in some hearts" despite the "rough ordeal of London life."[35]

Unlike the New York and London pounds, the Temporary Home presented itself as a beacon of compassion for stray dogs. Rooted in a concerned emotional stance, it gave lost dogs a true refuge from London's callous streets. The home, which moved to South London in 1871 and became the world-famous Battersea Dogs' Home, was an inclusive "Asylum" for "every homeless dog," whatever their "race or condition." Owners could retrieve their lost pets after paying for their upkeep there, while unclaimed or ownerless "waifs and strays" might find new owners and homes.[36]

Rehoming became a compassionate and restorative act. A "kind-hearted" lady who had visited Tealby's dog refuge bore witness to heartwarming scenes. She observed the arrival of a "poor little Scotch terrier, whose feet were bleeding terribly. He had worn them to that state in his efforts to find his home." With his bleeding feet providing evidence of the dog's desperation to get home and that dogs were unsuited to a life on the streets, his rehoming with a woman from Canonbury was "one of the many instances of the good we may do, and the sufferings we may relieve, of this most intelligent and affectionate of God's creatures—creatures so dependent upon man that they cannot possibly, in large cities, support life without our help."[37] The Temporary Home for Lost and Starving Dogs would mend the bond between dogs and humans that had been so strained by modern urban life. Such affective ties were at its heart.

The emphasis on the feminine and religious character of the Temporary Home accentuated its difference from the harsh, corrupting, violent, and uncaring masculine atmospheres of the New York and Paris pounds. Even writer Harold King, who mocked aspects of that facility, found it "a very useful and humane institution. Most of us are fond of dogs, and we owe them some slight return for the pleasure they afford us." He urged his readers to visit the "annual [fund-raising] bazaar" to "see what pretty things the agile and skilful fingers of fair lady dog-fanciers, animated by affectionate associations, can do, to relieve the distress of little Diarmid and his fellow-creatures."[38] Dog lovers could now take active steps to support strays.

The bazaar cemented the Temporary Home's domestic ambiance, and journalists compared the dog refuge favorably with the New York dog pound. Instead of cramped conditions and violence, London's lost dogs enjoyed "spacious pens," "an extensive exercise-ground," and a hospital. Stray dogs' dirtiness and wretchedness were no longer intrinsic traits but temporary characteristics that could be scrubbed away with care and compassion. Lost dogs thus became canine counterparts to homeless children, who still retained their innocence and could be redeemed through exposure to middle-class morality, guidance, and charity in benevolent institutions.[39] Stray dogs transformed from being hazardous, dirty, and diseased creatures into victims of urban life who, like London's downtrodden humans, deserved a degree of sympathy and support. Straying became a desperate yet noble search for a home rather than a disruptive activity.

Descriptions of canine emotional distress further legitimated the Temporary Home's mission. According to William Kidd, strays' "deflected tails" told "too plainly of their dejected spirit." The *London Reader* noted too that there is no more "mournful sight" than a "lost dog." It even extended compassion to the "many wretched wandering curs" who "probably never had a home" and whose "miserable existence" was generally terminated by "the wheel of a brewer's dray . . . or by a ''arf a brick' heaved by some human pariah."[40] Rather than stray dogs endangering humans, the city's workers and animalized human outcasts were now being portrayed as victimizing strays.

Yet similarities existed between Mary Tealby's dog refuge and the pounds of New York and Paris. Despite not paying individuals for bringing dogs to its gates, a whiff of corruption and financial impropriety hovered over the Temporary Home. Critics attacked its policy of selling dogs to new owners when it did not technically own them, thereby violating the original owners' property rights. Its more strident critics dubbed it a "prison," echoing the language used to describe the pounds. They dismissed its domestic image as a smoke screen for the internment and destruction of strays. There was some truth in these charges. For although the Temporary Home's supporters showed sympathy toward London's strays, they shared an underlying logic with the municipal authorities who ran the pounds: the dog's place was beside their owner. Dogs were domesticated animals who belonged in domesticated places. For their own well-being and that of other city dwellers, they needed to be removed from the streets.[41] Beneath the velvet declarations of love and compassion lay an iron fist.

Even largely favorable commentators noted the ambiguous mission of the Temporary Home for Lost and Starving Dogs. Harold King described how dogs entered this "temporary paradise," where they were "received and welcomed on a perfect footing of equality and fraternity—a model pantisocracy, which would have delighted the heart of the poet Collins, or Republican Southey, or his metaphysical friend Coleridge." The reference to late eighteenth-century Romantic political utopias might position the Temporary Home as a place of canine liberty and happiness. But King quickly debunked his image of a canine pantisocracy. The "aristocratic well-bred dog" and the "bourgeois dog" would quickly be returned to their owners or found new ones. Echoing Alexandre Roger's term from 1813, King noted how those dogs differed from the *canaille*, the "mongrels and curs of the very lowest degree" who are "of no use to themselves, or to others. Let them loose, and they would only live over again the same sans-culotte famishing life, kicked and cuffed and worried, to breathe out their last breath in the gutter, and to have their dead carcasses crushed and mangled by the ruthless wheels of Pickford's vans."[42] He distinguished between those dogs who had purpose through their connection with humans as pets or workers, and those without worth or utility who lived pointless and harsh lives and would be literally crushed by the modern capitalist economy.

Indeed, the Temporary Home divided dogs found on the street into two broad categories. Pets and valuable dogs who had strayed from their owner would be returned or sold, and ownerless ones would be destroyed after fourteen days. Its supporters did not hide this aspect of the facility. Kidd warned his readers not to "let it be imagined that every or any dirty little cur is indiscriminately to be admitted here, and kept in luxury. No! Morbid sympathy has no place in this establishment."[43] The compassionate treatment of dogs was conditional, based on their close companionship with humans and their conformance to middle-class values of respectability, domesticity, and cleanliness.

Such differentiation between valuable and valueless dogs once again aligned the Temporary Home with the pounds. In the Paris pound, dogs presumed to be pets were kept in better conditions than those considered ownerless: the former had eight days to be claimed, while the latter had only three. As one observer noted in 1873, the Paris Commune had neglected to write *Liberté, égalité, fraternité* above the pound entrance. Distinctions between canine "patricians" and "plebeians" remained. Observers of the New York pound noted too that "respectable looking dogs or high-blooded dogs are placed in a favored part of the pen" and fed "fresh meat," unlike their scruffier counterparts. They could be returned to their grateful owners (fig. 1.1).[44]

Like the pounds of New York and Paris, the Temporary Home confined and killed dogs. This aligned it with London authorities' efforts to contain canine straying. The Metropolitan Streets Act of 1867 gave police officers the right to capture presumably ownerless dogs and destroy them within three days if they remained unclaimed (these measures were extended to the rest of the country with the Dogs Act of 1871). The legislation treated stray dogs as obstructions, alongside cattle, shoeblacks, and hackney carriages, that needed regulating to ensure the smooth movement of goods and individuals around the capital's congested streets. But police commissioner Sir Richard Mayne and his men quickly found themselves housing and killing thousands of dogs whose numbers never seemed to diminish. Various initiatives to deal

FIGURE 1.1 W. A. Rogers, *At the Dog Pound—the Rescue of a Pet, Harper's Weekly*, June 16, 1883. Library of Congress, control number 93512104.

with the multitude of strays failed. Policemen in Chelsea, for instance, held auctions of the dogs they seized but struggled to find buyers. The Temporary Home offered a solution. A police order of July 6, 1870, allowed the police to seize "stray dogs whether muzzled or unmuzzled, seen in the streets and not under the control of any person," and take them to that facility. The partnership brought benefits to both sides. The police no longer had to house and kill captured dogs at police stations, thereby eradicating a "nuisance" to area residents. The Temporary Home, meanwhile, would eventually receive a threepence fee for each dog brought to its gates, according it a degree of financial security.[45]

Despite its aura of calm domesticity, the Temporary Home for Lost and Starving Dogs, like the pounds of New York and Paris, stirred emotions. It stood as a physical manifestation of care and love for dogs. But in practice it served the interests of dog haters who wanted strays off the streets. It was the embodiment of the emerging dogopolis. It demonstrated love for lost pets but revulsion to street dogs. The latter needed to be removed from the streets because they affronted middle-class sensibilities, but this had to be done in a manner commensurate with middle-class emotional norms of kindness and compassion.

In Defense of Straying

In removing strays from the streets in partnership with the police, the Temporary Home reinforced the notion that straying was a retrograde activity in the nineteenth-century metropolis. Yet middle-class defenses of straying as a healthy and useful canine activity made themselves heard, especially in France.

Influential French animal protectionists defended stray dogs as healthier than their housebound counterparts. Before the elaboration and eventual acceptance of germ theory, the suggestion that rabies could arise spontaneously in some dogs and then be transmitted through bites was legitimately held. For advocates of this view, a pressing question concerned the types of dog most likely to develop the disease. Some believers in spontaneous rabies questioned the whole premise that stray dogs were the source of the disease. One member of the Société protectrice des animaux (SPA [Animal Protection Society], founded in 1845), writer and lawyer Amable-Félix Couturier de Vienne, asserted that rabies was less common in "vulgar and roaming" dogs than in overweight, overprotected, and chaste pet dogs.[46]

The freedom apparently enjoyed by dogs in the Ottoman Empire informed such thinking. French writers displayed a marked fascination with and respect for the dogs of Constantinople (present-day Istanbul), who guarded their neighborhoods from human intruders and helpfully ate debris off the streets. The author and assistant administrator of the Salon art exhibition, Jules Maret-Leriche, highlighted how dogs in the Ottoman capital were "more numerous than disciples of the Koran," living "in an almost savage state" without any "constraints" on their freedom. Yet despite the city's oppressive heat, few of its dogs were rabid.[47]

What explained this resistance to rabies? Drawing from medical reports from Egypt and Turkey, SPA vice president, public hygienist, and philanthropist Dr. Henry Blatin observed that dogs who were free to follow their instincts were less susceptible to the disease. These "masterless and vagabond dogs" seemed healthier than French pet dogs; apparently, "liberty" was an effective prophylactic. The celebration of strays' freedom offered a way to critique what some saw as the cosseted world of bourgeois domesticity that stifled male sexuality as well as the repressive political atmosphere of Napoleon III's France. Blatin's veneration of canine liberty echoed and reinforced republican calls for greater human freedom under the Second Empire.[48]

Mirroring French concerns about the poor health of pet dogs and revisiting eighteenth-century condemnations of stifling indoor environments as physically and emotionally damaging to well-being, some British observers worried about the harmful effect on canine health arising from domestic confinement. The *London Illustrated News* even portrayed straying as a normal and necessary tendency in dogs: "every dog naturally and innocently desires to run out, once or twice a day, to visit the familiar street-corners of the neighborhood, and to see what is going on, with that vigilant curiosity which is characteristic of the race. A dog which constantly mopes indoors may be suspected of a morbid disposition." For psychologist James Sully, the "attachment" to humans had come late to the canine species: "the dog is by nature unattached and vagrant." Some dogs were incorrigible "rovers." George Fleming did not advocate allowing dogs to roam, but he similarly expressed concern that confining dogs to the home went against their "natural interests." The lack of liberty, in fact, might cause spontaneous rabies. Across the Atlantic and tapping into the highly gendered celebration of rugged masculinity and condemnation of feminine luxury, male American commentators attacked female dog owners who spoiled their dogs with tea parties, rich food, and domestic comforts. Such behavior, they alleged, would lead to rabid and unhappy dogs and civilizational decline.[49] Freedom kept dogs healthy, happy, and less susceptible to rabies.

Strays' general lack of pedigree even attracted some admiration. A contributor to *Leisure Hour* magazine in 1860 praised "mongrel" dogs as "all the more intelligent from the mixture of blood, and much better suited to a city life than animals of pure breed." Moreover, "we Englishmen are ourselves a mongrel race . . . and all the more active, enterprising, intelligent and efficient on that very account." Stray mongrels showed similar qualities, with the writer proving his point by describing the "vagabond mendicant life" of four resourceful dogs, Prowler, Snap, Ponto, and Smut, who roamed and ate their way around London. Other strays were more territorial, attaching themselves to a particular market, hospital, factory, workshop, or street. In its romanticized depictions of strays' nomadic lives, this narrative echoed sentimental accounts of human tramps.[50] Giving the dogs names also turned them into individuals with their own personalities and predilections rather than indistinguishable members of a frightening mass of strays.

There was some affection for stray dogs. But during the creation of dogopolis, condemnations of straying ultimately drowned out warm portrayals. The rise of dog breeding strengthened the justification to exclude stray dogs from London, New York, and Paris.

Pedigree vs. Stray

As the number and influence of dog breeders grew over the course of the nineteenth century, strays became anathema to the principles of pedigree dog breeding. Breeders hosted increasingly popular dog shows and created more and more dog breeding societies, which eventually fell under the control of national kennel clubs. In 1873 Sewallis E. Shirley, an aristocratic dog breeder, became the first head of the elite British Kennel Club, a model copied in the United States in 1876 with the founding of the National American Kennel Club and in France in 1882 with the establishment of the Société centrale pour l'amélioration des races de chiens en France (Central Society for the Improvement of Dog Breeds in France). In opposition to supposedly diseased, dangerous, and degenerate strays, kennel clubs and breeders promoted pedigree dogs as the pinnacle of domestication and evidence of human expertise and control over nature. The most discerning would-be dog owner was now encouraged to select only the best of the breed.[51]

Unlike strays, the breeding of pedigrees was controlled, and their ancestry was recorded in studbooks. At the same time, their physical appearance was judged, however imperfectly, according to its alignment with breed standards. Breed histories and standards may have been largely invented, particularly from the 1860s onward, but they transformed how dogs were understood and represented. The appeal of breeds lay partly in the financial rewards of displaying and selling pedigree dogs and the prestige such dogs conferred on their owners. For wealthy Americans, bloodhounds and collies represented European civilization, and the Westminster Dog Show at Madison Square Garden become the place for New York's elite to view these refined creatures.[52]

In urbanizing and industrializing societies, pedigree dogs symbolized an idealized rural past. For British breeders, foxhounds (and other rural breeds) embodied the lost stability and calm of pre-industrial Britain, while aristocratic French breeders celebrated regional hunting breeds as traces of prerevolutionary France. But although breeds represented national pasts, they were developed within networks of transnational cooperation and competition through dog shows and breeding publications. Female breeders and owners became major players alongside men in the breeding and selling of dogs, along with the showing of pedigrees at dog shows (fig. 1.2). Some, such as Gwendoline Brook, who imported spaniels to her farm near New York City, targeted wealthy Americans. Others, such as Mr. Jennings, a British

FIGURE 1.2 *Salle Wagram, Dog Show, Dogs [Chihuahuas] Belong to Mme Reiss.* Photograph by Agence Rol, December 14, 1923. Bibliothèque nationale de France.

immigrant who sold dogs and other animals from his house on Broome Street, Manhattan, catered to a less elite clientele.[53]

Dog breeding meshed with evolutionary theories on racial hierarchies, development, and difference. British surgeon Jonathan Hutchinson claimed that the transformation of wolves into dogs through domestication had immeasurably improved the animals, who had become "civilised and half-humanised." Just as modern Europeans were superior to "a Fiji," so "the moral and intellectual nature of the rude and savage progenitor of the dog" was inferior to his "ennobled offspring."[54] The domestication of the dog came to represent the journey from savagery and allegedly proved European superiority. Such thinking outlived the Darwinian debates of the nineteenth century. "The propagation of any creature in the animal kingdom by uncontrolled instincts results in degeneracy and a reversion to a wild state," claimed self-styled American dog psychologist Clarence E. Harbison in 1932.[55]

Dog breeders' emphasis on selective breeding, purity, and inherited traits further dovetailed with racist thinking about human racial hierarchies and difference. Arranging dogs and humans into breed and racial taxonomies helped make sense of variability in nature and in humans. Dog breeds also confirmed that nature was ordered and readable. An individual dog could be known through their breed, just as a human individual could supposedly be known through his or her race. Similar techniques of display and observation of breeds and races were also apparent, with human ethnographical displays sharing space with dog shows at the Crystal Palace in South London. Eugenicists, meanwhile, speculated that dog breeders' knowledge of selection and hereditary traits could be applied to humans, while physicians in New York asserted that pedigree dog breeding confirmed the necessity of racial purity and the dangers of racial mixing. L. L. Dorr, for instance, argued that hybridity led to social problems in humans and rabies in dogs. Scientific racism and dog breeding fed off each other to admonish the mixing of races in humans and breeds in dogs.[56]

Well-bred dogs supposedly had a greater capacity for emotional refinement than strays. Darwin's protégé Georges Romanes asserted that "curs of low degree" lacked the "moral refinement" and sense of "self-respect and dignity" enjoyed by "high-life" dogs, who could experience greater suffering due to their "constant companionship" with humans, a bond that had endowed them with greater intelligence and "emotional character."[57] The emphasis on strays' dull emotional life paved the way for them to be killed in the vivisectionist laboratory and in lethal chambers (see chapter 3). It also distanced them from the middle-class veneration of emotional refinement.

As breeding came to represent the zenith of human-dog relations, straying embodied its nadir. Stray, mongrel, and cur dogs became interchangeable. The "cur" morphed from being a dog of mixed origins in the early Victorian period who fulfilled useful domestic tasks, such as guarding homes, to a degenerate, dangerous, and undomesticated creature by the end of the nineteenth century. Lacking breed histories, displaying "indeterminate variability," and escaping the rational control of breeders, the figure of the stray cur challenged the nineteenth-century veneration of classification, pedigree, and improvement.[58]

The separation of dogs into stray and pedigree echoed and reinforced the late nineteenth-century narrative of degeneration. Physicians, psychiatrists, and others feared that urban environments, among other factors, would lead to individual and national decay. While anyone could degenerate, theorists of degeneration asserted that the depravity, vagrancy, and alienation of the poorest and immigrant classes of the modern metropolis made them most susceptible. The outcomes were mental diseases, immorality, and crime, all of which threatened the social order. Sexual relations between different classes and races would, according to racial theorists, weaken white racial purity and superiority. Hybridity was dangerous.[59] Like the human poor's demographic abundance, stray dogs' unrestrained reproduction was positioned as a potential threat to pedigree dogs. In this vein, Charles Darwin argued that poor laws and other forms of relief enabled "weak members of civilised societies [to] propagate their kind." Anyone who has studied "the breeding of domestic animals" cannot doubt "that this must be highly injurious to the race of man."[60] Degenerate and fertile strays seemed poised to defile and weaken refined and pure pedigrees.

Both the Temporary Home for Lost and Starving Dogs and the pounds reinforced perceived differences between stray and pedigree dogs, as the former could now be observed and described in more detail. Visitors to the dogs' home were struck by strays' variety as well as their physical differences from pedigree dogs. The street dogs seemed tough, noisy, and savage. Lennie Orme reported that the keeper at the Temporary Home "knows about a dozen of his large-headed, thick-limbed, gaping, shambling pensioners by the title of the 'wolves.'" They "formed the 'dangerous classes' of the Refuge." The rhetorical binding of strays and the human dangerous classes thereby entered that facility, with Orme's reference to wolves cementing strays' wild and savage character. Comparable observations were made in the New York pound. A journalist for the Chicago newspaper *Inter Ocean* observed a bitch suckling her litter: "there is neither strength nor comeliness, nor race about her . . . she is a pariah, a dog-waif, a canine flotsam and jetsam."[61] In a similar vein, another journalist visitor noted that

> the difference between dogs . . . who have been well educated and provided for, and the sneaking curs who contest with chiffoniers [ragpickers] for the contents of the gutter, is readily detected. The latter . . . are utterly destitute of self-respect, and shrink from observation with a manifest sense of shame and self-reproach; whereas the well-bred dog in the opposite pen . . . exhibits all the noble traits of sagacity, courage, and fidelity for which the race are [*sic*] distinguished.[62]

Despite their degrading experience in the pound, pedigree dogs supposedly held on to their positive traits and maintained their bond with humans, while breedless and ownerless dogs were dominated by harmful emotions and so remained elusive and wary of human contact.

Even concerned and sympathetic visitors struggled to see how ownerless and mongrel dogs could be redeemed and rehomed. Such was their unsavory character that a *Forest and Stream* journalist sent on an "errand of mercy" to the New York pound to adopt a stray dog for one of the magazine's Boston readers felt unable to select one from "such a wretched, miserable assemblage of dogs." This despite the journalist experiencing "a feeling of pity" and being drawn to the "mangy" dogs' "inquisitive, far, deep seeking eyes . . . which seemed to say, 'For pity's sake, keep us from death!'"[63] Feelings of disgust overrode those of compassion in this instance, and no dog was plucked from the pound. It was becoming increasingly hard to love strays.

The promotion of pedigree dogs reinforced strays' unsavory reputation, associating them with physical and emotional degeneracy and further reinforcing Westerners' aggressive emotional stance. Dog breeding's enmeshment with racial theories turned strays into backward creatures within London, New York and Paris, cities viewed as beacons of Western urban modernity and metropolitan centers of expanding colonial empires.

Straying Elsewhere

The rise of dog breeding transformed street dogs who lived beyond Europe and North America from freedom-loving and rabies-free creatures to living proof of cultural backwardness and racial inferiority. For A.-G. Beaumarié, writing in 1874, the stray was a "degraded being" and the "pariah of its species." Beaumarié compared strays in France to the dogs that inhabited Indian settlements, thereby stressing their deserved exclusion from the modern Western metropolis. Other supposedly backward places identified as haunts of "pariah dogs" who might attack the civilized traveler included Burma (present-day Myanmar) and Peru.[64]

Constantinople again loomed large in Western thinking about stray dogs. In a typical account, the *Times* of London's special correspondent described the city's strays as "masterless" scavengers who lazed around the streets during the day, encumbering pedestrians before becoming disruptive and noisy at night. They were loyal to their packs and neighborhoods but renowned for their hostility to pet dogs and Europeans. Local residents fed and tolerated these dogs. But they did not try to make them pets or eradicate them. This human-dog bond was an intriguing feature of the exoticized East but was ultimately framed as an inversion of the natural order. Such hard-to-categorize relationships between humans and dogs clearly distressed this observer: "this estrangement from our race of that most sympathetic of living species . . . is painful in the extreme."[65]

American author and dramatist Albert Bigelow Paine identified Constantinople's semisavage street dogs as evolutionary throwbacks. He believed that the dogs had "reverted to the original pattern—they are wolf-dogs." While not without their emotional and rational qualities (they were "the kindest, gentlest creatures of the dog family . . . and the most intelligent"), these "pariah dogs" were distinct from pet and pedigree dogs. In conflating Indian and Turkish street dogs by naming them pariahs, Paine asserted that the dogs' physical state was a direct reflection of Turkish society. They were often "mangy and motheaten and tufty," but the "Turks themselves are all of these things, and why should the dogs be otherwise?" Paine pondered.[66] The dogs embodied Turkish decadence and marked Constantinople out as an exotic and dirty city in sharp contrast to the urban areas of Europe and North America.

Stray dogs in London, New York, and Paris undermined the status of those cities as apexes of civilization. William Forsyth, MP, declared in 1878 that "London was getting very much like Constantinople in relation to useless dogs." Paine noted that "in America, two or three dogs will keep a neighborhood awake, but imagine a vast city of dogs, all barking at once—forty or fifty dogs to the block." The dogs may serve a social function by scavenging rotting food and other foul matter off the streets. But that was only necessary in a city that lacked the "great sewer systems of Anglo-Saxon civilization."[67] Strays were treated as superfluous in technologically advanced Western cities.

The identification of strays with supposedly inferior and uncivilized cities cemented straying as a retrograde activity in London, New York, and Paris. It rooted the creation of dogopolis within Eurocentric notions of white superiority and progress. If these three cities represented the pinnacle of modernity, stray dogs belonged elsewhere in purportedly less advanced urban societies, living among supposedly culturally and racially inferior people. Stray dogs became unwelcome reminders of degenerate and backward urban cultures within the modern metropolis, and they perhaps ignited elite worries that Western urban civilization was fragile, incomplete, and prone to degeneration. Branded dirty, diseased, and degenerate, the stray dogs of the working classes within the Western metropolis offered further evidence of the metropolitan poor's animalistic tendencies and their similarities to colonized subjects. The elimination of straying would, it seemed, improve bourgeois life in London, New York, and Paris by protecting the middle classes from the straying and snarling canine embodiments of urban poverty and civilizational decline while cementing these cities' superiority over non-Western cities. By rejecting strays, dog lovers increasingly turned their affection toward bathed and groomed pet dogs within the home.[68]

Loving Pets

Unlike strays, pet dogs were welcomed into dogopolis. Emerging during the Middle Ages, the word *pet* came from the French word for "little" (*petit*) and referred to the small dog breeds often owned by women. Pet keeping was informed by broader emotional histories: in eighteenth-century Britain, the elevation of sympathy to the height of human emotional refinement provided fertile conditions for pet keeping there. Unlike ownerless strays, pet dogs lived in households and were intended to be petted.[69]

Pet keeping grew in popularity over the course of the nineteenth century. This was due in part to rising living standards and the seamless insertion of pets into the middle-class domestic ethos that venerated private and comfortable houses and apartments, and found a spatial form in new architectural styles, such as the Haussmann-era Parisian apartment. Pet dogs were said to improve the emotional sensitivity of the humans who cared for them, and as emotional creatures they deserved kindness from their human family. Loving narratives and feelings clung to pet dogs within the enclosed space of the home.[70] Books, paintings, photographs, and newspaper articles celebrated these canines as loyal household members who comforted humans and protected the home from intruders. According to the editor of British hunting publication the *Field*, John Henry Walsh (known as Stonehenge), Saint Bernards made excellent guard dogs due to their "instinctive dislike to tramps and vagabonds."[71]

Strays—as dogs outside the home—troubled the middle-class veneration of domesticity and its associated feelings of security, love, cleanliness, and comfort. They exposed the limits of these emotional standards, as their very existence showed that dogs could survive, even thrive, outside the bourgeois interior world. As pets slotted into the middle-class ideas of domesticity and affection, strays without a human home were treated as openly aggressive to the idealized and loving family. Without human contact, strays were said to become "quarrelsome" and "aggressive." They set themselves on pet dogs, who, having become more "docile" in human company, fared poorly in street brawls with them.[72] Furthermore, some observers worried that allowing pet dogs to roam would undermine domestic stability and the balance between affection and domination within pet-keeping households. Warned one French authority, "*flânerie*" (strolling) would give pet dogs a "taste for independence," making them less submissive. A wayward pet dog exposed the fiction of the private and frictionless middle-class home cut off from the public world.[73] Straying undermined order inside and outside the home.

The practices of loving and caring for a dog changed over the nineteenth century. As pets became part of modern consumer cultures, the money spent on middle-class pet dogs' health and appearance further set them apart from ownerless strays. In addition to the treatment received from veterinarians, who increasingly retooled themselves to cater to the swelling ranks of pet dogs, the groomed pet dog looked and smelled differently from the street dog. A reader of *Le petit journal* claimed that it was easy to distinguish between owned and ownerless dogs. Echoing medical debates over the visual identification of cretinism and other perceived degeneracies in humans, the correspondent argued that it was possible to identify "at first glance" those dogs that "lived in a permanent bohemian state." Middle-class pet owners in Britain, meanwhile, looked down on the pet-keeping practices of the working classes, who had less money to spend on their dogs and gave them greater freedom to roam. The different fates of dogs of wealthy and poor owners continued after death. The former might find themselves buried beneath a headstone in the new pet cemeteries in Hyde Park, Asnières-sur-Seine, and Hartsdale, while the latter might be thrown onto the street or into a river (fig. 1.3).[74]

In the late nineteenth and early twentieth centuries, dog care experts—and

FIGURE 1.3 Entrance to the Asnières-sur-Seine pet cemetery on the outskirts of Paris, August 2008. Author photo.

companies with products to sell—turned grooming into a way of strengthening the bond between pet and owner. With dog combs, brushes, soaps, and flea lotions to market to American dog owners, a 1922 Q-W Laboratories catalog stated that "if you really love your dog, you will care for him so that he may keep healthy and happy. . . . Treat him decently, build up his self-respect and he will prove that a dog is not 'just a dog' but that he is dog plus something else. Just what that something else is no one can tell, but every real dog lover knows exactly what I mean. Dogs should be groomed regularly."[75] Washing, clipping, and brushing provided evidence that owners loved their canine companion, even if servants sometimes did the actual work of washing the family dog as part of the endless tasks they were charged with to keep the middle-class home scrupulously clean. Grooming was treated as vital to canine health. Veterinary professor Maurice Douville stressed that it would ensure the dog's "cleanliness, endurance, economy and health." Writer Paul de Grignon specified that owners should only use savon de Marseille on their dogs, while others recommended other brands or specialized dog soaps. The nineteenth-century fetishization of soap as a guarantee of purity, morality, health, and order, and the booming business of producing and selling soap, applied to canine as well as human bodies. In early twentieth-century Britain, meanwhile, the domestic science movement gave a scientific gloss to women's role in caring for canine members of the family.[76]

Grooming aligned dogs within the middle-class culture of cleanliness. But restraint was needed. New York veterinarian James Kinney and his coauthor Ann Honeycutt advised owners against overwashing their dogs, as it destroyed the vitality of their fur and led to skin conditions. Brushing or "dry-cleaning" with corn meal and applying alcohol or "bay rum" were their preferred options.[77] Of course, not all owners would have followed precise cleaning instructions, and it took time and money to keep a dog spotlessly clean. But the model pet dog was a clean one. With the middle classes increasingly prizing cleanliness, it was far preferable to pet a clean dog than a filthy one crawling with fleas. There was also less incentive to turn a groomed pet dog loose in the streets for the day, since they might roll in filth—a waste of the time, effort, and money spent on grooming.

Modern pet keeping also bound pet dogs and their owners through the leash. Dog care experts began to warn owners against letting their dogs roam the streets unaccompanied. Pets might fight and fornicate with ownerless strays or catch diseases from them, including the dreaded rabies. The advent of the motor car posed further risks for a free-ranging pet dog. Veterinarians and others therefore encouraged owners to keep their dogs either indoors or leashed. Legislation also pushed for using leashes. The 1867 Metropolitan Streets Act in London empowered the police to seize all unmuzzled and loose dogs. But leashed dogs were exempt from wearing a muzzle. A leash would henceforth save a London dog from muzzling, impoundment, and potential death. In Paris, a police ordinance of May 30, 1892, called for dogs to be leashed as well as muzzled after rabies outbreaks.[78] Once again, leashes would contribute to public safety and spare beloved and valuable dogs from impoundment. In early twentieth-century New York, leashed dogs could walk the streets without muzzles. The American Society for the Prevention of Cruelty to Animals therefore urged dog owners to use a leash when walking their pets.[79]

Many owners and animal protectionists now saw the leash as a less repressive technology than the muzzle and a way of safeguarding pet dogs. For some, however, it represented an infringement on their dog's freedom. But overall, owners recognized leashes as a way for dogs to be accepted within the modern city. Like grooming, leashing became a component of responsible pet keeping and—by physically attaching dogs and humans—cemented the difference between pets and strays.[80]

Pet dogs also received some bad press. Critical commentators argued that the pampered, selfish, and spoiled pets of the upper and middle classes consumed too much food, spread diseases, and bit innocent bystanders. British physicians asserted in 1878 that "the pleasure dogs kept by the richer classes are scarcely less a source of danger and extravagance [than those of the poor], for they appear very predisposed to rabies."[81] Dog loathers mocked what they saw as owners' excessive love for their pets. Critics singled out bourgeois women who fawned over their lap and toy dogs, overfeeding and underexercising them. And the supposedly spoiled and pampered pet dogs of wealthy women who dined in fancy restaurants like Sherry's in Manhattan were easy targets for male journalists and commentators. These men attacked what they saw as disproportionate female sentimentality that led women to treat dogs like dolls or children. More damningly, their overbearing love for their pets resulted in an inability to train their dogs effectively. Some female dog lovers also expressed concern. One was so aghast at how overly sentimental female owners spoiled their dogs that she published a book that aimed to correct their ways. These critiques of mawkish and emotionally deficient female pet owners shed light on the unequal gendered dynamics and divisions within the cult of domesticity. Middle-class women were charged with loving and caring for pets (and other members of the household) but were taken to task when their love and care seemed excessive, inappropriate, or harmful. The judgments heaped on them also exposed the fragility of the domestic private sphere by serving up their pet-keeping practices as objects of public deliberation and intrusion. Men may also have been unsettled by female dog owners' close bond with dogs, animals bound up in Victorian notions of masculinity. Female pet-keeping undermined the popular portrayals of hunting, sporting, and pet dogs as companions for men, with dogs and their male owners sharing the emotional qualities of chivalry, loyalty, bravery, steadfastness, and heroism.[82]

Pet keeping lent itself to mockery. But the pet dog nonetheless became the acceptable furry face of human-canine relations in the modern city as well as the deserved object of human attention, love, and compassion. Feelings of hostility therefore intensified against stray dogs, reinforced further by wider denunciations of human vagabondage.

Vagabond Humans and Vagabond Dogs

Rhetoric against stray dogs and human vagrants hardened in the fin-de-siècle period. As the American, British, and French economies struggled, unemployment and inequality rose. In the 1880s, declining prices and other economic woes in France's agricultural sector led desperate rural families to seek a better life in the cities, yet widespread urban unemployment increased begging there. In Britain, meanwhile, the number of homeless people doubled between 1865 and 1895. While there was some sympathy for their plight, tramps were commonly treated as unemployable scroungers who swelled the ranks of the poor deemed unworthy of aid from society. Concerns over increasing immigration levels fueled condemnations of vagrants in New York, where reformers, charity officials, journalists, and others placed them into the category of the undeserving poor.[83] The vagrants "crowding" and "swarming" through the city's streets were "the *enfants terrible* [sic] of civilization," wrote journalist Edward Crapsey. He claimed that "bestial parents" sent out their children each day "from the kennels which are their homes" to wander the streets. So wretched were these child vagrants that they reportedly ate food that even stray dogs refused to eat. Crapsey's less-than-subtle animalization of human vagrants helped underscore the notion that they were separate from respectable society.[84]

The apparent dirtiness, shiftiness, and restless movement of human and canine "vagrants" appeared to reflect and deepen the social problems associated with late nineteenth-century urban life. To their critics, both kinds of "outcasts" seemed flagrantly idle and economically unproductive. As the *New York Times* argued, "Homeless dogs find all the paths of honest canine industry closed to them . . . without any way of making a reputable living they fall in the habits of mendicancy." Like their human counterparts, "the wretched dog tramp . . . waylays people on the street, or sneaks around the back doors of suburban houses, begging for a crust." In anthropomorphizing language, the article derided their lack of "shame." These "mendicant dogs" were even more effective than human beggars in "appealing to our sympathies." Relying on their cunning, they reportedly manipulated passersby into giving them food by pretending to be lame or blind. In a nod to efforts to stamp out human begging, the newspaper called for a "Canine Employment Society" that would "give every vagrant dog an opportunity to become an honest, self-supporting, and moral animal." Similar attitudes were apparent on the other side of the Atlantic. So wily and independent were the "out-and-out gutter-bred street cur[s]" that British journalist James Greenwood declared that they survived by stealing food from butchers and persuading innocent pedestrians to give them a home for the night before running off at dawn to scavenge food waste.[85]

The condemnation of vagabondage intensified the loathing of ownerless strays. Without attachments to humans, vagrant dogs lost their essence. For A.-G. Beaumarié, the stray dog was a "satellite violently separated from its center of attraction [humankind] and evolution." Strays no longer represented their species, just as the human "vagabond" no longer "represented humanity." Without the "restraint" and guidance provided by human companionship, strays gave in to their base feelings. Alfred Barbou denounced their "deplorable behaviour," which included begging for food from cafés and "nocturnal revelling." He compared stray dogs ("the irregulars"; fig. 1.4) to those men who lived "outside society and displayed only limited respect for the law." As if to prove their interchangeability, Barbou suggested that vagabond dogs learned their cunning and "flair for evading the law" from their human counterparts.[86] Like human beggars, strays could not be trusted. They exploited and undermined the human-canine bond, unlike loyal pets, who strengthened it.

Nonetheless, some compassion toward strays survived amid the hardening rhetoric against them. American rural sports publication *Forest and Stream* argued that dogs were hardly responsible if they became "homeless and masterless," especially if they had poor owners. But such sympathy had its limits, and in blaming the poor for vagrant dogs, the magazine once again bound straying to poverty. Once loose on the streets, the dogs drifted into "vagrancy and outlawry," and the "incessant overflow of such vagrant animal life in the great cities" threatened to overwhelm the "health, peace and well being of the public."[87]

Some concern about stray dogs existed in France too. Animal protection-

FIGURE 1.4 *The Irregulars.* From Alfred Barbou, *Le chien* (1883).

ist Adrienne Neyrat claimed that human vagabonds could be hostile to them. She felt aggrieved by how bands of cruel poor children roamed Parisian streets terrorizing strays. Other dog lovers suggested that homeless people tracked these dogs down at night in order to claim a reward from the municipal pound.[88] The veracity of such reports is questionable, but they nonetheless represented a slender slice of sympathy for stray dogs, albeit at the expense of human transients.

But on the whole, fin-de-siècle narratives on both sides of the Atlantic treated strays as degenerate and incorrigible vagabond animals against which the rest of society needed to defend itself. This hardening of hostility toward strays was part of the wider Western problematization of nomadism and other forms of unregulated mobility viewed as threatening the well-being of the modern sedentary population. If human vagrants could expect police harassment, the withdrawal of public assistance, or deportation, strays were destined for impoundment and death. New York–based rural sports and racing journal *Turf, Field and Farm* welcomed this judgment, asserting that as "lazy curs" could "degenerate no further," they deserved elimination. Pet dogs needed protection from them. "A sense of duty to [that] noble and faithful animal," it continued, "should induce us to wipe out the disgrace by purifying the channels of blood." A British commentator similarly stated that "vagabond dogs, like vagabond men, thrive mischievously where they are tolerated. . . . We have nowadays no need for four-footed scavengers, and every master must find his dog or every dog find for himself a master. Unattached the dog is the most deplorable of outcasts."[89]

From this perspective, strays deserved eradication, as they lacked positive emotional connections with humans. Just as journalists and social investigators used emotive words to describe slums, such as *stench, dens, vice,* and *gloom,* to convince readers of the need for urban reform, so commentators' repeated descriptions of strays as vagrant and mendicant cemented their unsavory reputation and justified their exclusion from London, New York, and Paris. These dogs were classified along with free-roaming pigs, cattle, and other creatures as animals whose movement needed to be curbed, thereby creating a more ordered city in line with middle-class visions of urban civilization.[90]

Conclusion

The ever-intensifying feelings of revulsion to strays formed the foundation for building dogopolis. Strays, especially ownerless ones, represented all that was undesirable in dogs and city life, and an increasing number of middle-class urbanites wanted to remove them from the streets to assuage their anxieties about dirt, disorder, disease, and degeneration. Fear about, and revulsion to, strays led to impoundment and official and unofficial violence against them. Concern *about* the plight of stray dogs could still be found among some dog lovers, but this was mainly directed to lost pet dogs at the expense of canines living solely on the streets. Animal protectionists attempted to turn the stray dog into a victim of urbanization who needed human protection. But once again, they often distinguished between stray pets and street dogs. For many dog lovers, any affection for strays was submerged by their concerns *about* straying. Here they converged with dog loathers, as love and affection for dogs during the creation of dogopolis increasingly stuck to the pet and pedigree ones. These dogs conformed with middle-class norms and were considered as the most capable of bonding with humans. They were brought ever more deeply into the practices of middle-class domesticity.

Life on the streets changed for canine outcasts during the nineteenth century. Circumstances differed in each city, with strays subject to impoundment all year round in London and Paris and exposed to the most violence in New York, including being shot at in Central Park and attacked with swords

FIGURE 1.5 *The Pound: Arrival of a Vehicle Containing Dogs*. Photograph by Agence Meurisse, 1919. Bibliothèque nationale de France.

on the Coney Island waterfront in the 1890s.[91] But all three cities had become inhospitable environments. Even so, tougher legislation, impoundment, and hostile attitudes toward vagabondage did not eliminate canine mobility. In Paris, for instance, police introduced innovative impoundment methods. The introduction of horse-drawn (1904) and motorized (1912) vehicles to collect captured strays from the capital's many police posts was intended to make impoundment "more rapid and less onerous." The use of the *panier à salade* (the colloquial term for a police van) helped the police and pound personnel impound strays. The new vehicles apparently enabled the police to make some progress in removing stray dogs from the streets (fig. 1.5). However, the claim of *Le Monde illustré* in 1912 that Paris had been "as good as liberated" from rabies owing to the police's crackdown on strays proved premature, especially since many dog owners abandoned their pets at the outbreak of World War I.[92] Straying continued, and the presence of stray dogs in the cityscapes exposed the difficulty of containing a mobile and fertile population that drew a degree of sympathy from some dog lovers.

CHAPTER 2

Biting

In August 1878, the *New York Times* reported the gruesome death of a popular Yorkville resident, six-year-old John Clark. No detail was spared. John had played regularly with a local German Shepherd who allowed neighborhood children to sit on him and put their fists into his mouth. One day the dog uncharacteristically bit John severely on the face. The wound was washed and then "burned and blackened" with silver nitrate. As news of the attack spread, a crowd of area residents persuaded the local police chief to have his men kill the dog. Life returned to a degree of normality for John until a few days later, when he became ill and refused any liquids. A physician gave powerful sedatives to calm John's nervous system. They had little effect in preventing his spasms or foaming at the mouth. Realizing that the situation was hopeless, the doctor administered chloroform to ensure the boy's peaceful death. Hydrophobia was recorded as the suspected cause of death, and there was some debate as to whether John's intelligent mind had been so shocked by the dog's attack that it caused the disease to develop.[1]

The lengthy article formed part of the extensive press coverage accorded to rabies (also known as hydrophobia) in nineteenth-century New York as well as in London and Paris. It reveals the varied emotions that enveloped the disease: the bite's severing of the bond between boy and dog; the anguish of John and his family; and the possible emotional causes of the disease. The emotions were both individual and collective, from John's personal trauma to the crowd's fear and anger. We also gain a sense of physicians' helplessness before the advent of Pasteur's vaccine, a time when treatments were painful (cauterization

FIGURE 2.1 A mad dog on the run in London. Colored etching by T. L. Busby, 1826. Wellcome Collection, Attribution 4.0 International (CC BY 4.0).

or excision of the wound) or ineffective (including saltwater immersion, quack remedies, "madstones," and the "hair of the dog that bit you").[2]

Fears of biting and rabies were centuries old, and form part of the broader history of anxieties about disease. But they took on a pronounced emotional intensity in nineteenth-century London, New York, and Paris. If press reports are to be believed, the cry of "mad dog" was enough to make more timid pedestrians seek safety indoors and could provoke the more courageous onlookers to attack the animal (fig. 2.1). Invariably depicted as foaming at the mouth, a suspected mad dog sparked curiosity and excitement, capable of commanding large crowds even if the animal turned out to be hungry rather than rabid. While some commentators treated the anxieties surrounding dog bites as a justified response to the horrors of rabies, others dismissed them as excessive, and they deplored and mocked the disproportionate fears spreading from individuals to crowds with violent and unsavory results.[3]

Rabies claimed few lives compared with other diseases, such as cholera, and had little economic impact. But like other diseases in nineteenth-century cities, it raised concerns about rapid urbanization, physical and emotional suffering, social disorder, and death. Rabies' notoriety lay in the intensity of patients' suffering and its incurability. Public hygienists, physicians, journalists, and veterinarians repeatedly noted the "dread" that the disease inspired. "What could be more depressing than the knowledge of being doomed for a certain death, that would only arrive with horrible suffering!!!" pondered two French physicians. For rabies entailed the destruction of the rational and emotionally sound self.[4]

The apprehension about being physically, emotionally, and mentally consumed by rabies cast a shadow over London, New York, and Paris. To contain the disease, veterinarians and public hygienists in each city kept a close eye on developments in the other cities, with key texts translated from French into English and vice versa. More often than not, American physicians and veterinarians turned to their European counterparts for guidance.[5] Louis Pasteur's rabies vaccine, announced with much fanfare in 1885, heralded a transnational transformation in the understanding and treatment of the disease, and his methods were debated and copied in London and New York. As well as being a symbol of medical progress, supportive commentators presented his vaccine as a way of calming rabies anxieties. However, Pasteur's breakthrough did not fully quell the intense emotions stirred by the disease, and fears of dog bites persisted.

Throughout this period, fiery debates erupted about the effectiveness and ethics of muzzling. Supporters of muzzling viewed it as a necessary and rational measure to contain rabies and the anxieties it provoked. Opponents of the practice denounced it as a cruel, unnecessary, and dangerous practice that severed the bond between humans and dogs, causing the latter species much pain and contributing to the spread of rabies. Canine biting stirred emotions. Finding a way to contain its lethal potential and emotional impact was integral to the emergence of dogopolis.

Before continuing, it is worth noting that contemporaries sometimes used *rabies* and *hydrophobia* interchangeably to refer to the disease in animals and humans. Occasionally, however, they used *rabies* only when discussing the disease in dogs, reserving *hydrophobia* for discussions of the disease in humans. With the rise of germ theory at the end of the nineteenth century, *rabies* gradually replaced *hydrophobia*. For simplicity's sake, I will use *rabies* to refer to the disease in both humans and animals unless I am directly quoting from a historical source.[6]

The Horrors of Biting

Biting was a lacerating affront to the narrative that dogs loved humans. Canine aggression toward humans challenged the assumption that domestication had tamed the wild beast within dogs, perhaps reviving fears of wolves and other wild animals. Dogs, especially their jaws and teeth, had helped humans hunt for thousands of years. This heritage made them all too suited to spreading rabies, according to American physician Thomas Blatchford. The teeth of dogs and (wolves) "fitt[ed] them in a wonderful manner for seizing and holding their prey, and for rending and tearing flesh." Bites wounded, disfigured, and traumatized and, through mixing infected saliva with human flesh, spread rabies. For veterinarian William Youatt, rabies was "chiefly propagated by the dog, because with him the teeth are the natural weapons of offence." Once rabid, the dog has a "strange and irrepressible disposition to bite," allowing the "virus," with its "fatal energy," to spread.[7]

Some rabies experts had intimate experience with biting. The father of Louis-François Trolliet, a professor of clinical medicine, had been bitten by a suspected rabid dog. Trolliet *père* lost his appetite, could not sleep, and became delirious.[8] Bites had an uneven impact in that not everyone bitten by a rabid dog would inevitably succumb to the disease. Clothing might wipe the saliva off the dog's teeth and so lessen the risk of rabies transmission, and being bitten on the foot or lower leg was less dangerous than a bite on or near the head. But these facts were hardly sufficient to quell the public's fears.

Bites were not the only means of rabies transmission. The disease might enter the human body through a wound, an ulcer, or any other opening in the skin through less intrusive forms of contact. Youatt recounted cases in which humans had contracted rabies from dogs licking their mouth. The day after a nobleman's pet dog had licked his face and "insinuated his tongue" into his mouth, the dog displayed rabid symptoms. Licks, like bites, led to painful treatments. On Youatt's recommendation, a caustic was applied to the nobleman's tongue, lips, and palate "with great severity." More often than not, however, male physicians noted how women's overly sentimental feelings toward dogs placed them in particular danger of contracting rabies through licks and kisses. British surgeon Henry Sully recounted how "the elegant and accomplished Mrs Duff" allowed her beloved French poodle to lick a pimple on her chin and subsequently died from rabies. A Scottish Terrier who reportedly suckled their owner to remove milk from her breasts after her child was stillborn bit her hand, leading to her painful and protracted death, according to one American physician. True or not, these accounts show how women were more exposed to dog bites in the home than on the street due to the cultural restrictions placed on women's movement through public space. They also acted as gendered warnings that maternal love, for all its importance, needed to be controlled: dangers awaited when women's "potentially excessive emotionality" crossed species boundaries. Loving dogs excessively could be hazardous.[9]

Pet dogs in the home, unlike dogs on the street, posed a particular threat. French veterinarian and rabies authority Henri Bouley warned that a pet dog in the early stages of rabies was often drawn to their owner for affection and emotional succor. They might spread the disease through licks if the owner had a cut on his or her skin. Beware such "poisoned kisses," he warned his readers. Although experts and the press mainly blamed strays for disseminating rabies, a canine companion's loving contact with their owner could prove fatal. By bringing this disease into the home, rabid pet dogs threatened their owners' lives, and they disrupted the middle-class cult of domesticity and the emotional habits of pet keeping.[10]

However it was contracted, the disease had fearsome symptoms. Physicians and veterinarians recounted its gruesome, distressing, and often drawn-out stages in wide-ranging detail. Rabies caused emotional as well as physical pain. The aversion to water was perhaps its most dreaded and infamous aspect. Physicians and veterinarians outlined extensively the rabid patients' inability to drink water and the seizures and pain they experienced when attempting this once simple action. Similarly, the madness experienced by patients was much noted. Readers of the *Times* of London during the rabies scare of 1830 could learn about the "peculiar state of excitement of the nervous system," during which the "patient is pursued by a thousand fancies that intrude themselves upon the mind." In cultures celebrating the "manly will" that allowed middle-class men to control their bodies, minds, emotions, and sexual urges, rabies' ravaging of rationality posed an existential threat.[11]

Other emotional symptoms were also disturbing. The victims' "morale" changed, and they became "depressed, lonely, quieter and listless." Some of the afflicted fretted about the bite, and many became "irritable and ill tempered." They became distant and aggressive toward their family and friends. Experiencing an "exciting rage," some bit their loved ones and carers. In such instances, the disease seemingly destroyed the civilized self, turning the patient into a vicious wild animal. New York physician J. H. Griscom recorded one rabies patient's "terror and distress." When a nurse bought him a glass of water and an opium pill to calm his nerves, he "started up in a violent rage to spring at the throat of the nurse, spitting vehemently, with furious voice and gestures."[12]

Many physicians stressed that combating the disease necessitated an attentive and reassuring emotional management of the patient. Trolliet argued that because rabies was a disease of the nervous system, the patient should avoid exposure to strong sunlight and winds, along with abstaining from alcoholic drinks and smelly food. People looking after the patient should avoid anything that might cause a "disturbance of the soul" (*vive affection d'âme*). French veterinarian and animal protectionist M. E. Decroix believed that the best way to cure rabies was to remove the patient from all "sources of excitation" and give "nature the time to combat and sometimes defeat" the disease, in which the "imagination plays an important role." It was the physician's job to keep the hydrophobic patient calm and avoid words, such as *dog*, *bite*, or *water*, that might cause distress. Rabies authority George Fleming, too, placed much importance on the physician's "moral influence" in soothing the "patient's anxiety," as "mental emotions" affected the development of the disease.[13]

The horror of rabies justified overtreatment. Bouley advocated administering physically useless remedies if they served to calm the "terrors of apprehension." Horatio Bigelow duly repeated his advice: "no one would be accused of charlatanism who ordered his patient a placebo . . . which would induce mental quietude." The patient's sensitivity and character needed to be considered. Gordon Stables recommended that a "nervous subject" be given a "short alterative course of mercury, followed by tonics, exercise in the open air, and the Turkish bath, with plenty of amusement and genial society."[14] Tending to patients entailed attentiveness and a firm supervision of the disturbing emotions brought about by the disease.

Pain and madness were the forerunners of a certain and horrific death. According to one *Times* correspondent, "A man condemned to be hanged for his crimes is an object of envy compared to one under the tortures of hydrophobia." She urged the paper to publish examples of rabies deaths in "all their horrible" detail to spur physicians to find a cure. The *Times* duly obliged by publishing such a case directly after the letter. But some commentators criticized the lengthy press descriptions of rabies for stoking fears of the disease, echoing broader fears that reading such accounts could generate unwholesome emotions, especially among working-class readers.[15]

Biting unsettled dog lovers, as it threatened the human-canine bond. For veterinarians and physicians, it produced a troubling disease that required observation and management. For dog loathers, it provided ample evidence that dogs should be tightly controlled, if not eradicated, within the modernizing cityscape. Biting and rabies were emotionally intense topics, and they fueled discussions about human and canine emotional fragility.

Rabid Emotions

For much of the nineteenth century, the theory that rabies generated spontaneously jostled with the one holding that it was spread through a poison or virus. The spontaneous generation theory stressed the communality of human and canine emotions: emotional sensitivity made both species susceptible to the disease. Some physicians controversially argued that rabies was a *purely* emotional disease. Eminent Parisian doctor Édouard-François-Marie Bosquillon set the tone in 1802 when he confidently declared that rabies in humans was caused solely by terror. His observation that individuals were struck with rabid symptoms, including "loss of reason" and "convulsive movements," at the sight of a mad dog provided sufficient proof. Horror-inducing tales of rabies, fed to children from a young age, created fertile conditions for the development of the disease, particularly in "credulous, timid and melancholic" people. Gaspard Girard, Robert White, William Dick, J.-G.-A. Faugére-Dubourg, and Charles K. Mills developed this line of argument as the century progressed.[16]

In the 1870s, alienists (otherwise known as psychiatrists) lent greater intellectual credibility to theories of rabies' emotional etiology. They stressed the powerful sway that emotions and the mind held over individuals, especially in the enervating conditions of modern life. Physician Daniel Hack Tuke, a prominent British authority on mental disorders whose work was published in the United States, recognized that rabies could in some cases be transmitted by dogs to humans through biting and "morbid saliva." But he emphasized his belief that disturbing emotions and images could create rabid symptoms in susceptible individuals. Drawing from French examples, he argued that "such cases illustrate the remarkable influence exerted upon the body by what is popularly understood as the Imagination." The very act of being bitten by a dog and the "fearful anticipation of the disease" were enough to spark "hydrophobia," even if the dog was not rabid.[17]

Tuke suggested that, in some cases, excitement or other forms of mental, emotional, and sensory overstimulation could activate the virus years after a bite from a rabid dog. He drew from a striking case in the United States, as reported by the London *Daily Telegraph* in 1872. A farmer's daughter had been bitten by a farm dog when choosing chickens for slaughter. The wound healed, and no signs of rabies appeared until her wedding day two months later. The "mental excitement" of this life-changing event brought on a dread of water. After the ceremony, she experienced spasms and "died in her husband's arms." Tuke reproduced the newspaper's view—and more generalized gendered assumptions about female emotional delicacy—that such "nervous excitement" had a profound influence on the "gentler" sex, no doubt exacerbated by anticipation of her impending wedding night, which was often framed as an emotionally fraught sexual experience for women.[18]

The British alienists' depiction of rabies/hydrophobia as a predominantly emotional disorder made its way across the Atlantic. In the mid-1870s, Dr. William A. Hammond, president of the New York Neurological Society and leading American authority on mental disorders, stated that the evidence from Europe suggested that heightened emotions could cause rabies in humans. New York physicians and neurologists debated whether certain individuals had died from actual rabies or fears of the disease, and they discussed how fear could transform a bite from a healthy animal into a fatal accident. These theories cemented rabies as an emotionally charged disease and reinforced the dangers of dog bites: even a bite from a healthy dog could trigger a lethal neurological reaction in the swelling ranks of anxious urbanites.[19] But for dog lovers, these theories were potentially useful as they turned *human* fears of dog bites into the main issue to be addressed, not dogs themselves. Overactive human imaginations and nervous systems were the main problem.

Meanwhile, some physicians and veterinarians treated rabies as an emotional disease in dogs, linking it to their temperament and experiences. Proponents of spontaneous generation argued that excessive and disturbing emotions could foster the disease in dogs. British veterinarian Edward Mayhew's widely read book argued that dogs' "temperament" was one of "excessive irritability." They were under the sway of their highly developed nervous system, and their brains were constantly active: "no animal is more actuated by the power of the imagination." Rabies was a prime example of a canine disease of "nervous excitability," with afflicted dogs experiencing delirium and visions, just like human victims.[20]

Thomas Blatchford seems to have plagiarized Mayhew, bringing his ideas to American readers. Rabies arose from the canine "temperament" of "excessive irritability," he stated. Dogs' acute senses, active brains, highly developed nervous systems, and propensity toward anger meant that the rabies virus developed in their organs. Anger in some dogs was "so strong that they are enraged by the most trifling cause, so that they are constantly in a state bordering on madness."[21] Certain dogs were on an emotional knife-edge and could easily become rabid.

Sexual frustration joined anger and fear as a canine rabies trigger. Using animals as explanatory models for human bodies, French physician Julien-

Joseph Virey had highlighted the dangers of female celibacy in the early nineteenth century, arguing that it led to emotional disturbances, including spasms, "rage," and oversensitivity. French physicians François-Joseph Bachelet and Casimir Froussart applied such gendered thinking on the disruptive power of sexual organs and on the dangers of unfilled sexual desires to rabies. They asserted that sexual abstinence caused sexual and emotional disorders in humans as well as rabies-like symptoms, such as "sadness, despondency, fear of liquids, foaming saliva, grinding of teeth and a desire to bite." Canine sexual continence, more worryingly, led to actual rabies. In short, spontaneous rabies in dogs lay "solely in the privation of reproductive functions." A controversial report by M. Leblanc *fils* backed up this claim: rabies had developed in one unfortunate dog due to his frustrated sexual desires toward his mother, who was in heat.[22]

This theory connecting rabies with sexual privation informed official thinking. An 1878 French police report noted that canine "cerebral irritation" arising from "dissatisfaction," especially in the genitals, could foster the disease. "Testicles and ovaries can only produce worrying effects, violent desires, dissatisfaction, irritations, heightened anger, violence [and] sorrows," it noted. Physical and emotional conflicts were most likely to produce the disease in intelligent and sensitive dogs. Confining bitches in heat and neutering both sexes would prevent the disease developing, the report recommended. Bachelet and Froussart also endorsed canine castration. If done at a young age, it would cause little pain or emotional distress to the dogs, and although it might reduce their physical strength, it would not sap their "courage." British rabies experts concurred with French theories that sexual excitement could lead to rabies, but they could not bring themselves to recommend castration.[23]

Rather than seeing dogs as inherently emotionally unstable, dog lovers defended their steady and amenable temperaments and worried that cruelty might cause emotionally sound dogs to appear mad. Human provocation of dogs made them irritable and savage, exposing them to accusations of being rabid and the violence that entailed. "Dogs know when they are being laughed at," many dog lovers believed. While some might "walk out of the room in a huff," others turned to biting. Humans' bad treatment of dogs turned the "friend of man into his enemy." Wealthy owners should therefore take care to shield their dog from mischievous children and thoughtless servants to preserve their good nature and keep them safe, warned the *Pall Mall Gazette* of London. In their campaigns against cruel and unwholesome practices, such as dogcarts and dogfighting, British animal protectionists mobilized the belief that ill treatment of dogs among the working class could generate rabies.[24]

Dog lovers used the belief that rabies had emotional roots as further evidence of the need to treat dogs as emotional creatures and to shower them with compassion. Treating dogs with kindness would soothe canine emotions and so prevent rabies from taking hold. Alongside Darwinian theories of animal emotions and the affective narratives of pet keeping, as discussed in chapter 1, the existence of rabies seemingly confirmed that dogs were deeply emotional animals. In a similar vein, physicians, veterinarians, and public authorities presented a granular awareness of varied canine emotions as a line of defense against the disease and a way of dampening public anxiety.

Identifying Rabid Dogs

Newspapers, medical and dog care books, and police regulations all explained how to recognize a rabid dog. Official advice from the New York Health Department encouraged urbanites to pay attention to a sick dog's emotional distress, including their "RESTLESS" behavior, "DEPRAVED APPETITE . . . [and] DELUSION OF THE SENSES." Wise pedestrians would inform themselves on the physical characteristics of canine rabies. Dribbling, agitation, staggering, biting, convulsing, and howling dogs with shining eyes and their tail held between their legs should be avoided at all costs.[25]

A heightened awareness of canine emotional changes would enable owners and other urbanites to be alert to the two different types of rabies: dumb and furious. Giving evidence to the Committee on the Bill to Prevent the Spreading of Canine Madness in 1830, William Youatt explained that "furious madness" was easier to spot due to its growing emotional intensity. A marked "crossness" overcame the dog: "The eye becomes bright; there is a glare which is seen in no other disease, and in a large dog it is terrifying." Youatt claimed an insight into the pathological canine mind. The dog "labours under some delirium, watching imaginary objects, snapping at them, flying at them." Aggression overwhelmed the animal. Leading French veterinarian Henri Bouley observed such dogs held in cages at Alfort veterinary school; he, too, claimed an understanding of canine minds. The dogs switched rapidly between calmness and excitability. In the latter state, they would bite and rush "towards imaginary beings," and try to attack fellow dogs, who according to Bouley feared their mad canine companions and would seek to escape. Following the lead of Bouley, Youatt, and other experts, the press noted the emotional disturbances of the rabid dog, who "grows peevish and sullen,"

FIGURE 2.2 Furious rabies depicted in George Fleming, *Rabies and Hydrophobia* (1872). Wellcome Collection, Attribution 4.0 International (CC BY 4.0).

"angry," and "wild," while George Fleming provided his readers with a visual depiction of a dog stricken with furious rabies. With a wild look in their eyes and foam dripping from their jaws, this was a dog to avoid (fig. 2.2).[26]

The rabid dog became a creature who no longer conformed to how a dog should normally act and feel. For English sports writer John Henry Walsh "the first and most marked is a change of disposition and temper, so that the naturally good tempered dog becomes morose and snappish, and those which are usually fondling in their manners are shy and retiring." He witnessed this transformation firsthand when his Newfoundland contracted rabies. Owners' "emotional familiarity" with their pet dogs would potentially save them from rabies. They needed to closely observe changes in their dogs' disposition and be alert to rabid-like emotions, advice that was echoed in official French guidance.[27]

Deciding whether a dog was mad was no easy task, especially as so few people had clapped eyes on one who was certifiably rabid. Many physicians and veterinarians had never seen an actual rabid dog, and even those who had required an autopsy to confirm their suspicions.[28] The difficulty of identifying a rabid dog combined with the number of dogs roaming the streets of London, New York, and Paris did much to stoke fears of rabies and dog bites. The authorities in each city took steps to dampen anxieties and contain biting.

Teeth Blunting

One strategy to reduce the risk of bites was teeth blunting. In the 1870s, French veterinarian, public hygienist, and animal protectionist M. J. Bourrel advised blunting the flesh-tearing teeth of dogs. Converting their carnivorous teeth into those of herbivores would remove the threat of rabies. According to Bourrel, filing a dog's teeth was a quick and painless task, without any long-term side effects. To those who labeled the procedure barbarous, he countered that it was far preferable to the slaughter of dogs. But despite having received a medal from the Société protectrice des animaux (Animal Protection Society), Bourrel struggled to win over the Paris police and the veterinarians at Alfort veterinary school. Much to his annoyance, some of his French veterinary colleagues attacked his suggestion outright, declaring it impossible to file down the teeth of thousands of dogs.[29]

But Bourrel's idea traveled. New York sanitary inspector Charles P. Russel described his method as a "useful measure," and the New York Neurological Society was in favor: it displayed a dog with blunted teeth at one of its meetings. Fleming, too, argued that it could be useful as long as the dogs did not require pointed teeth to fulfill the tasks assigned them, such as hunting.[30] But despite this transnational support, the widespread filing of canine teeth did not materialize. Instead, the muzzle became the main way to constrain biting and alleviate the public's fears of rabies.

Supporting Muzzles

Muzzling advocates placed much faith in the power of leather and metal to restrain dogs' jaws. In theory, muzzling would calm fears of biting and prevent the spread of rabies. But its introduction did not pan out smoothly, and in an echo of mid-nineteenth-century British debates about the ethics and effectiveness of restraining measures in asylums, muzzling raised concerns. It was unclear whether the practice meshed with middle-class humanitarian concerns over cruelty to dogs.[31]

For a start, there was no consensus on when muzzling regulations should apply. Although many physicians disputed the popular assumption that rabies was more prevalent during hot weather, city authorities tended to introduce muzzling regulations in the summer months. Parisian police authorities reissued their ordinance of May 3, 1813, throughout the 1820s. It stated that dogs must be "locked up, muzzled or kept on a lead" or else destroyed. Although the measures applied all year round, the police issued the ordinances during the summer. These measures were reinforced by the ordinance of May 27, 1845 (see chapter 1). It ordered that all dogs on the street, leashed or not, wear a muzzle and collar or risk impoundment and death. Dogs who had bitten other dogs or humans were to be sent to the Alfort veterinary school for observation and, if necessary, destruction. Police prefects republished this order in the summer months up until 1878. Letters sent to the police prefect supported the use of muzzles to keep Parisians safe, with some correspondents suggesting improvements to the muzzling technology. For as well as spreading rabies, "atrocious bites" from large dogs endangered everyone, especially children.[32]

In New York, municipal authorities had passed ordinances against unmuzzled dogs since at least the 1830s. Unlike Paris, the laws only applied in the summer months. In July 1848, mayor William Frederick Havemeyer authorized the killing of unmuzzled stray dogs below Forty-Second Street. With the police paying a reward for each dead dog brought to their stations, this order unleashed the "Great Dog War." The *New York Herald* suggested that unscrupulous bands of dog-hunting boys roamed the streets, removing muzzles from dogs to collect the reward. With the opening of the pound each summer, unmuzzled dogs found themselves liable to impoundment as mayors reissued anti-straying and anti-muzzling ordinances each May or June. The creation of New York's Board of Health in 1866 gave fresh impetus to attempts to regulate nuisance animals. An 1867 law banned unmuzzled dogs from roaming the streets, and one in 1869 allowed the police to shoot any dog who looked rabid.[33] Policemen now had to judge whether a dog was rabid and act accordingly. Given the difficulty of identifying rabid dogs, and the emotionally charged scenes that ensued when a mad dog was spotted on the streets, the possibility for error was considerable.

In London, the Metropolitan Police Act of 1839 stated that the police should fine "every person who shall . . . suffer to be at large any unmuzzled ferocious dog, or set on or urge any dog or other animal to attack, worry, or put in fear any person, horse, or other animal." Muzzling, then, aimed to prevent physical and emotional harm to both humans and animals. Muzzling orders led to fines against owners, such as Mr. Moreby of Poland Street, Soho, whose unmuzzled dog bit John Clarke in 1867. Moreby's claim that his dog was usually calm did not sway the magistrate. But assertions that a dog's character was generally amenable could be convincing. Also in 1867, a magistrate dismissed the summons against John Pelman, a goldbeater from Walworth, whose unmuzzled Newfoundland had badly bitten the left ear of fourteen-year-old William Kebill. Pelman's response to Kebill's mother's understandable concerns that the dog could have torn off her son's ear—"That is of less consequence than a leg or an arm"—was hardly apologetic. But the dog was brought to the magistrate's court to prove their normally placid character, and the charges were dropped. Critics attacked this loophole in the law.[34]

The Metropolitan Streets Act, introduced on August 20, 1867, expanded muzzling in London. As police commissioner Sir Richard Mayne explained to the House of Commons, it was extremely hard for the police to find and fine the owners of unmuzzled and ferocious dogs under the 1839 act. Under the new legislation, he could issue a notice that dogs be muzzled on the streets when not led by their owner. The dog's comfort was to be taken into account, as the muzzle should allow it to breathe and drink freely. The unmuzzled and straying dog would be detained by the police until their owner arrived with a muzzle and paid the detainment expenses. Magistrates were also empowered to order a dog destroyed if the animal bit someone or attempted to do so. Middle-class dog owners largely welcomed the act, even if some worried that their dog might get caught up in the roundup of unmuzzled ones.[35]

Expert opinions legitimated muzzling. In 1878 Thomas Dolan, a British physician and poor law medical officer based in the Yorkshire town of Halifax, led a committee that supported the muzzling of dogs during rabies outbreaks. He urged the use of a modified version of the French Grauhan muzzle, as it allowed the dog to breathe. With some hesitation and after weighing evidence from Berlin, Brussels, Paris, and Toulouse, Fleming supported the use of well-designed and carefully fitted muzzles when rabies was epidemic, drawing heavily from Bouley's arguments (fig. 2.3).[36] As in New York and Paris, muzzling promised to dampen fears of the disease through human management of biting. But the muzzling edicts drew much criticism. Rather than settling emotions, they sparked them.

Opposing Muzzles

Critics of muzzling branded the devices cruel and dangerous. When Mayne issued muzzling orders under the 1867 act, he met with accusations of heavy-handedness. The press speculated that the public would vehemently disagree with the impoundment of unmuzzled dogs and that confrontations might ensue. Leading British dog expert Gordon Stables labeled the muzzle

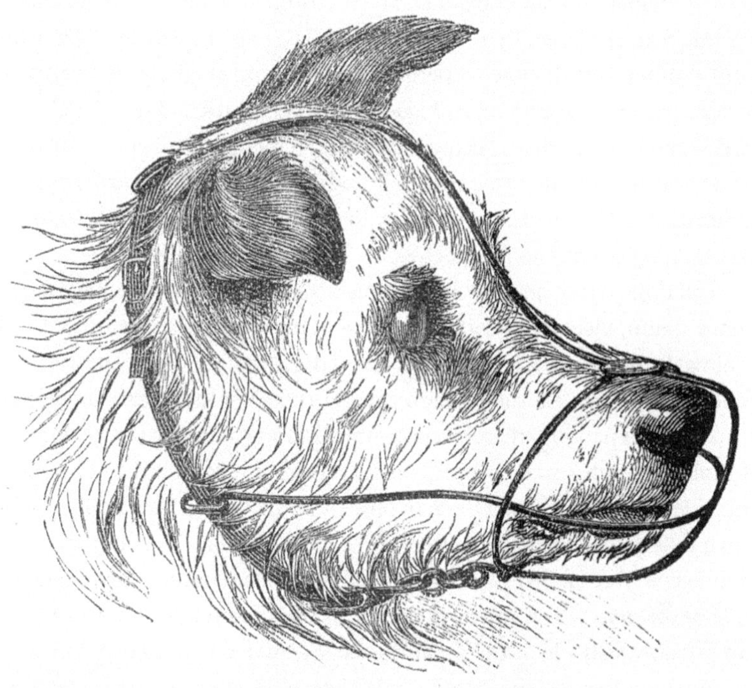

FIGURE 2.3 An example of a well-designed muzzle. From George Fleming, *Rabies and Hydrophobia* (1872). Wellcome Collection, Attribution 4.0 International (CC BY 4.0).

"disfiguring and cruel" as well as a grievous obstacle to the dog's ability to breathe. One correspondent to the *Daily Telegraph* dubbed the new law a form of "exquisite torture" before going on to lament over how a policeman had seemingly scapegoated his unmuzzled Newfoundland outside his home. As a wealthy owner of a pedigree pet dog, "Snarleyow" was surprised and horrified that the policeman had targeted his taxed dog while "vagabond curs" roamed the streets of Peckham. In what quickly became a widespread critique of muzzles, Snarleyow argued that the devices would promote the spontaneous generation of rabies by distressing dogs. George Jesse founded the Association for the Protection of Dogs and Prevention of Hydrophobia with the aim of ending the muzzling of dogs. Mayne himself expressed some concerns about the practice. He attacked the tin muzzles used in Paris, noting that many people believed that the contraptions could drive a dog mad.[37]

Cruelty to dogs also lay at the heart of the anti-muzzling stance in France and the United States. Bourrel observed that for the muzzle to work, it would have to be so tightly fastened to the dog that it would cause it such pain as to be "repugnant to our enlightened civilization." The muzzled dog's suffering was real, as shown by their disfigured face and "expression." Drawing from another French rabies expert (Bouley), Russel similarly attacked New York's muzzling law as cruel and likely to trigger rabies in dogs who already carried the virus. Perhaps keen to differentiate themselves from the medical professionals who supported muzzling and to assert their own expertise and authority, the New York Neurological Society passed a resolution denouncing muzzling as cruel and ineffective.[38]

In all three cities, animal protectionists joined the anti-muzzling stance. Henry Blatin, vice president of the Société protectrice des animaux (SPA [Animal Protection Society]), condemned the muzzle as one of the cruelties inflicted on animals in the modern age. It prevented them from breathing, drinking, and panting, thereby contributing to the spontaneous generation of rabies. French animal protectionists reported how muzzles tormented once friendly dogs, causing them to bite for hours on end. According to veterinary surgeon and SPA member M. L. Prangé, dogs, like humans, were born to live "free and without constraint" and did not deserve to be coerced "*à la prussienne*"—a pointed reference to the muzzling of dogs in Berlin and possibly a sly dig at the authoritarian Second Empire. For SPA member Eugène Meunier, meanwhile, muzzling evoked the worst excesses of France's revolutionary period. Suggesting that unwarranted fears of rabies had unleashed a "terror" against French dogs, he argued that the enforcement of muzzling orders by the police was actually a ploy to increase the risk of rabies so as to justify their "frenzy of extermination" against Parisian dogs. Muzzling would unleash dangerous emotions and risk public health. But some reluctant pragmatism emerged. In a bid to reduce the suffering caused to dogs, the SPA held competitions to find better muzzles, with members submitting their own designs.[39]

Concerns about cruelty prodded American animal protectionists into action. Using the findings of French and other European rabies experts to bolster his argument, Henry Bergh, president of the American Society for the Prevention of Cruelty to Animals, advised New York mayor John T. Hoffman—via the letters pages of the *New York Times*—that the emotional torments occasioned by muzzles led to the spontaneous generation of rabies, a warning Hoffman ignored. In London, the Royal Society for the Prevention of Cruelty to Animals, for its part, complained about the muzzling of "noble and faithful" dogs during the summer, and it concurred with those dog experts who stressed that muzzles must not "cause pain, or inflammation, or fever in the animal." It lobbied the Metropolitan Police to restrict their use.[40]

In addition to branding muzzling a form of emotional and physical torture, critics highlighted its ineffectiveness. Even pro-muzzlers lamented the many flaws in muzzling regulations. Paris had the oldest and most comprehensive muzzling laws of the three cities, but even these were often inadequate. The police admitted in 1830 that a "large number of [unmuzzled] dogs roam the public highway." Following the cholera epidemic of 1832, Gabriel Delessert, the prefect of police from 1836 to 1848, attempted to reinvigorate police action on everyday public health matters. He encouraged policemen and others charged with enforcing antirabies ordinances to ensure their "strict execution." In particular, he sought to tackle dog owners' "lack of concern." Once again, however, police action was ineffective, and Delessert was criticized for not dealing with the unmuzzled dogs, who "constantly expose[d]" the public to danger. An 1862 report estimated that only 1 in 100 dogs in France wore the muzzle, and many of them incorrectly. Moreover, most rabies cases were transmitted through bites in the home, where the muzzling laws did not apply. The muzzle had little impact in protecting humans from rabid dogs, it concluded.[41]

Against the backdrop of these various inadequacies, the summer of 1878 marked a move away from muzzling. In 1877 five Parisians fell victim to rabies, while twelve contracted it in the first half of 1878. These cases, and complaints from concerned Parisians, galvanized the prefect of police, Albert Gigot, who replaced the 1845 ordinance by publishing a new one on August 6, 1878. It declared that any collarless dog found on the street or any roaming dog of which the "owner is unknown in the locality will be seized and killed without delay." Henceforth, pet dogs that strayed from their owners, and all ownerless dogs, could be destroyed. Unlike the 1845 ordinance, muzzling was not compulsory. Instead, the new ordinance made owners identifiable and responsible for their dog's actions through collars and paved the way for the immediate slaughter of dogs suspected of rabies. These were the new weapons against the disease and a tacit recognition that the previous system of muzzling did not do enough to contain rabies and its associated anxieties.[42]

In New York, critics also highlighted the poor enforcement of muzzling. Newspapers and their readers noted many unmuzzled dogs on the city's streets. A *New York Herald* journalist counted seventy-three such instances from Spring Street to the corner of Broadway and Leonard Street. For Charles P. Russel, muzzling was completely ineffectual. Not only did it trigger the spontaneous generation of rabies, but the whole system was flawed. Dogs went unmuzzled at home, and a rabid dog was hardly likely to "present himself for muzzling as a preliminary to his elopement." Russel pointed to the "special absurdity" of only requiring muzzles in the summer, which was explained solely by the discredited belief that hot weather triggered rabies.[43]

The situation was little better in London. The 1867 Metropolitan Streets Act had multiple weaknesses. Owners could retrieve their dog from the Temporary Home for Lost and Starving Dogs upon producing a muzzle, but there was no guarantee that they would ensure that their pet was muzzled once they left the site. Nor did this legislation order the police to seize all unmuzzled and loose dogs: it merely *empowered* the officers to seize any such dog "found" on the streets. In addition, leashed dogs did not require a muzzle, even if the police commissioner had issued a muzzling order. The police themselves admitted that they lacked the resources to implement the anti-muzzling measure effectively, which, besides, did not apply throughout the whole Metropolitan Police area.[44]

Muzzling received bad press. Anti-muzzlers portrayed it as barbaric and dangerous. Those who adhered to the theory that rabies was a predominately emotional disease saw muzzling as raising the risk of rabies in dogs and stoking human fears of the disease. Dr. William Lauder Lindsay of the Murray Royal Asylum in Perth, Scotland, dismissed all antirabies campaigns as overblown, cruel, and misguided. It would be better, he said, to teach the public that rabies was rare, thereby dampening anxieties, particularly in individuals with "a morbid, or ill-regulated imagination."[45] Pro-muzzlers, for their part, decried the ineffectual muzzling measures that they believed were not up to the task of containing rabies and the fears it generated. Muzzling had stirred plenty of passions, but it failed to tame biting enough to allow the acceptance of dogs within the emerging dogopolis.

The Pasteurization of Rabies

Louis Pasteur's new treatment for rabies promised relief. After a distinguished career tackling a range of issues from beer brewing to silkworm diseases, the renowned scientist and germ theory pioneer turned to that disease in 1880. Along with Charles Chamberland and Émile Roux, Pasteur demonstrated that rabies could be transmitted by inserting infected material into a dog's brain. In 1884 he announced his development of a laboratory strain of rabies. Passing it through monkeys produced an attenuated virus, which he then used to immunize dogs against rabies.

Pasteur turned next to rabies in humans. At a meeting of the National Academy of Medicine in Paris on October 27, 1885, he revealed that he had produced a vaccine that could be administered to humans. His first step had been creating an artificial version of the rabies virus by inoculating infected tissue from a rabid dog into the brains of laboratory rabbits. Passing it through a series of rabbits produced a reliable incubation period of seven days and a "rabies virus of perfect purity," which had a stable virulence. Pasteur then weakened this *virus fixe* by removing the rabbits' spinal cords and hanging them in sterile glass jars. The dried cord was then macerated and mixed with sterile liquid before being injected into the patient. His treatment consisted of giving bite victims progressively stronger doses of the vaccine during the disease's lengthy incubation period to build immunity. He administered the vaccine in 1884 to Joseph Meister, a nine-year-old boy from Alsace who had been badly bitten by a rabid dog and faced certain death. Battling "lively and cruel worries," Pasteur oversaw the inoculation of increasingly strong doses of the vaccine to Meister (Pasteur was not a trained physician, so he could not give the injections himself). The boy survived.[46] Buoyed by this success, Pasteur successfully repeated the procedure on a young shepherd, Jean-Baptiste Jupille.

Despite immediate opposition from a combative and long-standing rival, surgeon Jules Guérin, Pasteur's speech at the National Academy of Medicine was greeted with rapturous applause. The news also delighted the press. Parisian weekly *L'illustration* declared that Pasteur had "definitively triumphed against this evil."[47] Although it carried some risk, Pasteur's procedure offered bite victims a chance of survival. It seemed poised to diminish the anxieties that shrouded rabies.

The public's sense of relief grew when Pasteur declared that he would treat rabies victims for free. Press reports of the calm inoculation of hundreds of rabies sufferers by Pasteur and his team in his laboratory at the École normale supérieure in Paris contrasted with previous accounts of physicians desperately inflicting painful and ineffective procedures on rabies patients. "It was difficult to imagine a more simultaneously grandiose and moving scene in its simplicity," observed *L'illustration* as Pasteur gave a "word of encouragement" to each of his patients. Instead of experiencing fear and anxiety, they left the treatment rooms with "serene" faces. Illustrations of the calm treatment rooms reinforced the sense of relief and hope. So, too, did the front cover image of *Le Don Quichotte* by Gilbert Martin, which depicted Pasteur as an angel calmly vaccinating a wild-eyed rabid dog who violently frothed at the mouth. These soothing images reached New Yorkers via the pages of the *New York Times* and other publications. Pasteur's treatment was also greeted with enthusiasm in Britain. Rabies deaths had reached sixty there in 1885. A rabid dog's biting of five boys in Poplar, East London, all of whom subsequently died, was one of many anxiety-provoking events that created openness to Pasteur's life-saving treatment. Newspapers devoted long and laudatory reports to his method and his offer of free treatment, and veterinarians and other dog experts cautiously welcomed his breakthrough.[48]

But disquieting emotions bubbled up. A visitor to Pasteur's laboratory might experience a pang of "pity" at the sight of the animals on whom he experimented. A dog's whole body "shook with a shudder of terror" before an operation, observed French journalists, and illustrations depicted the "agony and the end" of Pasteur's experimental dogs. Some of the rabies-infected dogs "were uncommonly affectionate, and implored me to take notice of them," reported a *New York Times* journalist.[49]

But such troubling emotions were insignificant compared with the optimism stirred by Pasteur and his treatment. The sense of relief intensified in 1888 with the opening of the Institut Pasteur in Paris, funded by donations. A sense of calm reportedly pervaded Pasteur's new premises. Patients had such confidence in Pasteur and his treatment that they went for inoculation "without the slightest fear." Pasteur's desire to prevent the suffering of children, his evident fondness of Meister and Jupille, and his generosity reinforced his reputation as a caring and committed scientist. Some British physicians who traveled to Paris to see for themselves placed their faith in the treatment because of the underlying scientific theory and method as well as Pasteur's calm and collected character. "He was not a savant who was led away by his enthusiasm," noted a doctor at the annual meeting of the British Medical Association in 1889. "The unwearied care, patience and intelligence" of staff at the institute impressed another.[50] Images of Pasteur as a noble savior of humanity who had conquered rabies reemerged after his death in 1895 (fig. 2.4). The pasteurization of rabies had the potential to neutralize the threat of canine biting and rabies, making the mid-1880s a key episode in the building of dogopolis.

Transnational Pasteurism

International travel strengthened the transnational feelings of elation that swirled around Pasteur. Five dog bite victims traveled from Britain to receive treatment at his institute between November 1885 and January 1886, with an additional seven from Bradford arriving in March 1886 under the auspices of Thomas Whiteside Himes, the town's Medical Officer of Health. They

Le Petit Journal

Le Petit Journal
CHAQUE JOUR 5 CENTIMES
Le Supplément illustré
CHAQUE SEMAINE 5 CENTIMES

SUPPLÉMENT ILLUSTRÉ
Huit pages : CINQ centimes

ABONNEMENTS

	TROIS MOIS	SIX MOIS	UN AN
SEINE ET SEINE-ET-OISE	1 fr.	2 fr.	3 fr. 50
DÉPARTEMENTS	1 fr.	2 fr.	4 fr.
ETRANGER	1 50	2 50	5 fr.

Sixième année — DIMANCHE 13 OCTOBRE 1895 — Numéro 256

A LOUIS PASTEUR

FIGURE 2.4 Louis Pasteur depicted on the front cover of *Le petit journal*, October 13, 1895, shortly after his death. Lithograph by H. Meyer. Wellcome Collection, Attribution 4.0 International (CC BY 4.0).

attracted extensive press coverage, and upon their return Himes promoted Pasteur's treatment to British audiences.[51]

Events in Newark, New Jersey, fanned American interest in Pasteur and his treatment. A public panic followed a suspected mad dog's biting of a group of boys on December 2, 1885. Policemen had taken to shooting suspected mad dogs. But the Newark policeman in this instance was not "an accomplished marksman," noted the *New York Times*, and officers often resorted to finishing off the dogs with clubs. Members of the public were, if anything, worse shots. One man shot his neighbor in the ear while trying to kill a dog. The *New York Times* arguably stirred up panic due to its extensive and sensationalist reporting of the events, yet it also berated the intense emotional responses to the biting. One article stated that "people should get it into their heads that this wretched scare is utterly without reason. There is no epidemic of rabies and no unusual danger." Amid the violence, the bitten boys' physician launched an appeal to raise funds to send them to Paris for treatment. The public obliged, and newspapers picked up the story, recounting in much detail the boys' transatlantic voyage.[52]

The journey to Paris provided further evidence of Pasteur's emotional qualities. "He has a tender and sympathetic heart," gushed the *New York Times* journalist who accompanied the boys. The trip was emotionally charged, from the boys' sympathetic reception among Parisians to the close analysis of their feelings during the treatment. This was an opportunity to foster and display American bravery. A journalist bribed one of the boys, Patrick "Patsey" Reynolds, to be stoic when receiving his injection so as "not to be outdone in pluck by a French boy." Upon their return to the United States, the boys were displayed in a Bowery dime museum, allowing New Yorkers a firsthand encounter with Pasteur's miraculous treatment. Alongside the extensive media coverage, the display led to public excitement about the possibilities of scientific and medical progress.[53]

Some New York physicians were so enthused by Pasteur's breakthrough that they set out to emulate his methods. Foremost among them was the father and son team of Drs. Alexander B. Mott and Valentine Mott, who came from a prestigious line of doctors in that state. Alongside members of New York's Francophone elite, including veterinarian Alexandre Liautard, who had translated Henri Bouley's treatise on rabies, the Motts established the American Pasteur Institute of New-York City in January 1886 to offer free treatment to rabies patients. After initial skepticism from Pasteur, Mott *fils* traveled to the Frenchman's Paris laboratory to learn about the rabies vaccination. After a month's study and observation, he returned with a rabid rabbit and—he believed—sufficient knowledge to start producing the vaccine. However, lacking laboratory training, the Motts struggled to replicate Pasteur's laboratory procedures and to produce the correct sequence of rabbit spinal cords. Valentine Mott's first patient was Harold Newell, a physician's son from Jersey City who had been bitten by an apparently rabid dog. The press held high hopes. But Newell could not complete the course of vaccination due to feeling weak and nervous after the initial injections and injuries sustained from falling down a flight of stairs and cutting his wrist. The initial excitement at Newell's treatment died out. But Mott did succeed in attracting New Yorkers who arrived in "an excessively nervous state," worried that they had contracted rabies. He reassured them and sent them on their way, "happy and contented." The emotional journey from panic to calm was an oft-repeated narrative of the new rabies treatment, and it enhanced the sense of relief that greeted Pasteurism. But the American Pasteur Institute was a small outfit, largely run and funded by the two Motts, and it experienced major financial problems. Mott *père* called on New Yorkers to get behind the institute, but they failed to heed his call. It closed in 1887, having treated a dozen patients.[54] The Motts' experience shows the difficulty in transplanting Pasteur's approach to rabies to the United States.

Three years later, in an unrelated venture, Dr. Paul Gibier, a much-decorated and well-connected French physician and rabies specialist with a large medical practice among New York's French community, founded the New York Pasteur Institute in February 1890. Having worked in prestigious Paris hospitals and the laboratory of the Museum of Natural History, Gibier had trained with Bouley and secured a doctorate from the Paris Faculty of Medicine. After immigrating to the United States, he presented himself as an urbane and kindly ambassador of Pasteurism and European savoir-faire: his institute would bring the benefits of French science to the United States. Unlike the Motts' venture, Gibier's institute was financially secure thanks to a more diverse range of revenue streams, including sales of pharmaceutical products across the United States and, from 1895, six thousand dollars per annum from the New York state government. In 1893 a substantial donation allowed Gibier to open a five-story building on Central Park West and Ninety-Seventh Street containing offices and laboratories, offering Americans the rabies vaccine without the cost and expense of Atlantic travel. At a time when some wealthy New Yorkers sought to reach out across class lines and create philanthropic places for reforming the urban poor and tackling social ills, Gibier stressed at the inauguration of the Pasteur Institute's Manhattan headquarters that the rich had a duty to care for the poor. In this vein, he charged rich patients for the rabies treatment but not poor ones.[55]

Although the closeness of Gibier's relationship with Pasteur is unclear, he had the latter's blessing for his institute, which became a physical manifestation of Pasteurism on American soil. Along with drawing legitimacy from his French connections, Gibier used the institute's resources and its in-house journal to attack anti-Pasteurians, such as Philadelphia physician Charles W. Dulles, as ignorant and dangerous retrogrades. By 1900 the institute had treated 1,367 patients, with nineteen dying (of which Gibier discounted ten, claiming they had arrived too late for effective treatment), yielding a mortality rate of 0.66%. But that year disaster struck when Gibier died in a horse-riding accident in the village of Suffern. The institute journal ceased publication, but the institute itself survived until 1918. Alongside the official Pasteur Institutes established in French colonies, the New York Pasteur Institute brought Pasteur's rabies treatment to new territories, somewhat blunting the fears posed by dog bites.[56]

In contrast, London did not host a Pasteur Institute. Instead, in July 1889 the lord mayor of London established a Mansion House Fund to send poorer Londoners to Paris for the treatment. This was proposed as a more cost-effective scheme, although antivivisectionist campaigns and chauvinism were perhaps the more likely reasons for this policy. Increasing numbers of British patients visited the Pasteur Institute in the 1890s, as its reputation solidified at the expense of other rabies "treatments." Physicians also considered a trip to the Pasteur Institute as an effective way to alleviate the rabies anxieties experienced by the most anxious patients.[57] Sentiments of hope and relief now countered the feelings of rabies-induced dread in all three cities.

Challenging Pasteur

Louis Pasteur's treatment seemed to have tamed biting dogs. But not everyone was convinced. Dissenting voices emerged amid the fanfare that greeted Pasteurian science. Debates raged in the American, British, and French medical, veterinary, and popular press as well as in the meeting halls of learned societies. The New York Academy of Medicine held a debate on rabies on October 16, 1890, at which new and old understandings of the disease were discussed. Prominent neurologist Landon Carter Gray, professor of nervous and mental disease at the New York Polyclinic, argued that serious emotional shocks were the most likely cause of the rare cases of rabies that existed in

New York. He drew from Daniel Hack Tuke's arguments to build his case, and like Tuke, he did not discount the possibility that rabies might be an epizootic disease. Charles Loomis Dana, professor of diseases of the mind and nervous system at New York Post-Graduate Medical School and Hospital, countered his views, arguing that rabies was solely a "microbic disease," even if a specific rabies microbe was yet to be found. Having visited Pasteur, he placed faith in the French scientist's experimental method and manipulation of the disease. He dismissed the "old-wives' tales" emphasizing "the power of the imagination to disorder and annihilate the body," along with the false claims made about hysterical "hydrophobia" killing patients: "the imagination alone cannot fatally inhibit the vital functions." Within the same clinical field, two conceptions of disease clashed—one stressing the power of the mind, the other the power of microbes. Other skeptical American physicians denounced Pasteur's nonmedical background, his laboratory techniques, and his inability to produce firm evidence of the rabies virus that anatomists and pathologists could see and verify for themselves.[58]

The New York debate was part of a national disagreement over Pasteur's innovations. A debate held at the Medical Society of Pennsylvania in the same year featured a heated contest between Dulles and a French professor of pathology, Dr. Ernest Laplace, of the Medico Chirurgical College, Philadelphia. Incensed at Dulles's critique of Pasteur, Laplace accused him of spreading lies. Dulles replied that "he didn't see what right Europeans had to come over here and tell Americans what to do." Anti-Pasteurism exposed the limits of transnational science as the tone of debate turned xenophobic and personal. Elsewhere, Dulles outlined his strident critique of Pasteur's experimental method. He argued that his treatment was dangerous and that its main influence had been to heighten fears of rabies and dogs. Backed by antivivisectionists, he and other anti-Pasteurian physicians continued to assert into the early twentieth century that rabies was a rare and largely emotional phenomenon, caused by overactive imaginations and faulty nerves. The Paris and New York Pasteur Institutes were particular bugbears, commonly depicted as torture chambers for dogs as well as factories that produced poisonous vaccines.[59]

In Britain, the opposition to Pasteur was the latest chapter in protracted medical debates about whether rabies was a predominantly emotional condition. Thomas Dolan, mentioned earlier in the chapter, played a leading role in attacking Pasteur, arguing that his claims were founded on shaky scientific ground. Dolan advised Britain to follow Germany's lead and introduce stricter dog control laws rather than be seduced by Pasteurism. Victor

Horsley, superintendent of the Brown Institution animal research laboratory and a surgeon at the National Hospital for Epilepsy and Nervous Diseases (both in London), passionately opposed Dolan in the *British Medical Journal*. Other believers in the theory that rabies was a largely emotional affliction joined Dolan in attacking the basis of Pasteur's research and its destructive influence. According to the dog-loving novelist writing under the pseudonym Ouida, Pasteur's intervention had heightened fears of rabies. At a time when the number of phobias and phobic patients was soaring alongside an expanding corpus of physicians, psychiatrists, and neurologists offering treatments, she argued that half the cases of "hydrophobia" in humans were the result of "hysteria-epilepsy, brought on by an excited imagination." "Fear" was a far greater illness than rabies, but "unfortunately it does not pay men of science to cure this malady and it does pay them to add to it." A better way to reduce rabies was to honor and protect canine emotional sensitivity. Dogs needed to be unmuzzled and free to indulge their "natural vivacity" and need for "sociability." Muzzles and "physiologists" were the main problems. In the London *Daily Mail*, one "eminent medical man" lamented over how the modern widespread and unfounded fears of microbes had fixated on rabies, which was actually a rare disease caused by fright. The resulting "kynophobia" swamped rational thinking and caused humans to torment dogs through muzzling and other tortures, thereby stoking canine rabies and human fears of the disease.[60]

The fact that some of Pasteur's patients died fueled suspicions about his treatment. Concerns focused on its intensive version, under which patients with multiple bites were given stronger doses of the vaccine. Following the death of one of Pasteur's Russian patients, the British Local Government Board appointed a commission in April 1886 to investigate his treatment, chaired by Sir James Paget and including George Fleming, Horsley, and other medical and veterinary luminaries. The commission submitted its report in June 1887, in the wake of two well-publicized deaths of two British men, Joseph Smith (Goffi) and Arthur Wilde. Despite these deaths, its findings came out in favor of Pasteur's treatment, to the consternation of British anti-Pasteurians.[61]

Pasteur's critics formed transnational alliances. A ferocious French critic, Auguste Lutaud, editor of the *Journal de médecine*, made no excuses for the "passion" with which he debunked the Pasteurian myth. He alleged that the treatment had become "dangerous." The new strains of the rabies virus created by Pasteur caused rather than prevented deaths. Antivivisectionists in Britain, like their French counterparts, were also horrified by the suffering that Pasteur's experimental methods inflicted on animals. Antivivisectionists Lizzy Lind Af Hageby and Leisa Schartau visited the Pasteur Institute and reported that "the light of the vaunted nineteenth-century civilisation seemed far away in this palace of artificial disease and well-paid quackery." They acknowledged that "mad dogs are dangerous, but this danger is nothing compared with that arising from the moral insanity of legally protected animal torturers." They seized on Lutaud's critique, inviting him to speak in London in July 1887, and endorsed his views in their publications.[62]

Citing Lutaud, Surgeon-General C. A. Gordon asserted that rabies was primarily a disease rooted in emotional disturbances. Emotional "self-command" was therefore a more effective treatment of rabies than Pasteur's. The "Pasteurian craze" whipped up fears of rabies, and those who underwent his treatment had their minds and anxieties focused on rabies while being injected with "morbid and morbific matters." Inspiration for anti-Pasteur commentary came from the United States too. British antivivisectionist organization the Victoria Street Society published Dulles's criticisms. From its perspective, the spread of germ theory, despite its slow and fragmented progression, had increased human and canine suffering and driven a wedge between the two species.[63]

The transnational attempts to discredit Pasteur were persistent and dragged on well into the twentieth century. Yet they failed to overturn his theory and method. Rabies came to be increasingly understood within the framework of germ theory, but its emotional charge persisted. Muzzling once again sparked conflict.

Parisian Muzzling Post-Pasteur

The pasteurization of rabies sparked further friction between pro-muzzlers and anti-muzzlers. With some notable exceptions, such as Dolan, pro-muzzlers greeted Pasteur's vaccine with relief. They treated it as a way of soothing anxieties over biting and rabies. In their view, the French scientist was a kindly benefactor whose modern scientific methods would provide a rational way to contain the disease and its emotional impact. For them, Pasteur had dismantled theories of rabies' emotional etiology, proving that muzzling could not provoke rabies and was instead an effective way of preventing its spread. They held this opinion despite Pasteur arguing that muzzles offered "no protection" (he instead suggested mass inoculation).[64] Anti-muzzlers, however, viewed Pasteur as a cruel man whose treatment stoked fears of the disease, and who circulated the erroneous view that rabies was spread by a virus rather than emotional disturbances. Pasteurism was a retrograde step that would increase the suffering of dogs.

Why, then, did muzzling persist? First, Pasteur's treatment was not completely effective, as shown by the death of some of his patients. Second, dog bites, especially to the face, remained dangerous, and delays in receiving the treatment added to the risk of a horrific death from rabies. And finally, the mass vaccination of dogs, Pasteur's preferred option, was deemed too expensive and impractical. Pasteur's treatment shifted, but did not transform, the management of dogs, providing a further reminder of the ambiguous impact of the Pasteurian revolution.[65]

In France, Pasteur's treatment had not quashed fears of rabies or ended the concomitant repression of dogs. Instead, during 1886, dubbed the "the year of rabies," "suspicion and terror" of dogs spread, according to French animal protectionists. Although the aforementioned 1878 ordinance had downgraded the importance of muzzling, police prefect Louis Lépine continued to order the close control of suspect dogs through leashing and muzzling while veterinarians strove to design more effective and less cruel muzzles. Policemen still captured aggressive and potentially rabid dogs, and they continued to receive bites in the process. The physical pain might have felt the same, but they could now go to the Institut Pasteur for the rabies treatment. Images continued to circulate of the institute as a beacon of medical progress against rabies where patients calmly received the vaccination (fig. 2.5).[66]

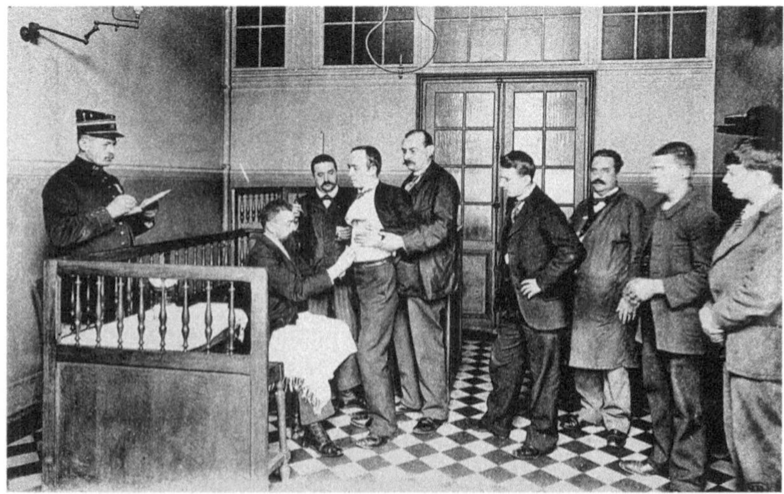

FIGURE 2.5 Inoculation hall at the Institut Pasteur, Paris. Photographic postcard, ca. 1910. Wellcome Collection, Attribution 4.0 International (CC BY 4.0).

If anything, the surveillance of dogs increased, with the police tracking the number of dog bites more closely. In 1892, for instance, dogs bit 999 humans. Of these dogs, 101 were confirmed to be rabid, leading to the death of two Parisians. In further echoes of the pre-Pasteurian era, concerned observers derided the police's ineffectual measures. A major problem, once again, was the unwillingness of dog owners to muzzle their dog or report them if they suspected rabies. Veterinarian Joanny Pertus sympathized with those owners who were loath to obey the law of July 21, 1881, that ordered the death of any dog suspected of being rabid. But he urged them to make this "sacrifice" to preserve their own and others' lives. Commentators made comparisons with other cities. "Docteur Ox," writing in the Paris newspaper *Le matin* in 1902, contrasted the situation in France—ineffectual muzzling and multiple rabies cases—with Britain, where muzzling was more extensive.[67] The tables had turned. London, not Paris, was now at the forefront of the muzzling campaign.

Stamping Out Rabies

Louis Pasteur's breakthrough did not dampen calls during 1885, the year of a rabies epizootic in Britain, to strengthen public health measures against dogs. Fleming supported Pasteur's theories and methods, but he asserted that sanitary measures, such as culling and quarantine, were the only the ways to stamp out rabies and prevent the ensuing panics.[68] Muzzling remained central to the prevention of biting, and it continued to cause divisions and stir passions. On June 14, 1886, Frances Ravell poured water over the head of a policeman who had tried to kill her neighbor's unmuzzled dog. Ravell was arrested and fined, stoking concerns about police heavy-handedness and arbitrariness. To defend her and other owners who ran afoul of the muzzling laws, veterinarian John Woodruffe Hill and George Candy, QC, the senior lawyer who represented Ravell in court, founded the Dog Owners' Protection Association in August 1886. (In 1892 the organization became the National Canine Defence League.) Woodruffe Hill and Candy furthered the long-standing anti-muzzling view that muzzles were cruel and created rabies through spontaneous generation, as rabies was a predominantly emotional disease. They recommended other antirabies measures, such as collars and the registration of dogs, which would serve to differentiate pet dogs from strays. Both men placed their faith in responsible middle-class dog ownership as the most effective public health measure. Unregistered dogs of the poor and street dogs, whom they blamed for spreading rabies, should bear the brunt of repression. The anti-muzzlers continued to treat the muzzle as a device severing the bond between dogs and humans. Prominent antivivisectionist writer and feminist Frances Power Cobbe opposed muzzles because they were "teaching the British public to regard with suspicion, dread, and finally hatred animals whose attachment to mankind has been a source of pure and humanizing pleasure to millions, and which has formed a link . . . between our race and all other tribes of earth and air."[69]

The pro-muzzlers also organized themselves. The Society for the Prevention of Hydrophobia and the Reform of Dog Laws was founded in September 1886 byVictor Horsley alongside biologist T. H. Huxley, zoologist E. Ray Lankester, physicist John Tyndall, and John Lubbock, MP. It opposed fervently the National Canine Defence League. Both sides charged the other with allowing emotion to cloud their judgment. The pro-muzzlers accused their opponents of misguided sentimentality about dogs, while the anti-muzzlers labeled Horsley emotionally unstable and panic stricken. They speculated that vivisection had corrupted his mind. Despite internal divisions, the Royal Society for the Prevention of Cruelty to Animals reluctantly joined the pro-muzzle side, as did the Kennel Club. So, too, did an 1887 House of Lords Select Committee, which took evidence from pro- and anti-muzzlers. It ultimately recommended muzzling when rabies was "prevalent" as well as the slaughter of strays.[70]

Also in 1887, the British government added rabies to the Contagious Diseases (Animals) Act. The Privy Council used this legislation to introduce two nationwide orders on October 1, 1886, and February 28, 1887, which gave local authorities greater powers to order the muzzling of dogs and required rabies cases to be reported. In addition, the council introduced a further muzzling order in London in June 1889, which the Board of Agriculture extended to the rest of the country six months later amid much controversy. The new Liberal government revoked the orders in November 1892, only for rabies outbreaks to recur, leading to their reintroduction in 1896. For government officials, muzzling seemed to work, as the reported number of rabid dogs decreased after the issuing of the orders.

But anti-muzzlers attacked the cruelty of the "muzzle maniacs." Their anger increased when Walter Long, the new Tory president of the Board of Agriculture, set out to eradicate rabies. He introduced further muzzling orders in London and other areas notorious for rabies, such as the North West of England. The order in London (1897) stated that "no dog shall be allowed to be in or on any public place unless such dog is efficiently muzzled with a wire cage muzzle so constructed as to render it impossible for such dog while wearing the same to bite any person or animal, but not so as to prevent such dog from breathing freely or lapping water."[71]

Long's orders stoked controversy. His opponents claimed that the number of reported rabies cases was exaggerated, and they decried the metal muzzles he prescribed. Female dog owners protested that their preferred lapdogs were now lumbered by cruel and restrictive muzzles, while the hunting dogs of rich men enjoyed a muzzle-free life. They likened muzzles to earlier male attempts to restrict female freedom and voices. They and other critics branded the muzzles inhumane and further spurs to rabies fears: "to inoculate a nation with cowardice, terror and fear is to injure it more than any bubonic plague."[72]

But Long stood firm. In September 1897, he introduced quarantine measures, and by 1900 rabies seemed to have been beaten. Outbreaks in South Wales in 1901 and 1902 suggested otherwise. But a case near Llandovery in November 1902 proved to be the last case of indigenous canine rabies reported in Britain. Long heralded the success of muzzling. His detractors minimized his achievement, pointing to more stringent testing measures that, they argued, showed that rabies had always been an extremely rare disease. The leading historians of rabies in Britain, Neil Pemberton and Michael Worboys, suggest that greater expertise and tighter surveillance and control over dogs' movements alongside owners taking more responsibility for their pets were also contributing factors to the stamping out of rabies.[73]

Muzzling and More in New York

American physicians closely followed muzzling measures in Britain. Some suggested that the British model of muzzling and quarantine could eradicate rabies from water-bound areas, such as Staten Island. But in New York, the system of temporary summertime muzzling continued as the main public health measure against rabies. As muzzling continued, complaints once again focused on dogcatchers' corrupt character and their unsavory and cruel methods of capturing unmuzzled dogs. Critics also attacked muzzling for stoking "cynophobia." Like its aforementioned British cousin "kynophobia," this condition afflicted emotionally sensitive individuals whose irrational fear of rabid dogs triggered spurious rabies and led to the unwarranted impoundment and slaughter of dogs. British alienists (psychiatrists), such as Daniel Hack Tuke, had already asserted that fears of rabies could create an imaginary manifestation of the disease. "Hydrophobia-phobia" demonstrated clearly the "action of mind upon mind." As physicians and psychologists on both sides of the Atlantic identified ever-more phobias in the fin de siècle, American dog lovers lamented over how muzzling multiplied fears of dogs. Humans had seemingly taken leave of their senses over canine biting, and dogs bore the brunt of this irrationality.[74]

But change was in the air. In 1894 the American Society for the Prevention of Cruelty to Animals (ASPCA) took responsibility for managing New York's strays and enforcing muzzling regulations. It created its own pound, and its powers were extended to Brooklyn in 1895, cementing its role in policing human-animal relations in New York (since its creation in 1866, it had been policing cruelty to the city's animals). By 1900 it had three "temporary shelters for lost, strayed, or homeless animals" (in Manhattan, Brooklyn, and Staten Island), and it portrayed its dogcatchers as humane and respectable agents who successfully and humanely regulated stray and unmuzzled dogs, in stark contrast to the corrupt dogcatchers of the previous regime.

The city's Department of Health then entered the scene under the leadership of Hermann Biggs, who had traveled to the Pasteur Institute back in 1885 and gained experience working in laboratories in Germany and the United States. Building on his transnational connections and buoyed by the greater acceptance of germ theory, Biggs created a Research Laboratory as part of the Health Department. He sought to integrate bacteriology within the city's public health program through the creation of a diphtheria antitoxin and a rabies vaccination scheme. In 1896 he sent Anna Wessels Williams, a talented bacteriologist at the laboratory, to the Institut Pasteur in Paris to learn about rabies diagnosis and the production of the vaccine. She returned with a rabies virus culture, and by 1898 she had developed ways of producing the rabies vaccine on a larger scale. In 1904 she devised a new technique for identifying Negri bodies, a classic sign of the presence of rabies, in brain tissue, enabling quick diagnosis of rabies through a microscope. With Williams's expertise gaining recognition at home (the American Public Health Association made her chair of the Committee on the Standard Methods for the Diagnosis of Rabies in 1907) and abroad (the laboratory received overseas visitors), the Department of Health expanded its treatment of dog bite victims from 28 individuals in 1900 to an annual average of 900 between 1908 and 1913. Meanwhile, its veterinarians examined ever-increasing numbers of dogs (over 4,600 in 1908). New York's public authorities had begun to take rabies and dog bites seriously, with Biggs determined to challenge the New York Pasteur Institute's expertise and authority on rabies.

But controversy was never far away. The Department of Health's 1903 proposal to muzzle *all* dogs on the city's streets (not just loose ones) brought it into conflict with animal protectionists. They downplayed the threat of rabies and continued to label it a rare and largely imaginary condition. In turn, the Department of Health and other medical professionals accused them of laxness and prioritizing dogs' well-being over human lives. Nonetheless, the establishment of the Research Laboratory cemented the pasteurization of New York City, both consolidating and challenging the groundwork laid by the two private-sector Pasteur Institutes in New York and Paris.[75]

For American Pasteurians, vaccination alone was not enough to tackle rabies, so a groundswell of support for muzzling arose. Despite feeling threatened by the Department of Health's growing dominance of rabies treatment in New York, Dr. George Gibier Rambaud of the city's Pasteur Institute similarly hailed muzzling as a rational and effective measure that had worked in Europe (he highlighted its use in Paris and Britain). Demands for increased muzzling in New York dovetailed with the recommendations issued by the United States Department of Health. Veterinary pathologist George H. Hart called for the muzzling of dogs nationwide, pointing to successful measures in Europe. Anti-muzzlers overlooked the annual rabies deaths of between one hundred and three hundred Americans, along with the "anxiety, mental terror, and suffering" of thousands of bite victims.[76] Human emotional anguish needed to be foregrounded.

Officials challenged the idea that muzzles were cruel and sought to counter the myths surrounding the human-dog bond. They challenged dog lovers' claims that dogs' faithful nature meant that they were not susceptible to rabies: a dog, "quite independent of his moral personality, becomes a menace to the welfare of his immediate associates and indirectly to the entire community." Even loyal and loving dogs posed a potential rabies threat. The emotional pain caused by rabies necessitated muzzling: "the very idea of an injury to the tender, soft skin of a child can not be entertained by a normal mind without causing a shudder."[77] Despite the widespread if incomplete discrediting of rabies' emotional origins, it remained a disease laden with emotional baggage.

Public scares led to calls for more action in New York. Residents of City Island in the Bronx felt terrorized by apparently mad dogs roaming their island in 1907. Echoing earlier concerns over stray dogs (see chapter 1), a resident likened the situation to Constantinople (present-day Istanbul). After a protracted dispute with the ASPCA and as rabies cases rose, in 1908 the city Board of Health succeeded in passing an ordinance requiring the leashing and muzzling of dogs from June to October. It created a dedicated police unit to shoot all loose dogs, many of whom would be strays. The order sparked outrage, but the board hailed it as a success in tackling rabies. American rural sports magazine *Forest and Stream* was far from alone in arguing that the "health, peace and well being of the public" justified the "necessity" of killing "vagrant" dogs. Humanitarian sentiment infused such views. The killing had to be humane, because causing animals to suffer would be "an act of inhumanity," and the spectacle of horrific public deaths would "debase the minds of a certain part of the community and disturb profoundly the larger and sympathetic part of it"[78] (see chapter 3).

Muzzling disputes broke out again in 1914. Rising numbers of rabies cases in the boroughs of Manhattan and Queens prompted health commissioner Sigismund Goldwater to call for year-round muzzling and a new dog pound. The ASPCA and animal protectionists again decried the cruelty of muzzling and accused Goldwater of trying to wipe out dogs in New York. In response, Goldwater declared himself a dog lover but argued that better canine control measures were needed to prevent unnecessary human deaths. He also sought to alleviate the concerns of dog lovers, as well as reproduce the stereotypes of sentimental female dog owners, when he stated that the police would not mobilize against "nervous old ladies carrying toothless lap dogs in their arms."[79]

The tactic of attacking anti-muzzlers' misguided and excessive emotional attachments to dogs once again came to the fore. In this vein, the chief of the Board of Health's Division of Veterinary Diseases, Dr. Archibald McNeill, dismissed resistance to muzzling as arising from "maudlin sentimentality." The city's mayor, the Veterinary Medical Association, and the *New York Times*, among others, backed the tougher muzzling policy, while the Board of Health sought to soothe the anti-muzzlers' concerns about cruelty to dogs. The Dog Lovers' Protective Association's qualms about canine suffering were reportedly assuaged after the board's demonstration of an effective yet gentle muzzle.[80]

The board declared that its tougher measures, including more extensive muzzling, had reduced the numbers of rabies cases. In 1917 only three New Yorkers died from rabies, and none of the victims had been bitten in the city that year. In 1918 there were no rabies cases. Muzzling, and the effective deployment of Pasteur's treatment, had apparently triumphed.[81]

But dogs continued to bite. The Board of Health recorded 2,873 bites in 1917, and the actual figure is likely to have been far higher. A rabies scare in 1937 in the Bronx and Brooklyn led to the imposition of muzzling and leashing orders and the capture of 8,000 strays. Between 1931 and 1937, the Department of Health recorded 135,203 bites from mainly unmuzzled dogs, with 9,011 people receiving the Pasteur treatment as a precautionary measure. The number of deaths remained low: between 1933 and 1937, there was one recorded rabies death.[82]

Rabies was under tighter control in New York, but concerns over biting dogs remained. This was also the case in London and Paris. In the French capital, the police prefect continued to issue edicts to impound and kill unmuzzled dogs. According to the Société protectrice des animaux (SPA [Animal Protection Society]), the edict issued in 1919 after a (contested) spike in bites and rabies cases provoked the "most lively emotions" among dog lovers. After receiving many anxious letters from dog owners, the SPA challenged the legality of the measures. In Britain, rabies cases followed the importation of diseased dogs (although British strays and muzzle order–avoiding British dog owners were often blamed for the outbreaks). In 1919, 140 cases were confirmed, with muzzling orders periodically introduced in affected localities.[83] Rabies and biting had been tamed, but they had not been eliminated.

Conclusion

Dog bites stirred emotions and led to divisiveness in London, New York, and Paris. Rabies—the main problem associated with dog bites—was treated as a deeply emotional disease in terms of its etiology, symptoms, and impact on these cities' residents. Two main emotionally charged stances coalesced around the issue of muzzling. The pro-muzzlers treated the device as a rational way of containing the disease and the dread it inspired. The anti-muzzlers viewed muzzling as cruel and dangerous. Louis Pasteur's rabies vaccine created new and profoundly transnational feelings of hope, relief, and gratitude. But the pasteurization of rabies ultimately hardened the divisions between the pro-muzzlers, who largely embraced his ideas, and the anti-muzzlers, who regarded him and his methods as cruel, misguided, and risky.

The pro-muzzlers reinforced the idea that dogs left to their own devices were too dangerous within the emerging dogopolis. The belief that dogs' biting and straying needed close management became a defining feature of human-dog relations in the modern Western city. Dogs would only be tolerated in London, New York, and Paris as long as the risks they posed to health and security could be contained through scientific knowledge, municipal regulations, and technology. Pro-muzzlers were able to claim some successes, especially in London. But like other risks in modern cities, such as natural disasters, new technologies, diseases, and pollution, those posed by dog bites were mitigated but not eliminated.[84] Nonetheless, Pasteur's vaccine, greater surveillance of dogs, and muzzling had sufficiently blunted the effect of canine biting to allow dogs to be integrated into dogopolis.

Despite its subduing, rabies continued to prompt the calls to remove dogs who did not fit the middle-class visions of a clean, ordered, and respectable city. Most pro- and anti-muzzlers agreed that ownerless stray dogs were dangerous and dirty, and so deserved elimination from the modern metropolis. In this vein, in 1908 the Board of Health branded New York's 150,000 stray dogs a "public nuisance dangerous to life and detrimental to health."[85] The vexed question of how to kill these unwanted creatures in accordance with middle-class humanitarianism is tackled in the next chapter.

CHAPTER 3

Suffering

Encounters with suffering dogs provoked intense emotional responses in London, New York, and Paris. The question of whether or not dogs (and other animals) were capable of suffering had sparked debate for centuries. The disagreements between French philosopher René Descartes and his detractors in the seventeenth century marked a particularly intense episode. According to the Cartesian worldview, animals were machines whose lack of reason and consciousness limited severely their capacity to feel and suffer. Many of the contemporary critics who attacked this perspective drew from their personal observations of suffering animals.[1]

Attitudes toward suffering shifted in the eighteenth century when philosophers and writers celebrated the human capacity to feel sympathy for the pain of others. In a departure from previous religious texts, pain and suffering were no longer considered God-given, necessary, or inevitable. This revolution in feeling was experienced in literature, medicine, and other domains. Middle- and upper-class white Europeans considered themselves to be the most emotionally refined humans and therefore the most sensitive to others' pain. This assumption motivated humanitarian efforts to alleviate the suffering of the poor, oppressed, and defenseless. Then, in the nineteenth century, social upheaval and misery ushered in by industrialization and urbanization gave humanitarian movements an added urgency.[2]

Animal protectionists saw themselves as part of this new humanitarian spirit. Antivivisectionists declared themselves "actuated by sentiment." Emotion acted as the glue that bonded civilized people together and ensured the smooth operation of modern societies. It was sentiment that prevented humans from carrying out quotidian social transgressions—from punching each other to smoking cigars in church—and was the wellspring of antivivisection. In fact, the ability to feel was "the sole safeguard that the individual possesses against the crude and ferocious instincts of the human animal." Sentiment was regarded as the basis of morality, as it tamed humans' potentially bestial natures.[3]

Animal protectionists and antivivisectionists considered dogs to be among those animals who deserved the most sympathy from humans due to their heightened capacity to feel and their close bond with humans. From countless tales of loyal pet dogs to suggestions that canine emotional pain caused rabies, the evidence for canine sensitivity was everywhere. Some dogs were even said to feel compassion for other animals. British veterinarian William Brown recounted the story of a Dandie Dinmont who nursed a cat back to health by tenderly licking a wound on his cheek. Although some animals could be cruel like humans, this dog showed that "there is this possibility of love and pity" in animals.[4]

This chapter explores a central conundrum in the emergence of dogopolis: how to get rid of unwanted straying and biting dogs in a way that chimed with middle-class humanitarian values. The manner in which these dogs were slaughtered had to be sensitive to canine suffering. Early killing methods outside and inside the pounds of New York and Paris as well as the London Dogs' Home were deemed barbaric and at fault for causing immense canine suffering. Change came in the 1870s due to the rise of Darwinism and antivivisection campaigns that highlighted dogs' capacity to suffer, alongside the hardening of attitudes toward strays. Within the emerging dogopolis, there arose an acceptance that a degree of canine suffering at the moment of death was necessary for the health of modern urbanites, as long as the suffering did not overtly challenge humanitarian principles. With most animal protectionists eventually aligning themselves with the assertions of public hygienists and municipal authorities that straying and biting dogs needed to be culled, the search was on for "humane" ways of killing undesirable dogs.

Killing on the Streets

As we saw in chapters 1 and 2, straying and biting dogs sparked anxiety and anger. Emotions ran high, leading to lethal violence, and dogopolis's exclusionary edge emerged. At times, individuals risked injury to confront free-ranging and seemingly rabid dogs. In September 1818, the *Times* of London recounted how "a poor man" named Denford had "bravely met, encountered, and KILLED" a "large and ferocious MAD DOG." Moved by Denford's bravery, which placed him in the hospital after he had been bitten by the dog, "some benevolent Gentleman" opened a subscription to the newspaper for him, which was intended to "stimulate others to similar exertions" in the "cause of humanity."[5] Opposing stray and potentially rabid dogs was thus elevated to a noble and heroic act of bravery for the public good that, in this case, cut across class divisions.

As fears of rabies raged in the summer of 1830, individuals and crowds sought to eliminate suspected rabid dogs from the streets of London and surrounding villages. Anxiety and anger morphed into aggressive action. In Lewisham, a large crowd attempted but failed to kill a foaming and roaming dog. A Clerkenwell constable, meanwhile, killed a stray by whacking it on the head with a metal bar. Elite fears of mob violence sometimes overrode anxieties about straying and led middle-class commentators to condemn the crowds that chased mad dogs, whom they saw as working-class mobs. Surgeon Richard Beal noted that "the senseless cry of mad dogs so often raised in Town does produce the most wanton cruelty to these faithful animals." A working-class man individually attacking a dog was laudable, as in Denford's case. But a working-class crowd was troubling, and it sparked fears of political protests and social unrest.[6]

Anti-stray violence was most intense in New York, reflecting and confirming the city's reputation as a brutal and chaotic place where inequality, racism, anti-immigration sentiments, rumors, and desires for political change fueled riots and violence. In Lower Manhattan in August 1830, a man felled a dog with an axe on Marketfield Street after the latter had harassed men, women, and children in the vicinity. Such activity reached a climax in July 1848 when a city law fixed a bounty on loose dogs. Dogs had nowhere to hide as juvenile dogcatchers reportedly tempted the animals from houses and yards to kill them and claim the fifty-cent reward. This "Great Dog War" was fought along class lines. The *New York Herald* took a partisan view and argued that the entry of "boys of the lower or loafer order" into the "dog-killing business" endangered public order. It reported that these boys, aged five to eighteen years, roamed in gangs ranging from 100 to 150 members, armed with "billets of wood, from the size of a lath up to the size of a piece of timber." The older gang members wielded the larger weapons to "give the finishing blow to the larger dogs." The gangs also threatened tradesmen by slaughtering the dogs of butchers, sausage makers, and apple sellers, and they stole firewood from cartmen as they improvised weapons on the chase. In between killing dogs and claiming their payment, the boys would stand on street corners, holding their bloodstained bludgeons "like the Mexican banditti in search of plunder." After the reported killing of seven hundred dogs in just two days, owners kept their pets close and ownerless dogs had reportedly quit town. The boys, rather than the dogs, had become a frightening presence on the violent streets of New York. But concerns over gangs of "rowdy" boys roaming that city were nothing new, so depictions of juvenile dog killers in 1848 essentially echoed and extended older apprehensions about unruly and aggressive youths.[7]

Perhaps haunted by memories of street violence during Paris's various revolutions, municipal authorities did not encourage citizens to chase and bludgeon strays. Lethal measures against these dogs were more discreet to avoid public outcry. In 1842 Police Prefect Delessert encouraged his police commissioners to distribute colchicine in those places where strays gathered. A Parisian pharmacist prepared this substance, sometimes known as *tue-chien*, derived from autumn crocus/meadow saffron and glory lily plants. Physicians used it to treat gout, but it was also highly toxic in large doses. However, poisoning failed to reduce the number of strays. According to one observer, rabid dogs, having lost their appetite, ignored the poisoned meat, and healthy strays found it unappealing compared with the other morsels available on the street. More worryingly, the poison endangered small children, useful animals, and ragpickers. In Britain, veterinarian and noted rabies authority George Fleming advised the authorities against using poison to combat strays. It could be effective, as he believed (wrongly) that its use in France had demonstrated, but it might harm other dogs and humans.[8]

At times, the Paris police resorted to more extreme action than poisoning. In June 1870, after strays reportedly attacked members of the public, the police shot one dog displaying rabies symptoms in front of hundreds of children in the Ranelagh garden of the wealthy 16th arrondissement. Having become accustomed to treating parks as familial sites of leisure and an extension of the home, Parisians did not expect to be exposed to violence in them.[9]

Killing dogs on the streets affronted middle-class sensibilities and heightened existing qualms about violent crowds and unruly children. The dog pound seemed to offer a more efficient and orderly alternative. It was poised to become a key site in the making of dogopolis by offering a more discreet and efficient way of killing unwanted dogs.

Killing in the Pound: Paris

The pound in Paris was an official site run by the city's police force. Yet the treatment of impounded dogs provoked some outcry in the 1820s. Dog lovers decried the site's existence and called for compassion. One of them even imagined a dog called Grognard making a speech at a police tribunal against the police's "canicide orders." At a time when bourgeois writers celebrated the quasi-spiritual bond between humans and dogs, Grognard's plight was intended to appeal to middle-class sensibilities. Dog lovers also linked the authorities' treatment of strays to the city's violent history. Invoking Paris's recent revolutionary past, one commentator bemoaned the "massacres," implying that the dogs had become the latest victims of ruthless and arbitrary state-condoned violence. Canine suffering was evident in the pound.[10]

However, these isolated protests failed to prevent stray dogs' exposure to violence in the pound and other locations. Private *écorcheurs* (dog renderers) made strays part of Paris's "blood and guts" economy. For instance, the Dusaussois rendering plant at Montfaucon had a dedicated room for processing dogs (and cats). Individual *écorcheurs* would also pay rag and bone collectors as well as dogcatchers to bring them strays. After hanging the dogs, they peeled away their skins and removed the fat to sell to glue makers. According to leading public hygienist Alexandre-Jean-Baptiste Parent-Duchâtelet, this commercial killing of strays was more effective than the pound, with renderers overtaking the police as the main exterminators (they reportedly dispatched ten thousand to twelve thousand canines a year in the mid-1830s). Thousands of dogs became lifeless commodities in accordance with public hygienist norms of improving urban cleanliness and boosting the economy.[11]

Nonetheless, confinement and slaughter within the relatively secluded enclosure of the municipal dog pound remained the main way of eliminating strays in the nineteenth century. Police commissioners were charged with taking bulldogs and valueless stray dogs to an annex pound at 11 boulevard de l'Hôpital, conveniently located near the rendering plant within the La Salpêtrière hospital complex. These dogs were to be killed immediately, while dogs thought to have some value were to be taken to the main pound at rue Guénégaud. The police authorities tried to hide the lethal character of 11 boulevard de l'Hôpital, reminding policemen not to give this address to owners hoping to reclaim their dogs. This system remained in place until 1851 when the prefecture opened a new pound at 13 rue de Pontoise (5th arrondissement) in a former Bernardine convent. No reasons for the secretive nature of 11 boulevard de l'Hôpital are explicitly outlined in police documents. But police authorities may have felt that this killing site would have drawn criticism from the emerging animal protection movement and offend bourgeois sensibilities at a time when cultural norms held that the living should be shielded from the dead. Perhaps public awareness of the location also would have made it even harder for the police to remove dogs from the streets if dog-loving Parisians were aware of their fate. Whatever its rationale, 11 boulevard de l'Hôpital represented a lethal and darker counterpoint to the more celebrated sites of Parisian modernity, such as the arcades.[12]

The growing influence of animal protectionists in the mid-nineteenth century paved the way for a more sustained critique of the pound. Animal protectionists, who came from mainly middle-class backgrounds, cast the pound as a merciless site of incarceration and cruelty. Rejecting the notion that animals were senseless machines, they promoted the view that dogs experienced emotional distress, and they denounced the pound as a site of canine suffering. One member of the Société protectrice des animaux (SPA [Animal Protection Society]) regretted that dogs were kept like "prisoner[s]," with an average of eight to ten to a cage. On busy days, up to thirty dogs were held in the same cage, leading to suffocations.[13] Such suffering was but the tip of the iceberg.

Hanging, the mid-nineteenth-century method of killing in the pound, repulsed humane sentiment. It was an unwanted reminder of capital punishment during the ancien régime. The staging of the drawn-out suffering of the criminal on the gallows had disappeared from French public life with the introduction of the guillotine in the aftermath of the 1789 revolution, partly because legislators worried about the emotional impact on the spectators who gathered around the hanging body. In the 1840s, between 12,000 and 13,000 dogs were killed annually through hanging, and 14,600 reportedly met their end this way between 1865 and 1875. In 1875 the SPA tried to save dogs from hanging by parading the condemned canines in front of a crowd in the pound's courtyard in the hope that onlookers would take pity and rehome them. As *Le Figaro*, a Paris newspaper, noted darkly, it recalled the former tradition of a condemned man being saved if he could find a woman to marry him.[14]

The emotional and sensory impact of hanging dogs required containment. Once the pound moved to 13 rue de Pontoise in 1851 (fig. 3.1), the police prefect ordered the private renderer who carried out the slaughter to "avoid all unnecessary cruelty" and for killing to be conducted in such a way so as not to disturb the neighbors. An illustration in the Paris police archives hints at the work involved in hanging dogs. One man is shown dragging two dogs into the room where the hanging took place; one dog looks fearfully at what awaits them. Another man hangs a dog from a pulley suspended from a wooden beam, and two men cart away dead dogs. The atmosphere is one of grim, but calm and determined, work. The image of life draining out of

FIGURE 3.1 The municipal pound at rue de Pontoise, Paris. Photograph by Agence Meurisse, 1919. Bibliothèque nationale de France.

the dangling dogs starkly challenged celebrations of the human-dog bond. In contrast to the contemporaneous efforts to devise more efficient and humane slaughter in French abattoirs, the hanging of dogs appeared crude and retrograde. A more efficient and humane method of slaughter was required.[15]

Killing in the Pound: New York

From a humanitarian perspective, the situation was no better in the New York pound, where dogs met a watery death. As well as supplying New York with fresh drinking water upon its opening in 1842, the water supply system from nearby Croton facilitated the slaughter of the city's stray dogs. In 1859 a Massachusetts newspaper described how the pound's management kept two barges on the East River, from which workers pushed dogs into a large tank, drowning "200 at a time, a Croton pipe letting the water in." Once the bodies were removed from the tank, a gang of "butchers" removed the dogs' skins for boots and gloves. Dead dogs were also taken to malodorous Barren Island, the dumping ground for much of the city's waste and animal corpses, to have their fat removed. The drowning reportedly started at 5:00 a.m. and finished at 1:30 p.m., the time at which new dogs arrived at the pound. This arrangement could kill over two thousand dogs per week.[16]

By 1877 a new system of drowning was introduced, under which up to forty-eight dogs at a time were herded into a cage and submerged by a crane into the East River. Some dogs were reportedly aware of their fate and put up "a most ferocious and dangerous resistance" (the danger was presumably for the pound staff who coaxed or forced the dogs into the cage). Thousands were drowned each summer: in 1885 alone, 6,292 had been killed by the end of September. The canine carcasses were then taken to the city's "offal dock," where along with other dead animals they were dumped in the river or taken to a renderer. These were dismal scenes. *Harper's Weekly* advised that "no person of sensibility" should visit the pound, even if "drowning in the dumping cage . . . is as merciful a way as can be devised for putting them to death." The sounds of drowning dogs were "pitiful to hear. From their tremulous whines one can tell that they are perfectly conscious of the impending doom." The policeman stationed at the pound reportedly got himself out of "earshot" during the drownings, as he could not bear the sounds.[17]

The killing was criticized abroad. Just as the *New York Times* condemned hanging in French pounds as barbaric and cruel, so Europeans denounced drowning in New York as "lamentable and disgusting." For the *Revue britannique*, the "canicide bathtub" was reminiscent of the "republican drownings" at Nantes during "the Terror," when Jean-Baptiste Carrier had drowned suspected counterrevolutionaries in 1793 and 1794.[18]

Other sights in the pound were even more distressing. A reporter described how one of the brokers who brought dogs to the pound would club to death any who were too big or dangerous to be drowned (fig. 3.2). He struck "reckless blows and tortur[ed] them by breaking their legs and gashing them unnecessarily, and taking a most fiendish delight in his cruel work. He spattered the blood and brains on the spectators." Dog-catching boys witnessed the scene, and they very much enjoyed turning on the tap to drown the dogs. An accompanying image showed one of them gleefully performing this task. According to humanitarian narratives, such killing was horrific for the animals and dehumanized humans (although the boys in this example seemed jubilant rather than brutalized).[19] The sights and sounds of canine suffering were almost unbearable for middle-class commentators.

Killing in the Battersea Dogs' Home

Drowning and strangulation were among the reported ways that London's dogcart owners killed their dogs, whom they no longer considered useful

FIGURE 3.2 *Slaughtering the Dogs—"Andy" in His Glory*, *Frank Leslie's Illustrated Newspaper*, August 14, 1858. Library of Congress, control number 2004669991.

after their vehicles were banned in Central London in 1839. Moreover, policemen had the power to bludgeon with their truncheons dogs whom they deemed dangerous. Witnessing a bludgeoning "spoil[ed] the life of the sensitive," lamented travel writer and animal protectionist Isabel Burton. Gruesome details of how dead dogs were lugged off in carts to be boiled down at a rendering plant underscored the barbarity of bludgeoning. Occasionally, workers would hear a whine from the pile of dead dogs and finish off survivors with a pole axe. "One feels quite proud of such a Christian and humane country as ours!" noted satirical journal *Fun*.[20]

Such methods were deemed too cruel for use at Battersea Dogs' Home, which portrayed itself as a profoundly humane institution (see chapter 1). But death lurked behind its humanitarian sheen. Its employees used prussic acid (hydrogen cyanide) to kill unclaimed dogs. This fate was mainly reserved for ownerless street dogs who had little chance of being rehomed and thereby integrated within the emerging dogopolis. As one writer glossed it for young readers, prussic acid would end the miserable life of unwanted creatures: the "very useless and ugly curs, who *will* never find masters . . . have to take prussic acid, and their poor little troubles are over." The slaughter of undesirable and miserable animals thus slotted into middle-class humanitarian narratives and campaigns that tried to turn children away from cruelty to animals. This was a necessary and merciful killing, compatible with nurturing feelings of care and compassion toward animals in British children.[21]

But this method of exterminating dogs was thought to cause too much suffering. Anesthetist and public hygienist Benjamin Ward Richardson observed that the home's staff had become skilled at administering prussic acid by mouth to each condemned dog, leading—on the whole—to a painless death. But the toxin was dangerous to handle, and this killing method exacted an emotional "tax" that was difficult to bear. Moreover, prussic acid did not guarantee death. Reports surfaced of dogs reviving themselves as they were carted off to the countryside to be turned into manure. Alive or dead, stinking carts of rotting dogs offended rural nostrils.[22] This was far from a humane and dignified end, and the act of giving poison by hand was too intimate.

Other commentators were concerned that the pet and pedigree dogs of middle-class owners would get caught up in the "massacre." The London *Standard* worried about "Carlo" slipping out of his owner's house and "revelling in the indulgence of a truant stroll," only to be hunted down and "ultimately converted into manure for the provinces" via the dogs' home and a rendering plant. Echoing the criticisms leveled at dogcatchers in New York, rumors circulated that policemen seized pet dogs from outside their homes. Writer Charles Reade accused them of acting in this way in a letter to the London *Daily Telegraph*, which was reproduced in the *New York Times*. He argued that the "slaughter of innocents" at the dogs' home meant that it was stretching the English language to call it a home.[23]

Overall, however, middle-class commentators supported the killing of straying and biting dogs in London, New York, and Paris. They viewed it as a necessary measure to cleanse the emerging dogopolis of these dogs, commonly perceived as ownerless, repulsive, and dangerous. But the methods of slaughter exacerbated the canine suffering that so affronted humanitarian sensibilities, and owners worried that their beloved pets might end up hanged, drowned, or poisoned. The stakes became even higher after Charles Darwin's elaboration of dogs' varied and sensitive emotional repertoire.

Emotional Dogs

Before the nineteenth century, humans had treated dogs as emotionally sensitive creatures. But from 1800 onward, dog owners and experts reinforced the idea that dogs were emotional creatures, which constituted an important step toward their eventual integration into dogopolis. Veterinarian William Youatt, the leading British authority on dogs in the mid-nineteenth century, declared that "hatred, love, fear, hope, joy, distress, courage, timidity, jealousy, and many varied passions influence and agitate [dogs], as they do humans." Canine and human emotions were of the same "character," even if human emotions and intelligence were more refined.[24]

Some rabies experts believed that the powerful "attachment" between pet and owner would protect the latter if his canine companion became infected. According to Henri Bouley, such was the "affectionate feeling" of dogs toward their owners that it overrode their urge to bite, even in the disease's final stages. The owner's "presence" and "voice" kept the dog "quiet and gentle" and under control. Bouley also described rabid dogs' much-noted tendency to run away from home to die as an attempt to protect "those they love" from their rabid rage. Heavily influenced by Bouley, George Fleming asserted that "the unparalleled affection for mankind, which forms so remarkable a trait in the dog's character, can scarcely be disturbed by the agonies of so excruciating and maddening a disease as rabies." The assumption that canine love could override the horrors of rabies cemented dogs' reputation as emotionally sensitive animals.[25]

Charles Darwin's theories of evolution lent further scientific credibility to the idea that dogs were profoundly emotional. According to Darwin, evolution formed the foundation of canine fidelity: the "love of man has become instinctive in the dog." Most notably in *The Expression of the Emotions in Man and Animals* (1872), he suggested an emotional communality between humans and dogs. They shared bodily behaviors and movements, such as snarling and trembling, which were linked to internal mental states. These emotional expressions were rooted in the deep past and had since become inherited habits. Snarling in humans—the exposure of a canine tooth—was the remnant of an ancient animal past that served no real purpose in the modern world (fig. 3.3). Darwin used dogs (and other animals) to develop his theories and promote them to contemporary audiences. Dogs roam through *Expression of the Emotions* as they do in many of his other works. The movement of canine heads, tails, teeth, ears, and eyes all gave an indication of their emotional states, including joy, anger, pain, fear, surprise, and affection. As a dog lover, Darwin tended to highlight how canine affection for humans drew the species together (fig. 3.4). Licking, for instance, was a sloppy sign of canine love. Dogs were lively creatures capable of feeling, not the animal machines depicted by René Descartes in the seventeenth century. The accessible and anecdotal style of *Expression of the Emotions*, its many illustrations,

FIGURE 3.3 A snarling dog. From Charles Darwin, *The Expression of the Emotions in Man and Animals* (1872). Wellcome Collection, Attribution 4.0 International (CC BY 4.0).

and its frequent reference to domestic animals made it a quasi field guide for aspiring observers of canine emotions.[26]

Darwin's ideas were far from universally accepted, not least in French scientific circles. Some Christians also accorded animals an emotional life because God, not evolution, had given them the ability to feel joy and kindness and even enjoy a degree of spiritual life. Nor did Darwin eradicate all differences between humans and animals. He insisted, for instance, that blushing was uniquely human. But his works did prompt extensive reflection on the emotional capabilities of dogs. They also lent scientific legitimacy to those who believed that dogs and humans shared analogous emotions. In the wake of Darwinism, even those commentators who denied dogs comparable intellectual abilities to humans were prepared to admit emotional similarities. *McClure's Magazine* contributor Edwin Tenney Brewster talked down his collie's intelligence but argued that "when it comes to the fundamental impulses of our lives,—fear, anger, curiosity, sex, parenthood, hunger, fatigue, the joy of battle—we are all of us, men and beasts together, pretty

FIGURE 3.4 Dog caressing their master. From Darwin's *Expression of the Emotions* (1872). Wellcome Collection, Public Domain Mark.

much on a level."[27] Darwinism breathed fresh life into the assumption that dogs were highly sensitive creatures whose emotional palette enabled them to bond with humans. It bolstered animal protectionists' attempts to prevent cruelty to animals.

Combating Cruelty

As discussed in chapters 1 and 2, animal protectionists aimed to reduce or even eliminate unnecessary animal suffering. They led many campaigns against cruel practices such as animal combat sports and the poor treatment of urban horses. Before Darwinism, they had sought to educate, cajole, and discipline the public away from cruel behavior, as they were deeply concerned about the impact that cruelty to animals had on human bystanders. In France, in this vein, the Grammont Law (1850) prohibited public violence and cruelty to domestic animals. Animal protectionists and antivivisectionists tried to change people's emotional responses to animals. They aimed to foster sympathy and empathy for innocent, defenseless, and voiceless creatures who, they claimed, shared emotions with humans. In New York, this belief was enshrined in the 1866 anticruelty law: animals had a right to protection because of their ability to suffer, not just because they were property. Compassionate and humanitarian attitudes toward animals would create a civilized society by spreading emotional and moral uplift. Cruelty and "maudlin sentiment" would be banished from this utopia.[28]

Animal protectionists elevated the ability to feel compassion toward animals as evidence of an individual's humanity. French feminist and animal protectionist Maria Deraismes stated that "sensibility is the condition of life. To live is to feel; to feel is to live; to feel is to think." Feeling was the "impulsive force that determines all our acts." By implication, people who could not feel compassion, as shown by their inability to sympathize with animals, were deficient humans. This idea had longevity. French animal protectionists stated bluntly in 1927 that owners of animals who treated them cruelly had a "hard heart" that constituted a "pathological anomaly."[29] Being cruel to animals became evidence of human failings and emotional deviance.

Among animal protectionists, antivivisectionists did the most to highlight canine suffering. The mistreatment of dogs, especially when it led to their torturous death in the vivisectionist laboratory, marked a rupture in the affectionate ties between dogs and humans, along with a betrayal of *canis familiaris*. Dogs were central to the vivisection experiments conducted in the laboratories of London, New York, and Paris. They were plentiful, reasonably easy to obtain, and pliable in the laboratory, and their physiology was sufficiently similar to humans for comparisons to be made between the species (although antivivisectionists challenged this claim). Vivisectionists outlined the various experiments that could be conducted on dogs. *Handbook for the Physiological Laboratory* by John Burdon Sanderson, professor of practical physiology and histology at University College London, included sections on asphyxiation, secreting bile, and electrocuting the sciatic nerve.[30]

Women led the charge against vivisection in Britain, with feminist Frances Power Cobbe at the fore. With the Royal Society for the Prevention of Cruelty to Animals mired in disagreements over vivisection, Cobbe secured a Royal Commission in 1876 and founded the Victoria Street Society for the Protection of Animals from Vivisection. But the ensuing Cruelty to Animals Act that year, which introduced a regime of licenses and laboratory inspections, overrode many of the Victoria Street Society's demands in favor of those of scientists. Although it was the first legislation of its kind in the world, Cobbe saw it as deficient and began to campaign for the total abolition of vivisection.[31]

At a time when women from across the globe forged transnational activist networks, female British antivivisectionists, in particular, campaigned beyond national borders. Cobbe gave advice and encouragement to Philadelphia animal protectionist Caroline Earl White, who established the American Anti-Vivisection Society in 1883. The creation of the New York Anti-Vivisection Society followed in 1908. Cobbe also published an exposé of vivisection in the United States, which highlighted particularly cruel experiments. Featured here was a Jersey City physician, B. A. Watson, who dropped an etherized dog from the ceiling onto iron bars to research concussion of the spine. Cobbe pleaded with Americans to rise against the "new vice of scientific cruelty" that was taking root in their country. Whether or not they directly heeded Cobbe's call, American female antivivisectionists joined their French and British colleagues in seeing themselves as part of a crusade to save humanity, even if they tended to situate themselves within Christian and social reform movements rather than feminism.[32]

Antivivisectionists advanced the belief—bolstered by Darwinism and popular dog-loving narratives—that humans and dogs shared similar emotions (even if Darwin and many of his disciples supported vivisection). For Cobbe, two of these shared emotions—faith and affection–were manipulated, exploited, and degraded on the vivisection table. Antivivisectionist physician George Hoggan emphasized, too, the emotional confusion and suffering experienced by sensitive dogs. As a laboratory assistant, he had witnessed two dogs "seized with horror as soon as they smelt the [laboratory's] air." They then "made friendly advances" to the researchers, and they held their ears, eyes, and tails so as to "make a mute appeal for mercy." In a distressing scene common in antivivisectionist literature, when the dogs were held down on the table they licked the experimenters' hands "as their last means of exciting compassion." Hoggan's upsetting personal encounter with canine suffering reinforced the sense that dogs experienced vivisection as a form of emotional torture.[33]

As dogs held such emotional resonance, antivivisectionists frequently published detailed descriptions of experiments on them to convince the public of the evils of vivisection. The apparent similarity between the defenselessness of dogs and children, which underscored much humanitarian work in the United States, added to the sense of anguish. Echoing concerns within the broader humanitarian movement, the antivivisectionists worried about the potentially troubling emotional and moral effects of the graphic descriptions of suffering animals. But they stuck with the distressing accounts, because they wanted to shock their readers and provoke a visceral emotional reaction that would spur humanitarian action. The revulsion felt by readers would, they hoped, move them to act, as would printed images of dogs begging the vivisector for mercy (fig. 3.5).[34]

Some vivisectionists admitted that animals could experience emotional and physical pain, which they could successfully dull by using the anesthetics that had transformed human medicine. Anesthetics also had the advantage of allowing them to perform more delicate procedures on still rather than writhing animals. The *British Medical Journal*, for its part, approvingly quoted the claims of New York experimental physiologist John C. Dalton that the "exhibition of pain in an experimental laboratory is an exceptional occurrence" due to the use of anesthetics. Expressing the common slur that female antivivisectionists were overly sensitive and emotionally deficient, one provivisectionist argued that anesthetics meant that the "only pain given is that to the feelings of tender-hearted people ignorant of physiology." For Dalton and other vivisectionists, scientific progress could eliminate canine pain and suffering and affirmed their belief that they were emotionally healthy individuals who represented all that was best in humanity.[35]

The emotionally charged debates in scientific journals and antivivisectionist publications spilled out into the mainstream press, putting canine suffering in the public eye. For antivivisectionists, vivisection represented the ultimate betrayal of the human-canine bond, and university and hospital laboratories became sites of torture that challenged the status of London, New

FIGURE 3.5 Engraving by D. J. Tomkins, 1883, after a painting by J. McClure Hamilton. Wellcome Collection, Attribution 4.0 International (CC BY 4.0).

York, and Paris as beacons of civilized urban modernity. For the vivisectionists, these sites were humane centers of progress and modern science where anesthetics would ease canine suffering. The vivisection debates intensified the deliberations on canine emotions and dogs' ability to suffer. They also raised the possibility that scientific and medical developments might diminish suffering.

Public Hygienists Call for Culls

The prospect of killing dogs with reduced or even no suffering offered a potential solution to the slaughter of straying and biting dogs who seemed increasingly abhorrent within the emerging dogopolis. From the 1870s, a broad consensus coalesced around the culling of strays. Public hygienists and municipal authorities portrayed exterminating these dogs as a necessary public health measure to protect the well-being of humans and pet dogs. It was also an oft-mentioned solution to the problem of biting dogs. With the "bare possibility" of contracting rabies "sufficient to appal the stoutest heart," the *Brooklyn Daily Eagle* called for the impoundment and killing of ownerless strays: "these ill-fed, ill-favoured curs are the animals most liable to rabies, and form par excellence the 'dangerous classes' of the canine race." Calls for the impoundment of strays invariably intensified after rabies outbreaks. In 1877 Britain experienced the most certified numbers of deaths from rabies in the nineteenth century. In response, a committee headed by Thomas Dolan, a physician and poor law medical officer, urged the "capture and, if need be, destruction of vagabond or stray dogs" to remove the source of contagion.[36] The committee was far from alone in conflating straying and biting dogs, as concerns over rabies, vagabondage, and disorder stuck to these animals.

In Paris, meanwhile, the 1878 police ordinance strengthened a crackdown on dogs, which the chief police veterinary surgeon Camille Leblanc dubbed a "hecatomb." The police seized 3,383 dogs in July of that year and 1,334 in August, of which 4,500 were killed. Leblanc affirmed that the number of reported rabies cases in animals (mainly dogs) had subsequently fallen from 613 in 1878 to 285 in 1879, while human deaths had fallen from twenty-four to twelve. Despite this apparent success, Leblanc still worried about the number of stray dogs on Paris's streets, whom he blamed for spreading rabies. He bemoaned the lack of personnel to enforce the city's antirabies ordinances.[37]

In all three cities, animal protectionists, public hygienists, and pound/shelter managers sought for a way to kill straying and biting dogs that would not offend humanitarian sentiments. Echoing the search for more humane methods of executing criminals, the search was on for a humane method of canine slaughter. Efficiency, bloodlessness, suffering reduction, and hygiene were guiding principles, as was the need to place more distance between the killers and the killed through technology.[38]

The Search for Humane Killing

Asphyxiation, which had been proposed as a humane way of executing humans during the French Revolution, found favor in London and Paris for exterminating dogs. Having already outlined to the Royal Society for the Prevention of Cruelty to Animals how anesthesia could reduce suffering for animals during operations, Richardson applied this idea to animal death by devising a lethal chamber. After struggling to keep up with dispatching the number of dogs crossing its threshold in 1882 and 1883, Battersea Dogs' Home installed Richardson's chamber in 1884. The sealed brick chamber had a sliding door through which up to two hundred dogs at a time entered, contained in a two-tiered cage wheeled in on tram rails. Before the dogs' entrance, staff filled the chamber with chloroform and then added carbonic acid. Death took place within two minutes and was reportedly painless because anesthesia, rather than asphyxiation, killed the dogs. In the words of sporting and hunting journalist Basil Tozer, "The animals sleep into death . . . no sign of a spasm or struggle being ever presented by their dead bodies." The system was more efficient than administering prussic acid, dispatching 206,000 dogs between 1895 and 1896. An onsite crematorium then provided a more dignified way of disposing of the canine corpses than boiling, rendering, or transforming into manure. The novelist Ouida, however, decried the Battersea Dogs' Home's killing of dogs and their allegedly ongoing "profitable manufacture of sensitive living creatures into manure."[39]

Despite Ouida's concerns, the lethal chamber allowed Battersea to portray itself as a merciful institution. "We kill in a painless and humane manner," stated its secretary, Matthias Colam. In line with its domestic ethos, canine death became unthreatening, even homey. The dogs' bodies even "present[ed] after death the familiar appearance of dogs curled up asleep on the hearth-rug before the fire." Canine death had been domesticated.[40] The celebrated anesthetization of humane surgery was thus extended to canine death. Medical and technological progress had dovetailed with humanitarian sensibilities, public health objectives, and anti-stray sentiments.

French observers noted with interest Battersea's adoption of Richardson's lethal chamber. But when the Paris police abandoned the hanging of stray dogs in the 1880s and switched to asphyxiation, they used illuminating gas instead of carbonic acid and chloroform, perhaps because it was cheaper and more readily available (its main use was for street lighting). As in London, the dogs were rolled into a lethal chamber within a wheeled cage. Commentators portrayed the move to asphyxiation as a "less barbarous" way of killing dogs than hanging, during which the animals had perished in "terrible agony." Asphyxiation ensured that dogs died without "any suffering." French commentators troubled by the bloody and public spectacle of executing humans with guillotines watched these developments with interest. Physician and writer Armand Corre suggested that asphyxiation could be used on human criminals as well as stray dogs.[41]

Asphyxiation enabled the police pound to kill more dogs. The year 1892 was the most lethal for Paris's strays. The police impounded 26,502 dogs after an upsurge in rabies cases, most of whom were killed. However, echoing Ouida's denunciation of Battersea, some French animal protectionists labeled this method of asphyxiation inhumane. Upon visiting the pound in 1899, animal protectionist Adrienne Neyrat observed up to eighty panicked dogs crammed into an iron cage, "tearing into each other" as they were delivered to the lethal chamber. She reported many problems. Owing to the number of dogs and the deficiencies of the killing machine, it could take up to ten minutes for the dogs to die. Some traumatized dogs even emerged alive, to be finished off by the renderer's hammer.[42]

Neyrat's hopes for a more "modern machine" that conformed to "scientific progress" were met in 1902 when the animal protection organization Assistance aux animaux donated a "cynoctone" to the police pound. Following the recommendations of public hygienist Edmond Nocard, this British-inspired machine asphyxiated condemned dogs with carbonic acid once they had been lowered into an underground chamber. Eyewitness reports described how the dogs seemed to "sleep from weariness." Echoing the language of drowsy death at Battersea Dogs' Home, this was an end "without pointless suffering." Despite its designers having been inspired by a visit to Battersea, the French press portrayed the cynoctone as evidence of French technological savoir-faire.[43]

Human suffering diminished too as the pound's personnel no longer had to listen to the agonized and protracted sounds of dying dogs. Most now died in less than two to three minutes, confided pound manager Monsieur Hébrard to Paris newspaper *Le matin*. Despite this improvement, Hébrard admitted to some troubling emotions. Since working in the pound he had become a dog lover, and it was a "real suffering to see their eyes demanding mercy as they were lowered into the pit." Yet such concern about dogs had its limits, and the pound continued the commodification of strays by selling dead dogs to glove makers.[44]

By aligning the pound with the preference of animal protectionists for efficient, hygienic, and humane animal killing, the cynoctone legitimized it as a site of slaughter that was necessary to secure Paris for the rest of the population. But despite its positive reception and its scientific and modern credentials, the lack of an effective anesthetic damaged the cynoctone's humane reputation. This was remedied in 1904 when the *New York Herald* donated a Richardson lethal chamber to the pound. In a front-page splash, the newspaper celebrated how its generosity banished canine suffering and transformed the Paris pound into one of, if not *the*, best-equipped facility for humane slaughter in the world. But pound officials suspended its functioning during World War I as the price of chloroform had become too expensive due to its use in operations on wounded soldiers.[45]

Not everyone was convinced by humane killing. With confirmed rabies cases low in 1916, Ernest Coyecque, former vice president of the Société protectrice des animaux (SPA [Animal Protection Society]), argued that the slaughter constituted an attempt to "suppress a race," recalling the Ottoman Empire's measures against Armenians and the dogs of Constantinople (present-day Istanbul). As well as echoing nineteenth-century reflections on Turkish stray dogs to understand human-dog relations in Paris (see chapter 1), Coyecque's comments indicate how more radical members of the SPA felt that the death of any dog was unjustified, regardless of the risk it posed to human health.[46]

Animal protectionists were also heavily involved in observing the killing of dogs in New York. In 1874 pound officials experimented with carbonic acid as a means of slaughter, with the American Society for the Prevention of Cruelty to Animals carefully monitoring the proceedings. ASPCA Superintendent Hartfield reported that the ensuing canine suffering was too great. Placing his ear against the box in which the dogs had been placed, Hartfield heard "a terrible struggling, as though the dogs were deprived of their voices, but were engaged in a death struggle to avoid breathing the carbonic acid gas." The ordeal lasted for twelve minutes. Upon opening the box, Hartfield saw a "mass of backs and legs." The dogs had buried their heads against their neighbors' bodies, presumably in a futile attempt to avoid suffocation. The ASPCA took urgent action, and its president, Henry Bergh, arrested pound master John Marriott. A leaky tank hindered a further attempt to kill dogs humanely with carbonic acid. This time, some dogs were still alive after two hours. After consulting the ASPCA observer, Marriott decided to drown the survivors. However, after the tank was opened, some of the dogs scrambled out "to the intense consternation and terror of the several officers and spectators present." Marriott and his men, along with the ASPCA observer, finished off the agitated dogs with guns and clubs. The extent of suffering convinced the ASPCA that drowning was in fact the most effective and humane means of slaughter, and the pound continued in this way.[47]

But drowning remained cruel and inefficient. The ASPCA wrote to New York mayor Abram Hewitt in March 1888, demanding that he find an alternative to this "barbarous" system. Stray dogs needed to be removed on the grounds of public health, noted the organization, but they still deserved "charity." In fact, the misery of their existence and their "helplessness and sufferings" meant that they should be killed in the most "painless and merciful [way] as science can devise." The ASPCA recommended testing two more humane extermination methods: gas, as used in Britain, and electricity. The latter was its preferred option. Its reasoning was perhaps influenced by Thomas Edison's experiments on dogs to examine the effects of alternating and direct currents, the construction of the first electricity station in New York in 1882, and the portrayal of use of the electric chair in New York State as a modern, painless, and humane execution technology.[48]

Technology seemed poised to meld with humanitarian sentiment to provide a humane end to the suffering stray, who was simultaneously cast as an urban victim and a pest. The mayor and the Department of Health approved the search for a new slaughtering system, with the latter also favoring an electric shock as the surest and most humane method. An experiment with electricity took place at the municipal pound in August 1888 with experts from Bellevue Hospital and Cornell University in attendance. But electricity was ultimately deemed too expensive and dangerous, and chloroform emerged as the preferred method. By December 1888, the Health Department had installed a machine for killing dogs in the pound that could use chloroform vapor or illuminating gas. Its chief inspector, Cyrus Edson, had struck on the idea of using illuminating gas after learning that this was the Parisian method. Unlike drowning, "no evidence whatever of pain appeared," he reported, even if some dogs experienced "erotic excitement" in the moments before death. The *New York Times* depicted the new system as more humane: it was a way of "killing dogs scientifically." Gas also had the advantage of being cheap, as it was taken from the city's main gas supply. Up to forty-eight dogs could be killed at a time in a large zinc box, where they seemingly fell asleep. The death-by-sleep narrative thus made its way across the Atlantic and extended American notions of the Good Death, which was peaceful and dignified, to dogs. The killing of dogs thus became part of New York's much-heralded modernity. Modern public health norms justified the killing, and illuminating gas—a symbol of security, progress, and civilization—provided the means.[49]

But *Harper's Weekly* was not wholly convinced. An article admitted that "really it seems too dreadful to relate, but there before your very eyes is the great ominous looking airtight box that takes the place of gallows or electric chair or guillotine, into which . . . the unrescued ones will go, to be put out of the world quickly, painlessly, humanely, by asphyxiation with gas. And then? Well, it isn't very pleasant to think about, but their bodies and bones will be made into commercial products, and their pelts into ladies' muffs and capes and boas."[50] The arrangement was more humane than previous ones, but unsavory elements from the days of drowning continued to surface.

Nonetheless, lethal chambers were depicted as efficient slaughter machines and came to be regarded as a humane, necessary, and progressive way of eliminating unwelcome canine life. Technology, condemnations of straying and biting, humanitarianism, and public health objectives coalesced to facilitate and rationalize the extermination of dogs. Humane killing enabled those that did not fit the dogopolis mold to be removed from London, New York, and Paris.

The Spread of Humane Killing

A new wave of more radical animal protectionists viewed the death of any animal as immoral and intolerable. But the use of lethal chambers spread, and mainstream animal protectionist societies welcomed them into their shelters. In Paris, James Gordon-Bennett, publisher of the *New York Herald* and long-term supporter of animal protectionist causes, funded a refuge at Gennevilliers, to the northwest of Paris, where dogs were sheltered, rehomed, or killed in a Richardson lethal chamber. The animal hospital run by the Assistance aux animaux also had a cynoctone to kill dogs and other animals whom it was unable to treat. Although the more traditional male members of the SPA had attacked what they saw as the misguided sentimentality of the often female refuge managers, the organization eventually swung behind the institutions and took over the Gennevilliers refuge in 1917. It encouraged refuge owners throughout France to display on their premises a poem written by an SPA member that captured the humanitarian atmosphere of refuges where dogs received a "maternal welcome." They were places were "life was

FIGURE 3.6 Animal refuge, Gennevilliers, France. Photograph by Agence Rol, 1927. Bibliothèque nationale de France.

better, [and] where death was kinder" (fig. 3.6). Yet however humane the killing might have been, it still caused emotional distress for refuge owners who had to put dogs to sleep. At her boulevard Sérurier refuge, which the SPA eventually took over, Madame Blanchard was reportedly in tears each time she had to prepare a last meal for one of the rescue dogs: her "heart and head were worn out."[51]

The SPA justified the killing of dogs at its refuges as a better fate than being "tortured abominably" by a vivisector (the city pound passed strays on to laboratories). But it was clearly ambivalent about the humane slaughter of dogs. In 1917 it rejoiced that its lobbying had finally persuaded the government to draft dogs from the Paris pound into the army and so save them from asphyxiation. Potential death in the trenches trumped certain death in the lethal chamber.[52]

Like its French counterpart, and once it took over the licensing and policing of New York's dog population in 1894, the ASPCA combined combating cruelty with humane slaughter. It turned the Manhattan pound into a shelter at 102nd Street and East River, and it established shelters in Brooklyn and Staten Island once those boroughs were incorporated into the city. In these refuges, lost dogs could be rehomed or "mercifully destroyed," it declared. "Vagrant animals" had thus been spared "much suffering." ASPCA reports noted with delight how children no longer captured dogs to sell to the pound but brought strays to the shelter for retrieval, rehoming, or humane destruction. Families could indeed bring their old or ill pets to be killed, such as the family who conveyed their beloved collie to the Brooklyn shelter. "Sniffles dominated the scene," reported the ASPCA's publication *Our Animal Friends*. But it was the right thing to do, as the "faithful" dog's "suffering was at an end."[53]

The term *shelter* sheds light on the ASPCA's evolving objectives. Its premises were seen as sheltering dogs from suffering on the streets or from ill health and old age. Like *home*, *shelter* gave a humanitarian gloss to a site of slaughter. This helped mask a transformation in the ASPCA's mission. It had gone from protesting inhumane killing in the dog pound to overseeing the destruction of Gotham's unwanted canines. To further justify this change in mission and reflecting his more conservative approach to animal protection than his predecessor Bergh, organization president John P. Haines described killing in 1896 as a "necessity" to avoid the transmission of rabies, distemper, parasites, and mange between unhealthy strays and healthy pets. Recognizing that many of the destroyed dogs had poor owners in the city's tenements, he claimed that the removal of these diseased and decrepit dogs would benefit their owners, whose homes would be cleaner and less diseased. Destruction was the healthy and humane thing to do. He contended that "the animals . . . are removed absolutely without pain, from a precarious existence which is full of hardships, and is often attended with great and unrelieved suffering."[54] The middle-class condemnation of stray dogs and working-class pet keeping (see chapter 1) once again justified their slaughter.

But if the sheltering narrative did not cut it, humor offered another defense against the killing of dogs. John Read, superintendent of the first ASPCA shelter in 1894, observed that the "putting to death of dogs is not exactly a pleasant pastime." But it had a "humorous side," because "lower"-class New Yorkers asked him for skin and hair from black dogs as a rheumatism cure, and dog fat for "bronchial troubles." Jokes at the expense of poorer New Yorkers perhaps appealed to the ASPCA's middle-class supporters and helped numb the emotional pain of systematically destroying the city's stray animals. Between 1894 and 1908 alone, the organization killed 1,515,513 small animals (a figure that included cats as well as dogs).[55]

The rate of capture and destruction increased during a rabies scare in 1908 when the ASPCA "humanely destroyed" 185,398 small animals. The following year, it recorded 222,468 deaths and 318,615 in 1910. Its then president, Alfred Wagstaff, justified this slaughter as necessary to avoid the "misery these animals would have endured from exposure and starvation, disease and injuries." Under the "protecting arm of the Society," a humane death was better than an inhumane life on the streets. The *New York Times* approved of the mass slaughter of dogs, who were killed as "painlessly as possible" (even if the ASPCA could not afford to use chloroform when it was killing 1,000 dogs a day). The organization's superintendent, Thomas Freel, further justified the killing of "mongrel curs living from garbage cans or sewers. It is surely in the interest of the community to put a snapping, mangy cur which no one claims, out of the way. And it is also in the interest of the good, desirable dogs."[56] Street dogs lived in the dirt (unlike pets), spread rabies, and had no immediate connection with human New Yorkers. The separation of strays from pets and the fears of biting and straying continued to pave the way for the mass culling of stray dogs and the advent of dogopolis.

The ASPCA's leadership viewed the humane killing of stray dogs in its shelters as evidence of progress and efficiency. Two images in its fiftieth annual report contrasted the pre-1894 ramshackle dog pound jutting into the East River with its "modern shelter." A further image juxtaposed drowning to its lethal chamber, which was "a modern and humane method of destroying animal life." The absence of animals and humans in the latter image reinforced the technological and bloodless nature of modern killing. By the 1920s, ASPCA reports did not carry images of lethal chambers or statistics of the number of small animals the chambers destroyed: they had perhaps become too controversial and distressing. But in 1923 the organization still celebrated its "merciful destruction" of cats and dogs over the last thirty years as a "civic as well as a humanitarian task." It was a "humane service to God's creatures never before undertaken and never paralleled."[57]

Challenging Humane Killing

This is not to say that humane killing did not divide animal protectionists. Some, particularly women, challenged the whole premise of humane killing. They refused to kill any dog unless the animal was too sick or wounded. Inspired by a visit to a refuge in Paris in which all dogs were homed rather than killed, Flora D'Auby Jenkins Kibbe set up the Bide-a-Wee Home on Lexington Avenue in New York in 1903. It dealt with far fewer dogs in the city than the ASPCA and faced financial difficulties, yet it still managed to save 1,871 dogs in 1906 (fig. 3.7). In a glowing description of the facility, journalist Elizabeth Banks noted the excellent care given to the dogs—who ate scraps from the Waldorf-Astoria Hotel—and recommended that owners who

FIGURE 3.7 Bide-a-Wee Home, New York City. Photograph by Joseph Byron, ca. 1907. Library of Congress, control number 2011661012.

no longer wanted their pet dog (or cat) take the animal to Bide-a-Wee rather than turn the pet out to face suffering and destruction on the streets. She also pointed out the facility's key difference from the ASPCA shelter. Bide-a-Wee would not put pets to sleep, although it might provide some advice on the subject.[58]

Kibbe and her supporters faced criticism. Although they plucked stray dogs from the streets "with sympathy and zeal," according to one *New York Times* article, they were inefficient in this process. In addition, the barking dogs at their shelter constituted a "public nuisance." One of the newspaper's readers agreed that the city's priority should be removing and destroying strays; Bide-a-Wee hindered this objective. The ASPCA was also unimpressed with Bide-a-Wee. In a gendered insult more commonly directed toward rather than uttered by animal protectionists, it dismissed many of the shelter's female supporters as "uncontrollable sentimentalists." An editorial in *Our Animal Friends* compared the "principled humanity" of the ASPCA with the "inherent feebleness" of the Bide-a-Wee project. Even the whimsical Scottish-inspired name, which meant "stay a little," smacked of "sentimentalism." The editorial went on to say that ASPCA inspections of the Bide-A-Wee home had indicated that although Kibbe was well-intentioned, she lacked adequate knowledge of dogs. It concluded that sentiment without "common sense" and knowledge had produced a "canine inferno."[59]

The barking dogs at Bide-a-Wee eventually attracted the attention of the city's Department of Health. In June 1908, it ordered Kibbe to transfer the dogs to her rural shelter in New Jersey. The simmering disagreement between Bide-a-Wee and the ASPCA now boiled over, as the latter's vans turned up outside the shelter in the expectation that they would have to take the dogs to an ASPCA shelter for destruction if Kibbe was unable to complete the transfer. The dogs eventually reached New Jersey, but the two anticruelty organizations' different approaches to animal suffering and humane killing had been laid bare. The divergent attitudes toward canine death clashed again in 1909 when Bide-a-Wee distributed muzzles and leashes to the dogs of the poor to prevent them from being seized by the ASPCA and destroyed.[60]

In London, views clashed within the same organization. A committee within Our Dumb Friends League, an organization originally created in 1897 to care for London's horses, disagreed over the number and type of dogs that should be humanely destroyed in its North London Dogs Home. Founded in 1912, the home took three thousand strays a year from the police by the early 1930s.[61]

Opinions concerning the best killing methods also varied in the shelters that held contracts with the London Metropolitan Police for processing strays: prussic acid injections at the East Ham Dogs' Home; chloroform at Our Dumb Friends League; and chloroform and carbolic acid gas fumes at Battersea. All the methods had their supporters and detractors. Battersea declared its method the "most humane." Meanwhile, the National Canine Defence League and the Royal Society for the Prevention of Cruelty to Animals derided the use of prussic acid at the East Ham Dogs' Home even though the dean of the Royal Veterinary College declared it quick and painless.[62]

Whatever the process their facility chose, the homes' managers concurred that the killing of strays was a humane and necessary, if difficult, task. The National Canine Defence League bemoaned an increase in stray dogs in London in the mid-1920s. Its Bethnal Green shelter had become a "dump for the surplus canine population of the East End" as dog owners who could no longer afford to look after their pets brought in their dogs for destruction. It confessed to struggling to cope with the canine "submerged tenth," yet saw its duty as giving a "painless passing" to the East End's diseased, weak, hungry, suffering, and unloved dogs. In an echo of the linking of strays with the "dangerous classes" in the nineteenth century, and taking up late nineteenth-century concerns about unruly and uprooted underclasses (the "submerged tenth"), loose dogs were once again associated with the poor and supposedly problematic sections of urban society. Humane slaughter, rather than social reform or emigration, was the agreed response to the canine underclass.[63]

Due to its long-standing and extensive collaboration with the Metropolitan Police, Battersea Dogs' Home remained London's main site for the humane destruction of strays. In the fifty years since its move to Battersea, the home had reportedly received over a million "canine outcasts," most of whom had met a "merciful death." Care and killing went hand in hand at the facility. According to the *London Journal,* "kindness is the keyword of the Home" and infused its various activities. Donations from the public to reconstruct its lethal chambers, as one "lady dog-lover" had done in 1910, became an act of compassion and kindness. After this woman's donation, and challenging the *New York Herald*'s aforementioned claims about the Paris pound, the *Journal* declared that Battersea now had the "most humanely perfect lethal chambers for the painless destruction of animals in the world."[64]

Kindness was also the watchword at the Our Dumb Friends League home in North London. According to its superintendent, E. S. Kennedy, the "maternal instinct" of its female staff made them the best handlers of dogs: "dogs respond most to a sympathetic human voice. Kindness is far more effective than bullying. They require much the same treatment as a child. We are very keen on managing dogs by love." The perceived canine understanding of human emotions and dogs' "mental attitude" made it imperative that the staff were calm and inspired trust. "When a dog *trusts* you," Kennedy revealed, "although the experience you are giving him may be quite unusual, he feels that you must be doing the right thing." Love had a lethal edge.[65]

Yet such assertions failed to quell unease about humane killing. The antivivisectionist Animal Defence Society organized an international conference on animal euthanasia at Caxton Hall, London, on June 14, 1933, with veterinarians, antivivisectionists, and animal protectionists in attendance. Conference delegates worried about the "mass destruction" taking place at Battersea. Some of the dogs died from asphyxiation (a "distressing death") rather than narcosis, and the more intelligent dogs seemed aware of the "impending disaster" awaiting them in the lethal chamber. This latter circumstance was against the "principle of humane slaughter in that as far as possible the victim should be kept in ignorance of his fate." British, European, and American delegates and correspondents also stressed the importance of skilled veterinarians in overseeing the process of slaughter, whether by carbon monoxide, chloroform, or electrical current, and emphasized that those doing the killing needed to be "really and truly imbued with the humane spirit" so as to treat the animal kindly and reduce its fear of death.[66]

Dogs' emotional sensitivity and strength made their deaths that much harder for them to bear. Lizzy Lind Af Hageby, the head of the Animal Defence Society, told conference delegates that "there is difficulty and resistance . . . animals do not like to be killed. They are apt to sense and smell danger. They will resist if they do. They will, so to speak, make a fight to retain consciousness, and when consciousness is gone the subconscious will continue the fight." Along with applying concepts about human psychology to animals, Lind Af Hageby, who also chaired the Society for the Prevention of Premature Burial, implied that as in humans, the boundaries between life and death in animals were fluid and mysterious. Another attendee at the conference, veterinarian J. Wakefield Rainey, similarly stated that the "putting to sleep idea is often a myth." Dogs at Battersea did not go to sleep but faced a "hard struggle against a powerful narcotic poison." The search for a swifter form of death—in which the loss of consciousness was instantaneous—was ongoing. Wakefield Rainey recommended the use of electricity, which was used at the National Canine Defence League shelter in Croydon. Battersea followed suit, introducing an electrical slaughter facility in 1934.[67]

Conference participants dismissed the charge that they were overly emotional. Lind Af Hageby denied that she and others concerned about humane killing were "one-sided sentimentalists." Instead, they were "promoting something of vital importance to civilisation and to peace between nations. . . . Cruelty and brutal treatment of animals are obstacles to that refinement of the human mind upon which alone true civilisation and international co-operation can be built." Based on what we now know came later in the 1930s, such a sentiment can seem naïve. But Lind Af Hageby's speech nonetheless spoke to wider female efforts to build international cooperation, and it underscored how the fostering of humanitarian sentiments and the encouragement of humane treatment of animals were transnational endeavors. Furthermore, she declared that the humane killing of animals was far removed from "drawing room" animal protection. Instead, it was raw and challenging work.[68]

Dispersed Killing

Despite such unease, animal protectionists promoted humane killing beyond the pounds and shelters. As part of its campaign to reduce the number of stray dogs, the SPA encouraged Parisian owners of bitches to kill newborn puppies through drowning (in an unconscious echo of the earlier practice in New York). This was an "act of pity to be conducted by all those who truly loved animals." In London, an early death was also preferable to a life of misery on the streets, the prospect of impoundment, or ending up in the hands of vivisectors. E. S. Kennedy advocated for "painlessly destroy[ing]" unwanted puppies to prevent future suffering. So, too, did the National Canine Defence League, which recommended that owners drown "mongrel" puppies, making sure to bury them deep enough to stop their mothers from digging them up. It also issued guidelines on how to kill unwanted pets, warning owners not to ask a "man or boy" to get rid of their dog but to take it to a shelter for humane destruction or to a chemist for an injection of prussic acid.[69]

The ASPCA, meanwhile, advised policemen on how to kill injured dogs (and cats) humanely with a gunshot. In addition, in line with the growing number of motor cars in the United States, which often injured small animals on the roads, animal protection society agents nationwide improvised portable lethal chambers. They suggested attaching a small metal barrel with the wounded animal inside to a car's tailpipe to create an al fresco lethal chamber.[70]

But calls for killing to be conducted more humanely sometimes fell on deaf ears. Despite receiving complaints from members of the public and animal protectionists, the London police turned down a suggestion, supported by Our Dumb Friends League, that its officers be equipped with portable lethal chambers to kill injured dogs on the streets. It also declined to adopt the recommendation from the Royal Society for the Prevention of Cruelty to Animals to use Greener "Safeti" captive bolt pistols for stunning animals before killing them, arguing that its existing methods were humane enough.[71] Nonetheless, mobile humane killing showed how much the destruction of unwanted dogs had become part of the fabric of urban life as it got dispersed throughout the emerging dogopolis.

Conclusion

The growing humanitarian intolerance of pain and suffering, the advent of Darwinism, and the rise of animal protection and antivivisectionist movements made canine suffering an explosive issue. There was a growing consensus among public hygienists and other authorities that straying and biting dogs needed to be culled, but that this had to be done in a humane and efficient manner. Hanging, drowning, and poisoning failed to meet humanitarian standards. The invention of humane killing ultimately made canine suffering a disquieting but ultimately acceptable element of human-dog relations in modern London, New York, and Paris. In removing many straying and biting dogs, humane killing was essential to the building of dogopolis, in which dogs closest to humans—pet and police dogs—would have the figurative keys to the city, while straying and biting ones would be largely excluded.

CHAPTER 4

Thinking

In March 1907, a reporter for the Paris newspaper *Le matin* paid a visit to Max, a police dog living with Madame Thirouin on rue Nationale. Despite Thirouin's assertion that this dog was an "intelligent animal," the journalist concluded that Max was "no psychologist." The police dog had mistaken him for an "Apache" criminal and had barked and strained on his lead. Despite his training at the hands of one of France's foremost police dog trainers, the dog could not, at least in this instance, distinguish between a criminal and a law-abiding citizen.[1]

In addition to offering a rare insight into police dogs' domestic arrangements, *Le matin*'s visit fed into a fascination with Paris's first police dogs, creatures who seemed to mark a new episode in its urban policing. Alongside concurrent developments in the training of customs and army dogs, police dog advocates saw an opportunity to reshape the human-canine bond to further urban security. Rather than confronting smugglers or enemy troops in the relative seclusion of the Franco-Belgian border or the battlefield, the experiment with police dogs took place on city streets, where public and media scrutiny was unrelenting.[2]

The introduction of police dogs in Paris marked a new stage in the relationship between dogs and law enforcement there as well as in London and New York. After decades of police chasing straying and biting dogs, a "natural antipathy" had developed "between dog and constable," noted satirical journal *Fun* in 1868.[3] But at the beginning of the twentieth century, police dog handlers were training canines for police work. This was specialized canine labor that gave a select handful of dogs social purpose within the emerging dogopolis. It stood in contrast to the use of relatively unskilled dogs to pull, say, New York ragpickers' carts, the sort of canine labor animal protectionists associated with working-class cruelty and rabies and succeeded in banishing. It also cleared the way for the interspecies bond that lay at the heart of highly skilled guide dog partnerships that developed after World War I. Alongside pedigree pet dogs, police dogs had the potential to be welcomed into dogopolis as dogs who were affectively bound to humans and who would help the middle classes thrive within the emotionally unsettling modern city. Police dogs might become part of the modern police force, which was integral to the rise of "bourgeois civilization" based on liberalism, capitalism, and the protection of private property.[4]

Police dog advocates paid careful attention to events in other cities, and specially trained dogs traveled across the Atlantic to patrol New York's streets. Echoing other developments in modern policing, police dogs emerged as a response to local conditions and circulated through transnational exchanges.[5] Supportive middle-class observers placed great faith in these dogs' thinking abilities. Unconsciously returning to debates about sagacious watch dogs who guarded private premises in Georgian London, journalists, dog lovers, and police dog trainers celebrated the important role that well-trained intelligent dogs could play in securing London, New York, and Paris from crime, thereby making wealthy citizens feel safer (fig. 4.1).[6] As middle-class fears of crime plagued all three cities, the police dogs' capacity to think, alongside their courage, loyalty, and strength, seemed poised to quell these anxieties. Their emotional attachment to their handler, developed during training and echoing the revered bond between pet dogs and their owners, would enable them to fulfill their crime-fighting potential. That, at least, was the hope placed on them.

The debate over whether dogs could think was hardly novel. Police dogs became embroiled in centuries-old deliberations on instinct and intelligence dating back to arguments over human rationality and animal impulses in ancient Greece. Fast forward to the seventeenth century, and René Descartes's philosophical model of animal machines famously denied animals reason and made rationality the defining feature of humanity. Cartesian philosophy became an influential yet disputed means of separating intelligence and instinct, splitting humans from animals. Then nineteenth-century evolutionary theories unsettled Cartesian assumptions and blurred the boundaries between instinct and intelligence.[7] Rather than boundaries, Charles Darwin and his protégé Georges Romanes depicted interlinked and fluid categories, an approach that influenced French psychologist Pierre Hachet-Souplet.

FIGURE 4.1 *Police Dog and Arrested Man*, New York City. Photograph by Bain News Service, 1912. Library of Congress, control number 2014680001.

In response, comparative psychologists Conwy Lloyd Morgan and Edward Lee Thorndike sought to reestablish the boundaries between animals and humans by denying the former intelligence.

At the same time, Darwinism unsettled the assumed superiority of human rationality. Darwin's emphasis on the animal roots of emotions in *The Expression of the Emotions in Man and Animals* (1872) made humans more like animals in being described as beings who were sometimes governed by hard-to-control passions. Darwinism also inspired Cesare Lombroso and other criminal anthropologists to depict criminals as instinctively driven and animalistic evolutionary throwbacks. Such claims, and the search for the biological causes of madness and delinquency, increasingly challenged notions of moral responsibility, human rationality, and free will. As physicians, anthropologists, psychologists, and psychiatrists animalized criminals, police dogs became thinking and socially useful creatures in ways that made them quasi-human.

Of the various kinds of animal intelligence identified in the nineteenth century, that of dogs was seen as having been most nurtured and enhanced through centuries of domestication.[8] This chapter explores how humans comprehended canine intelligence and sought to harness it through training, which was understood to be an emotional process designed to augment the dogs' thinking capacity and direct their biting instinct toward criminals. But misgivings soon surfaced. Were the dogs smart enough for police work? And could the emotional connection with their handlers ever tame the beast within? Was training enough to counter centuries of worries about canine biting? These questions animated a skeptical stance toward police dogs' crime-fighting abilities that was marked by doubt and anxiety. The instrumentalization of the human-canine bond to fight crime and the integration of police dogs' biting instinct into the emerging dogopolis were far from assured.

Mapping Crime

Stoked by lurid stories in newspapers, magazines, and novels, fears of crime haunted London, New York, and Paris. These cities gained reputations as perilous places in which murders, robberies, and assaults could happen anywhere and to anyone. Press reports depicted Parisian criminals as dangerously mobile and violent, with Apache gangs bursting out of their haunts in the city's parks and suburbs to wreak havoc in the city center. These gangs were first named Apaches in 1900 to denote their supposed savagery and refusal to conform to civilized norms. The term framed them as obstacles to social progress and Paris as a wild urban space of hunters (the police) and hunted (Apaches). British and American journalists and police officials deplored the Apache gangs' hold over the French capital and their global reach: New York police commissioner Theodore A. Bingham bemoaned the involvement of these "absinthe-consumed perverts" in New York prostitution rackets.[9]

Crime rates may have been falling in London (as they were in Paris), but British journalists and writers similarly served up shocking accounts of violent crimes to appall and entertain their readers. Their sensationalist narratives included tales of violent and drunk working-class men and women assaulting their neighbors, strangers, and policemen. Reported murder cases, including the Regent's Park and Whitehall murders in 1888, and the hooligan panic of the late 1890s reinforced the impression that the capital's streets and parks were plagued by solitary murderers and armed gangs of "roughs." Even though very few Londoners were likely to encounter a gang member, let alone a murderer, criminals seemingly threatened the city's law-abiding and respectable citizens.[10]

Fears of crime in New York fixated on the Lower East Side of Manhattan, including Five Points and the Bowery, as well as difficult-to-police suburban areas. Generated and sustained by public health and police reports, slum fiction, and newspaper articles, the image of slums as sites of poverty, misery, and crime in need of reform and containment crystallized during the nineteenth century. Immigration from southern and eastern Europe and East Asia intensified anxieties. More so than in London and Paris, observers understood these crimes with respect to their perpetrators' ethnicity. Bingham singled out Italians as the most violent of New York's criminals: "the audacity of these desperadoes is almost beyond belief."[11]

Jacob Riis and other slum investigators believed that the environmental and social roots of crime could be tackled through religion, charity work, the suppression of vice, temperance, better sanitation, and housing reform. Yet Riis also depicted criminals and other slum inhabitants as instinctual and animalistic: the gang member's "instincts of ferocity are those of the wolf rather than the tiger." He drew from Darwinist ideas in his classification of New York's immigrant populations, ranking them according to his appraisal of their ability to evolve and assimilate to white, middle-class, and Protestant ideals. According to Riis, life in the slums transformed human biology. The New York "tough" was "less repulsively brutal in his looks" than his "London brother," as the "breed is not so old. A few generations more in the slums, and all that will be changed." He posited that "the whole strain of tenement-house dwellers has been bred down to the conditions under which it exists. . . . This is the familiar law of nature."[12] Riis's language of instincts, animals, strains, breeds, natural laws, and survival spoke to new—if far from universally accepted—understandings of criminality in the United States, Britain, and France in the post-Darwinian era.

Instinctive Humans and "Born" Criminals

Doctors, including French physician and psychologist Prosper Despine, had linked criminality to heredity in the first half of the nineteenth century. By the end of that century, influential physicians, psychiatrists, and psychologists increasingly saw instincts as observable explanations for human behavior. They identified strong continuities between human and animal minds, instincts, and conduct. Alongside stressing the emotional aspects of rabies (see chapter 2), Scottish physician William Lauder Lindsay argued that crime, especially theft, was common among animals. Dogs could be trained out of their thieving inclinations, but criminals could also train them to steal. Humans, meanwhile, had retained bestial characteristics: "there is always a bestial tendency in man, however civilized, a liability to the development of theroid instincts, an aptitude for reversion or, in morals and intelligence, in passions and appetites." If even the most developed humans could degenerate, then those who were identified as having low intelligence and poor morality were particularly susceptible to bestial instincts. This perspective downplayed free will and rationality, and it often turned criminals into creatures governed by harmful instinctual impulses. It seeped into journalistic reports that explained criminal behavior and insanity as hereditary. In this vein, newspapers in the United States branded the infamous Chinatown criminal George Appo as "Born to Crime."[13]

Nineteenth-century evolutionary thinking about instinct informed this approach to criminality. Charles Darwin avoided offering a precise definition of instinct in *On the Origin of Species* (1859). Instead, he identified a widespread understanding of instinct as an action that individual members of the same species performed "without their knowing . . . [the] purpose." He developed his theory through observing dogs. Retrievers and sheepdogs had inherited, rather than learned, their instinct to retrieve or herd, he believed. Darwin's comparative method blurred distinctions between humans and animals, and he transformed instinct into a cross-species entity when he speculated that human intelligence had its origins in animal instincts. In *The Descent of Man* (1871), he argued that humans and animals shared certain instincts, including "self-preservation" and "sexual love." In both humans and animals, social instincts drew individuals together and formed the basis of cooperation. Differences, however, existed. Certain animals possessed far more complex instincts than humans—a spider knew instinctively how to spin an intricate web—while humans had a greater capacity to learn than animals. They alone could reflect retrospectively on their actions and hold in mind what others thought of them, both of which modified their instinctual behaviors.[14]

Darwin's evolutionary theories influenced criminologists. Most famously, Italian criminology pioneer Cesare Lombroso advanced an influential theory in *Criminal Man* (1876) that some criminals were "born with evil inclinations." Through an examination of skulls, brain size, height, hairiness, and facial features, criminal anthropologists claimed to be able to uncover criminals' animalistic, violent, and instinctive traits. In their view, criminals differed emotionally from the rest of society. They lacked "sympathy for the misfortune of others," were insensitive to pain, and displayed "precipitous passions." They were abnormally motivated by revenge, and their emotions were marked by "instability, impetuousness and often violence." In reviving long-standing literary representations of bestial criminals, Lombroso gave a pseudoscientific gloss to the animalization of criminals. And although the fourth edition (1889) of *Criminal Man* paid more heed to the role of environmental factors in shaping criminals, Lombroso became best known for his identification of the atavistic born criminal.[15]

As with Darwin, dogs provided evidence for Lombroso. Echoing the association of straying with degeneration, he stated that "the dog left to run wild in the forest will in a few generations revert to the type of his original wolf-like progenitor." Domestication and civilization were traits that could be reversed in certain environments. Wildness could return. Drawing legitimacy from reports on scientific experiments, Lombroso claimed that "under special conditions produced by alcohol, chloroform, heat, or injuries, ants, dogs and pigeons become irritable and savage like their wild ancestors. This tendency to alter under special conditions is common to human beings." Rabies might also spark criminality, he noted. He claimed to show how one of his subjects, Giuseppe Fissore, had already displayed signs of criminal tendencies, such as somnambulism, as a young boy; these tendencies were then aggravated by the bite of a mad dog.[16]

Lombroso's theories were far from universally accepted, with critics attacking his relative neglect of environmental causes of crime. Nonetheless, his books were published in Britain, France, and the United States, and his biological explanations for human behavior and pathology were discussed at international congresses on criminal anthropology. This new discipline found a particularly warm reception in the United States, where it helped establish criminology as a respectable science under the auspices of the American Institute of Criminal Law and Criminology (founded in 1909) and eventually legitimized restrictive immigration laws.[17]

French physicians, such as Hubert Boëns, had already begun to apply heredity theories to criminality. They animalized instinctive criminals who, like dangerous and worthless animals, needed containment. Prominent French criminologist Alexandre Lacassagne may have distanced himself from some of Lombroso's bolder assertions on born criminals, yet he still claimed French roots for the discipline of criminal anthropology and ascribed to its perspective on heredity. New police techniques also dovetailed with criminal anthropology, especially Alphonse Bertillon's method of identifying individual criminals through physical features. Transnational connections spread these techniques, with Bertillon demonstrating his method to delegates at the 1889 Congress of Criminal Anthropology on their field trip to the Paris police prefecture.[18]

Criminal anthropology was less influential in Britain, where environmental theories of crime persisted even among Lombroso's biggest supporters, such as Havelock Ellis. Nonetheless, some British criminologists depicted criminals as animal-like savages unable to control their violent urges. Even before the publication of *Criminal Man,* Edmund Du Cane, chair of the Directors of Convict Prisons, had argued that habitual criminals "approach those of the lower animals so that they seem to be going back to the type of what Professor Darwin calls 'our arboreal ancestors.'" But not all British physicians and psychologists depicted instinct as an uncontrollable and intrinsically destructive force in humans. Intelligence and morality were said to restrain animalistic desires. Surgeon and psychologist Wilfred Trotter, for his part, treated herd instinct—or the innate need to associate with other humans—as a foundation of social life and survival.[19]

Nonetheless, the image of instinctive criminals against which society needed to defend itself took root in Britain as well as in France and the United States. With many physicians, psychologists, and psychiatrists animalizing criminals, other middle-class commentators proposed that canine intelligence might serve society in combating robbers, gang members, and murderers.

Thinking Dogs

The question of animal intelligence dates to at least the Aristotelian distinction between rational human souls and sensory animal ones. René Descartes strengthened this vision of unthinking animals with his depiction of animal machines. Sensationalist philosophers, including Abbé de Condillac (1715–1780), argued against Descartes, believing that animals could act reasonably in response to their sensory environment by drawing from memories and imaginative associations. Darwin continued the sensationalist argument in his belief that thinking comprised a series of images that arose from sensations, memories, and associations. He claimed that animals were capable of thought, could learn from experience, and could act rationally: "instinctive actions may lose their fixed and untaught character, and be replaced by others performed by the aid of the free will. On the other hand, some intelligent actions, after being performed during several generations, become converted into instincts and are inherited." In identifying mental continuities between species, Darwin blurred human-animal boundaries as well as those between instinct and intelligence.[20]

In reinvigorating the question of animal intelligence, Darwin paved the way for the discipline of comparative psychology. Georges Romanes continued in his footsteps. He collated and synthesized a vast number of anecdotes in *Animal Intelligence* (1882), ordering animals on an evolutionary scale from protozoa to primates. More so than his predecessors, Romanes sought to define instinct and intelligence and their relationship to reflex actions. Reflex actions were hereditary and physiological, and they could be triggered by environmental stimuli. In contrast, an organism displayed intelligence when it learned "by its own individual experience." To varying degrees, certain animals were intelligent, as they were capable of "balancing relations, drawing inferences, and . . . forecasting probabilities." For instance, some creatures could infer a relationship between action and consequences. Instinct sat between reflexes and intelligence. It was "antecedent to individual experience, without the necessary knowledge of the relation between the means employed and the ends attained, but similarly performed under the same appropriate circumstances by all the individuals of the same species." Crucially, Romanes argued that some instinctive actions contained an "element of mind," by which he meant that they entailed "*mental* operations" or "consciousness." The organism could choose a course of action in response to stimuli. It was the "amount of conscious deliberation" that separated instinct and intelligence. Despite their differences, reflexes, instincts, and intelligence sat on the same spectrum and arose from the same "nervous processes."[21]

Dogs recurred frequently in the debates on animal intelligence. The notion that they were intelligent animals reinforced wider understandings of them as clever and capable creatures at the end of the nineteenth century. In 1870 dog breeder and writer Thomas Pearce (whose pen name was Idstone) argued that "mongrel" and working dogs, such as rat catchers, circus dogs, and poachers' lurchers, were among the most intelligent kinds of dogs. Sheepdogs transmitted their "shrewdness" to their offspring, while Idstone's own crossbred terrier Havelock was so intelligent that his "eye was actually eloquent, and like that of a human being. It looked through you. As you watched him you couldn't help believing in the transmigration of souls." Pet keeping not only provided evidence of dogs' emotional qualities but also laid bare their intelligence. British writer Harriet Anne de Salis was far from alone when she observed that "there is no doubt that [pet] dogs must be endowed with something more than instinct."[22]

Even if dogs lacked human levels of intentionality, consciousness, and reflection, their capacity to think struck observers as remarkable and seemed to cement their connection with their human companions. One anecdote in *Harper's Weekly* had it that a dog saw his master drop a gold coin, picked it up in his mouth, and refused to eat anything "for fear he should drop the treasure" before the master returned. This dog seemingly possessed foresight, an understanding of the value of money, and unstinting loyalty to his owner. Another dog was said to "distinguish at a glance a tramp or a swell-mob's man from a gentleman, even in the most soiled attire." Canine intelligence mingled with sensory adroitness and emotional depth to allow them to understand human difference.[23] The much-remarked-upon ability of dogs to ascertain social variation helped legitimize their eventual police work.

In France, animal intelligence also became a much-discussed topic. Although ignoring the scientific debates that animated comparative psychology, Charles Delattre and other writers similarly collated stories of clever animals, including bears, lions, tigers, foxes, and, of course, dogs. Throughout the nineteenth century, French dog owners also reported on their pets' intelligence in both the mainstream and the specialist press.[24]

French psychologists sought to ground the discussion of animal intelligence in experimentation and research. In 1901 the General Psychological Institute established a group charged with studying animal intelligence and psychology. Pierre Hachet-Souplet became the first director of its Institute of Zoological Psychology and spearheaded efforts to better understand animal intelligence. In line with evolutionary theories, he placed human intelligence at the top of the evolutionary scale and treated it as a more complex manifestation of animal psychological abilities. He claimed that dogs and monkeys possessed a sense of self, dreamed, and were capable of abstract thought. Dogs also possessed reason. And like humans, they could lose their minds and be driven to suicide. However, Hachet-Souplet identified limits to canine intelligence: human intervention and guidance were required for it to emerge in a useful way, just as schoolchildren needed effective teaching to become intelligent adults. The abilities of dogs and other domestic animals developed and revealed themselves through training relationships with humans.[25]

Disputing Canine Intelligence

Yet the question of animal intelligence remained controversial. American natural historians deliberated on the topic, and not all were convinced. Naturalist John Burroughs, alongside president Theodore Roosevelt, attacked so-called nature fakers, those writers who made spurious claims about animal intellects and abilities. Revisiting Descartes, Burroughs claimed that animals were nothing more than "machines in fur and feathers."[26]

Psychologists on both sides of the Atlantic similarly challenged the notion of animal intelligence. Georges Bohn of the École des hautes études in Paris aligned the discipline of psychology with those of chemistry and the biological sciences, and he deplored the "more or less fantastical stories of the old psychology" of Darwin and Romanes.[27]

In Britain, Conwy Lloyd Morgan cautioned against claiming too much knowledge of animal minds in *Animal Life and Intelligence* (1890). He argued that dogs could dream, form "highly complex [mental] constructs," and understand some basic human words, but they could not reason or analyze. His skeptical attitude toward animal intelligence hardened by the time he published *An Introduction to Comparative Psychology* in 1894, a book that contained his much-quoted canon: "*In no case may we interpret an action as the outcome of the exercise of a higher psychical faculty, if it can be interpreted as the outcome of the exercise of one which stands lower in the psychological scale.*" Although he continued to admit the possibility of higher mental faculties in some animals, he now stressed the "breach" between the "mental development" of humans and animals. "The step from consentience, or sense-experience, to reflection and thought" was uniquely human.[28]

Morgan's caution had a major impact on the development of comparative psychology in the United States. Strengthening Morgan's opposition to Romanes and inspired by German experimental psychology, Edward Lee Thorndike claimed that his puzzle boxes, which he developed as a psychology PhD candidate at Columbia University, showed that animals were far from intelligent. In his wooden contraptions, hungry cats, dogs, and chicks negotiated loops, levers, bolts, and platforms in their search for food while Thorndike timed them and plotted the results on a time-curve graph. He used his findings to dismiss the very idea of animal intelligence as misguided, subjective, and anthropomorphic: "dogs get lost hundreds of times and no one ever notices it or sends an account to a scientific magazine. But let one find his way from Brooklyn to Yonkers and the fact immediately becomes a circulating anecdote." Thorndike argued that his experiments proved conclusively that animals could not reason and that they only had a limited capacity for learning through imitation. Instead, they learned to make associations between actions and consequences "merely by the accidental success of [their] natural impulses." These acts were repeatable not due to memory but because the animals found themselves in a similar situation that generated the same impulse and subsequent pleasurable sensory experience. Humans, on the other hand, made far more frequent and complex associations through thought, inference, and comparison.[29] Morgan's canon and Thorndike's puzzle boxes had an enormous influence on the establishment of comparative psychology in the United States, which became an academic discipline founded on experimentation and the denouncement of anthropomorphism.

Yet the question of animal intelligence was far from settled within scientific circles, as Robert M. Yerkes and Lawrence W. Cole challenged Thorndike's dismissal of animal intelligence.[30] The debate also burst from the country homes of British evolutionists and spilled out of the laboratories of French and American psychologists onto city streets. Dogs sat just below primates on evolutionary scales of animal intelligence in the post-Darwinian world, but were they intelligent enough to be trained for police work? Could training direct canine instincts and intelligence against instinctual criminals to reduce the public's fear of crime? Would the emotional connection between trainer and dog be enough to contain the latter's bestial passions? These questions animated the development and deployment of police dogs, and the attempts to integrate them within dogopolis, beginning with bloodhounds.

Bringing In the Bloodhounds

Bloodhounds seemed to offer an effective and specialized way of tracking down elusive criminals. London was their initial testing ground, with the New York press closely following developments. Charles Warren, chief commissioner of the Metropolitan Police, called in two bloodhounds—Barnaby and Burgho—to hunt the serial killer known as Jack the Ripper in 1888. Buoyed by the promises of the dogs' owner, Edwin Brough, and a successful trial run in Regent's Park, detectives hoped that the dogs' ability to track scents would transfer from the British countryside to the slums of East London. Brough was not alone in framing bloodhounds as canine detectives whose extraordinary intellectual and olfactory powers would enhance policemen's ability to solve crime—commentators compared the sleuthing hounds to Sherlock Holmes. These human and nonhuman detectives shared good breeding, extraordinary environmental sensitivity, and high levels of independence and initiative.[31]

Yet concerns immediately arose about the dogs' savage instincts. British journalists had already reported bloodhounds' unprovoked mauling of children across the Atlantic in New Jersey. They now worried that the dogs would mistake innocent Londoners for a murderer and attack them. Even dog lovers noted bloodhounds' potential for ferocity. Renowned dog expert Gordon Stables related his own "uneasy" experience of being tracked by a bloodhound on a training exercise. These were intelligent yet potentially vicious dogs. They could show aggression to their "captive"—"the horrible savageness of the fixing [of the captured criminal] will hardly bear thinking about"—yet there was also a "scrutinising calmness and dignity about the eye of a well-bred bloodhound." Stables further noted that "if you are a perfect stranger to the [bloodhound], it is evident he is regarding you not with hatred by any means, nor with affection, but with thoughtfulness mingled with a little suspicion of your intentions." He concluded that this intelligence ultimately controlled bloodhounds' aggressive instincts. The mixture of instinct and intelligence alongside careful breeding and training would, he felt, enable them to track down criminals.[32]

In line with his status as dog breeder, Brough stressed the importance of breeding to control bloodhound ferocity. Overlooking the earlier British use of bloodhounds to track and oppress slaves in Jamaica, he contrasted the well-bred English pedigree bloodhound with the "savage" Cuban bloodhound used by slave owners in the southern United States to track down fugitive slaves. Breeding and training would, he asserted, ensure that his dogs acted in a civilized, safe, and useful fashion.[33]

In the end, Barnaby and Burgho did not get a chance to pursue Jack the Ripper. But the debate on bloodhounds' intelligence, instincts, and suitability for police work continued on both sides of the Atlantic. Brough exhibited his dogs at shows in the United States, where his promotion of the breed's aristocratic lineage chimed with the aspirations of elite American dog fanciers. Dr. Louis H. Knox, a Connecticut supplier of bloodhounds to police forces in the United States, asserted that "they're the cleverest dogs you ever saw." Echoing Brough and trying to dampen concerns over their ferocious instincts and brutal past, Knox claimed that his purebred dogs had nothing to do with the crossbreeds once used to track slaves. Glossing over bloodhounds' enrollment in the violent defense of slavery and racism, he highlighted their tender and kind character: "why the bloodhound has a friendship for man so intense that the victim he quarries or tracks to earth is fondled with caresses and never molested, unless the dog is specially trained to do him injury."[34] According to Knox, pedigree bloodhounds' instincts were fundamentally benign, and their love for humans could be harnessed successfully for police work.

Criminal anthropology provided the intellectual framework to justify the deployment of bloodhounds. Leading New York police analyst Leonard Felix Fuld presented the Lombrosian view that criminals were identifiably different from the rest of society. They smelled unlike "ordinary" men due to the increased perspiration triggered by their heightened feelings of "fear or rage" or state of "intoxication." Fuld's identification of criminals' supposedly intense odor resonated with bloodhound breeders' claims that white and upper-class men possessed the subtlest and most elusive scent that only highly trained dogs could follow.[35] Malodorous criminals would, in theory, be easy to track down.

Others, however, argued that bloodhounds would not be able to tell the difference between criminals and innocent citizens. A commentator in *American Lawyer* questioned the legality of using a bloodhound's identification of a criminal in court, as the dog could not be sworn into court or cross-examined. During a Nebraska Supreme Court case in 1905, one lawyer argued that a bloodhound pursuit is "an act of a dumb brute, proceeding from no intelligence, with no realization of the importance of his act or the consequences that might follow it." Such animal machines had no place in the courtroom. And despite his identification of a distinct criminal smell, Fuld concluded that "the mere pointing of the dog to a person is not sufficient to determine that he is the criminal. There must be additional evidence."[36]

Despite these arguments, the New York police force contemplated deploying bloodhounds. After a tour of European cities—and even with opposition from inspector James McCafferty, who believed that the dogs would be unable to follow scents in the urban environment—deputy commissioner Arthur Woods recommended their mobilization. This decision followed the murder of Amelia Staffeldt near Long Island City in May 1907 when detectives believed that a bloodhound would have helped locate and arrest her killer. Woods charged Lieutenant George R. Wakefield, a dog enthusiast, with preparing a study on the usefulness of bloodhounds in tracking suspects in the American metropolis. Like McCafferty, Wakefield concluded that bloodhounds would be of limited use, as they would lose a suspect's scent in the event that they jumped onto a street trolley. Modern urban infrastructure would confuse bloodhound noses. Former New York police chief "Big Bill" Devery put it bluntly: "Bloodhounds in this great metropolitan city? It is to laugh." Nonetheless, the Long Island Railroad decided to deploy bloodhounds. It subsequently reported that English bloodhounds recruited by superintendent Robert E. Kerkam had helped reduce murders and burglaries at its stations. The Long Island hounds had even reportedly tracked down an Italian gang of copper bond wire thieves from the "cold steel rails" to an "East New York liquor shop."[37]

Yet concerns about bloodhounds' inability to reason and bloodthirsty instincts persisted. In June 1908, one of the bloodhound guard dogs at the prison in Mount Holly, New Jersey, "jumped" at their handler's throat and then took "full possession of the jail yard all day." Neither guards nor prisoners proved willing to approach the dog. Legacies of racialized violence also informed the debate. Memories of slaveholders' use of bloodhounds to track runaway slaves continued to fuel reservations about the appropriateness of tracking humans with dogs. For the *Los Angeles Times,* it was "too much of a reminder of those dark days of slavery, when the animals were the terror of those who tried to make their way to freedom." Despite such concerns, bloodhounds were still deployed to stalk African American suspects, including on George Vanderbilt's Biltmore estate in Asheville, North Carolina, in August 1907. This breed of dog thus continued to play a role in the racialized policing of African Americans as humanized "sleuth hounds" tracking down animalized humans. But they proved too unsuited to the modern cityscape and too burdened by their violent past to find a place within dogopolis.[38]

Promoting All-Purpose Police Dogs

Bloodhounds were not deployed on the streets of Paris. Instead, the city's police force, like its continental European counterparts, promoted multipurpose police dogs. As with British experiments with bloodhounds, these developments attracted the attention of American observers. William G. Fitz-Gerald identified "little Belgium" as the main police dog innovator. He reported how the police commissioner of the City of Ghent, E. Van Wesemael, had deployed "powerful and sagacious" Belgian sheepdogs in the 1890s to make up for the force's manpower deficiencies. Van Wesemael had harnessed the dogs' "sense of smell, their instinct that all was not right, and their remarkable jumping and swimming powers" to great effect. As press attention focused on his animals, Van Wesemael told the *New York Times* that "a dog is always alert: eyes, ears and nose are constantly at work to detect any one or anything strange." In addition to these sensory powers, dogs could better traverse and investigate dark corners of the city than their human companions, and "when it comes to close quarters [with a suspect] he would be a more dreaded antagonist than a policeman." The London *Daily Mail,* meanwhile, noted the dogs' impressive intelligence and physical prowess. They could "generally achieve feats which the ordinary policeman would not think of attempting."[39] The canines' combination of instinct and intelligence seemingly destined them for police work.

France's first police dogs arrived in 1905 when the police commissioner of Pont-à-Mousson (Meurthe-et-Moselle), inspired by accounts of Belgian and German police dogs and encouraged by the Eastern Canine Society, deployed a couple of dogs to help control the town's many "brigands." The next year, the Eastern Canine Society organized a police dog show in Nancy at which Belgian and German dogs, along with the two from Pont-à-Mousson, were judged on their abilities to find a hidden man, defend their master from a stick-wielding assailant, and jump over obstacles. The display impressed Lalloué, a policeman from Epinal (Vosges), who subsequently obtained some German shepherds to train for police work. The dogs' sense of smell, intelligence, trainability, and physical strength seemed to offer an effective solution to urban policing deficiencies. Like uniforms, police dogs would give policemen greater visibility on the streets and underscore the state's commitment to fighting crime. In this vein, Lalloué argued that the "four-legged policeman" not only offered human policemen physical protection, especially at night, but accorded them more "dignity and authority" because they felt "stronger." Echoing pet-keeping narratives, he promoted close affective companionship as ennobling and socially beneficial.[40]

Henri Simart, police commissioner of the Parisian suburb of Neuilly, similarly drew inspiration from Belgium during his visit to Ghent. Hoping to better protect his men after the murder of Brigadier Fleurant, he secured approval from Neuilly's municipal council in February 1907 to use dogs to "purge" the Bois de Boulogne, a large public park, of "disreputable people." With newspaper reports portraying the Bois de Boulogne as a poorly policed and therefore dangerous space plagued by Apaches, the dogs' potential contribution to policing seemed significant.[41]

French police dog promoters held high hopes for these canines. Dogs ostensibly possessed the necessary physical and mental attributes to become effective police auxiliaries. They might even counter some of the nefarious effects of urban life on the human population. In line with medical theories stressing that modern life in cities caused individual and national degeneration, social problems, alcoholism, and crime, and with the American Wild West in mind, writer René Simon claimed that 95 percent of modern city dwellers had lost the physical strength and keen senses possessed by "ancient Indian tribes," "valiant pioneers," and "hardy hunters." These people were under constant threat from silent yet deadly criminals who had retained the savage strength of uncivilized peoples. In some areas, "the bourgeoisie dared not go out at night." Consciously or not, Simon echoed Darwin's racialized belief that certain instincts, as well as powers of intuition and "rapid perception," were stronger in "lower races" and provided evidence of "a past and lower state of civilization." Dogs would mitigate the physical and sensory deficiencies of the civilized urbanite. For Simon, they had the "muscular suppleness, sensory sharpness, instinctive sense of smell, [and] alert attention" that the French middle classes no longer possessed.[42]

Local initiatives took precedence over centralized programs during the early stages of police dog work in France, replicating the weak centralization of French policing. However, national societies and clubs soon emerged that spearheaded the integration of police dogs into dogopolis. The Police, Game-Keeper, and Customs Dog Club, founded in 1908, brought together members of the French Kennel Club and individual dog breed societies as well as politicians and police officials (including Simart). The club established a police dog training kennel on rue Chevaleret in Paris's 13th arrondissement. Its membership made it somewhat elitist, however. In contrast, the Union of Guard and Police Dog Enthusiasts in France, founded in 1910, portrayed police dog training as a useful "recreational sport" suitable for all and an effective form of self-defense fit for a democratic republic. The union organized shows in which police dog skills could be judged and showcased. It was believed that the ideal police dog contained a mixture of instinct and intelligence as well as emotional fortitude. Judges gave dogs points for their "general attitude" and such qualities as "love of work, shrewdness, brilliance, intelligence, instinct, atavism, will [and] courage." Esteemed figures such as president Armand Fallières frequented the shows, which were also the object of enthusiastic press reports.[43]

Paris's municipal council eventually budgeted eight thousand francs to create a police dog service on December 30, 1908. Although the police prefecture purchased seven dogs of its own, six of its other dogs were privately owned and lodged with individual policemen. It also hired twenty-six dogs from the Police, Game-Keeper, and Customs Dog Club and accepted twelve others donated by writer, philanthropist, and entrepreneur Henri de Rothschild. Whatever their provenance, the dogs were to patrol Paris's outer arrondissements and suburbs, where open and abandoned land was commonplace and considered crime ridden.[44]

British and American police officers, dog lovers, and journalists keenly followed developments in France. In his survey of European police dogs, British police and army dog enthusiast Edwin H. Richardson identified French ones as the most violent, which he explained by the ferocity of their criminal opponent: "the low, skulking, murderous, Parisian Apache." Dubbing the Paris police dog shows "contest[s] in sagacity," the *Daily Mail* was similarly impressed by the dogs' displays of strength and intelligence as they successfully chased men playing the "role of hooligan." The *Brooklyn*

Daily Eagle portrayed Parisian police dogs as a vital measure against the city's violent Apache gangs, noting with approval that "a strong jawed mastiff had a courage far beyond that of any man, and a detective skill almost human. Moreover, the dog could frighten the Apache, which is more than can be said for a policeman, detective or gendarme." The dogs also combined with other innovations in French policing techniques. They helped the police "make a sudden descent on the Parisian equivalent of a Bowery lodging house," reported the *New York Times*, guarding the suspects until the police arrived to conduct Bertillon checks.[45]

Impressed by developments in continental Europe, the New York police force established its own canine unit. Upon the orders of Deputy Commissioner Woods, Lieutenant Wakefield secured five puppies from Ghent in 1907. He trained them at a dilapidated mansion in Fort Washington Park in Upper Manhattan, assisted by patrolmen Berrman and McDonnell. The training program was based on Wakefield's attendance at a police dog training course in Ghent and his experience with breeding and training dogs. Following their French counterparts, wealthy American canophiles promoted the use of privately trained dogs. In 1915 Benjamin H. Throop established a police dog training college at West Hempstead, Long Island, to train German shepherds for sale to municipal police forces.[46]

Richardson, who also visited Ghent as well as Paris and Berlin on a fact-finding mission, advocated the use of British police dogs against the hooligan, "a murderous scoundrel, who renders our constable's night-beat in the slums a dangerous one." Apparently unaware of Morgan's and Thorndike's critiques of anthropomorphism, he suggested that the police could harness canine characteristics, including "sagacity," determination, and a "keen sense of humour," to scout out empty houses and nocturnal streets for "suspicious characters." Like bloodhounds, all-purpose police dogs needed a good sense of smell. But their main role was to protect their handler and physically apprehend criminals. Richardson trained Airedales as police dogs at his home in Harrow and loaned them to police forces around Britain. One of his dogs, Bob, had reportedly helped reduce the number of burglaries in Glasgow. Yet despite Richardson's encouragement and the deployment of dogs in Liverpool, Nottingham, and Manchester, among other cities, the London Metropolitan Police remained unconvinced and chose not to establish a police dog service. Concerns about the potentially lethal violence of police dogs may have preyed on commissioners' minds. Richardson attempted to downplay such qualms: "the death of the criminal is never desired, and these dogs while they can hold on can never kill."[47]

Instead of creating a centralized service, police commissioner Sir Edward Henry allowed policemen patrolling sparsely populated areas at night to take their own dogs with them, as long as they paid for the dogs' licenses and upkeep. Unlike New York and Paris, the onus rested on individual policemen to deploy pet-police hybrid dogs. Often regarded as a model of innovation, the Metropolitan Police force lagged behind Paris and New York in the deployment of police dogs, even as British authorities in South Africa (from 1908) and Palestine (from 1935) spearheaded their use in tracking down Black South Africans and suspected Palestinian terrorists. The dogs' potential for violence was treated as less of an issue in the colonies than in the metropole.[48]

Police Dog Breeds

There was no consensus on the best type of dog for police work. Instead, trainers and journalists assessed the mental, emotional, and physical attributes of various breeds. They divided dogs into categories and established a hierarchy of their intelligence, abilities, and potential for police work. These rankings resonated with the growing if controversial interest in measuring and assessing human intelligence, as pioneered in France and the United States during the early twentieth century by Alfred Binet and other psychologists.[49]

The invention, standardization, and promotion of dog breeds during the nineteenth century (see chapter 1) gave police dog trainers and handlers an array of breeds to consider. In harmony with arguments put forward by increasingly vocal and organized pedigree dog breeders, one French observer advised police commissioners that pure breeds were superior to mongrels: training was not everything, and just as good servants could not be found in "vagabond asylums," so dog pounds and refuges were poor places to obtain police dogs. In line with breeders' claims that purebred dogs were the product of rational selection, expert knowledge, and prestigious ancestry, Robert Gersbach—a German breeder whose police dog training manual was translated into French in 1911—advocated the careful examination by police forces of any potential police dog's breed, particularly its "history and development," and for trying to secure dogs from among the breed's "elite subjects." Better still would be to favor the offspring of successful police dogs, since they would have inherited the "moral qualities" of their parents.[50]

Some experts recommended particular breeds. Richardson favored Airedales due to their suspicious attitude toward strangers, loyalty to their masters, and excellent senses. However, in a rare expression of doubt about the desirability of purebred dogs, he warned against Airedales bred for the "show-bench." It was best to have "a dash of collie, sheep-dog, bull-mastiff or retriever" to help "with character." Lalloué also identified Airedales as a suitable breed, alongside Alsatians, Dobermans, and Belgian and French sheepdogs. Each of these had their advantages and disadvantages. Dobermans were highly trainable but could be hostile to other dogs, while Airedales offered policemen a heightened sense of security but were poor at jumping and running long distances. Of all of them, Lalloué concluded that the Alsatian—or German shepherd—was the "ideal" police dog due to the breed's excellent sense of smell, trainability, loyalty, and "very developed intelligence."[51]

Across the Atlantic, Throop's Swiss-born trainer Rudolph Hauri similarly praised the German shepherd, who "takes kindly to the most rigorous training and it's not long before we have them perfectly fitted for police work." Joseph Couplet, whose police dog training manual was praised by police analyst Leonard Felix Fuld in a glowing review in the *Journal of American Institute of Criminal Law and Criminology*, also claimed that shepherd dogs were best, due to their historical role of protecting sheep from wolves. The breed now embodied the perfect combination of canine emotional, physical, and cognitive abilities, forged through centuries of protecting productive human communities from dangerous outsiders. The journal *L'eleveur belge* offered a lone voice of dissent against German shepherds, arguing that they were hesitant to bite. Since the French police wanted dogs for protection, they were hardly an "ideal" choice.[52]

Some police dog experts, however, cared more about personality than pedigree. Pierre Saint-Laurent agreed with the suitability of German shepherds for police work. But he emphasized that the individual dog's "personal qualities" were more important than their breed, especially since dogs of the same breed differed substantially. In contrast to the quantifying aspirations of the Binet-Simon human intelligence test, many police dog experts recommended subjective assessments of individual dogs and placed major emphasis on the affective connection between handler and dog. Lieutenant Wakefield noted that "dogs, like men, vary in intelligence, and have their special adaptabilities." Simon, moreover, argued that trainers should only work with one dog to develop the "most perfect" understanding of each partner's "will." In such a way, training would take into account the "psychology of each animal," since every dog had a "particular soul." By this Simon meant a "character, a collection of qualities and flaws which are unique [to the individual dog] and distinguishes him from his peers."[53] Once again, the preferred police dog–handler partnership mirrored the model of middle-class pet keeping promoted within the developing dogopolis.

The lack of expert consensus on breed partly explains why French and American police forces used a variety of dogs. Belgian sheepdogs and a Groenendael, which Wakefield imported from Belgium, comprised the bulk of the official New York police canine unit. The *New York Times* stressed their suitability: "the faces of these dogs have a keen fox-like expression, and they are noted for their courage, intelligence, and endurance." Jean Lembach, a sailor on the boat that had ferried the dogs across the Atlantic, confirmed that they were indeed hardy, intelligent, and eminently cut out for police work due to their mistrust of strangers—a quality journalists experienced firsthand when they approached the dogs on the quayside only to be greeted by growls.[54]

Dogs of other breeds joined the force in more haphazard ways. When one of the Belgian dogs died, Wakefield replaced him with an Airedale. Recruitment also took place informally. Jim, a dog "born with the detective instinct" and "of no particular breed known to fanciers," showed such an interest in the police dog training taking place in Fort Washington Park that his owner allowed him to join the unit, as "he had lost interest in everything but detective work." According to a journalist who was presumably not acquainted with Morgan's and Thorndike's assertions that animals could not educate each other, Jim "was soon training the other dogs." It seemed he had "an almost uncanny wisdom that placed him head and shoulders above" the other dogs.[55]

The first two police dogs in France—Achate and Argus—were mongrels trained in Pont-à-Mousson in 1905. Although the Eastern Canine Society had recommended purebred canines to the town's police commissioner, he accepted a spontaneous offer of the mongrels rather than seeking funds to buy expensive pedigree dogs. In contrast, Commissioner Simart used Belgian shepherd dogs in Neuilly's canine unit, and when the Paris police force obtained ten dogs in 1909, nine of them were German shepherds (the tenth was a French shepherd).[56]

As with breeds, there was no consensus on the desired sex of police dogs. Although male dogs took the top three places at a police dog competition in August 1908, two bitches, Foullette and Mordienne, came in fourth and fifth. And though the names of certain dogs—Garcon and Moustache—contributed to the Paris police force's culture of masculinity, police units also deployed bitches. Female dogs proved themselves effective agents in the field. They included the German shepherd Lucie, who reportedly used her intelligence and sense of smell to pick out two fugitives from a crowded bar.[57] Rather than sex or breed, the dog's individual capabilities, and their response to training, were treated as paramount.

Training Canine Recruits

A host of manuals laid out detailed and extensive programs for police dog training, resonating with the more in-depth training that policemen underwent. They also echoed the advice offered in pet care books: owners needed to train their dogs carefully to cement the bond with their pet, and the trainer's emotional stance toward the dog should be calm, gentle, and firm. The training manuals often traversed national boundaries. Fuld urged that Couplet's book, which had drawn inspiration from the French translation of Pathfinder and Hugh Dalziel's training manual, be translated and distributed to all policemen in the United States.[58] These manuals promoted police dogs as intelligent animals whose emotional bond with their trainer could be effectively harnessed to alleviate crime and related fears.

The guides presented dogs as creatures who possessed varying degrees of intelligence and instinct. They were not animal machines but adaptable and responsive animals whom a methodical, sensitive, and patient trainer could train to perform a range of complex policing tasks. In making such claims, the trainer-authors followed in the footsteps of Charles Darwin and Georges Romanes in treating instinct and intelligence as reciprocal and flexible qualities.[59] But in contrast to comparative psychologists of whatever persuasion, trainers sought to better understand animal minds, not to prove or disprove arguments about the relationship between humans and other animals in the post-Darwinian world, but to mobilize dogs to more effectively fight crime. This was practical animal psychology tested on the fraught city streets.

Gaston de Wael, a Belgian trainer, placed much emphasis on canine intelligence. He noted that the "marvels" of dogs' intelligence were becoming more and more apparent. Drawing from the anti-Cartesian strands contained within the writings of Gottfried Wilhelm Leibnitz (1646–1716), de Wael argued that although instinct often governed dogs, they could be trained to act intelligently. Instinct was a property that belonged to a species and could not be developed, only suppressed. Intelligence, on the other hand, was a "faculty" that could be cultivated in individual animals through training and rewards. So even though de Wael believed that dogs "cannot reason," he argued that the well-trained dog would learn to associate finding a "wrongdoer" with receiving a treat from their owner and become less governed by those instincts that inhibited police work, such as chasing cats and fighting. Trainers could also help dogs to "reflect" on what to do in certain situations. De Wael's recognition of canine intelligence placed him in opposition to Descartes. But, he pointed out, neither was he a follower of Montaigne, who "lauds animals to bring down humans." It was, after all, "human intelligence" that enabled "progress" in animals.[60] The police dog would enter dogopolis firmly under human control.

Alongside intelligence, police dog training manuals asserted the importance of the emotional connection between dog and human, and they emphasized that trainers needed patience and kindness to transform dogs into police dogs. Lalloué preferred "caresses" to "the whip and violence," since training was an emotional and reciprocal process in which dog and trainer became attuned to each other. A well-trained dog would feel "happy" when they successfully completed a task, because they could sense their owner's satisfaction. Furthermore, the trainer had to "love" his dog. Even if a dog failed to achieve the task set, their trainer should only consider punishment if the dog was disobedient. The trainer should use punishment sparingly because it could physically harm the dog and damage their character, undermining their suitability for police work. Gersbach warned that violence would create a "slave that seemed obedient" but who would never become a "loyal companion" ready to "share danger and sacrifice themselves." Such thinking dovetailed with humane societies' recommendation that animals and children be disciplined and controlled through kind and emotionally attuned exercises. Not only would such a strategy reduce suffering, but close affectionate emotional bonds would create more responsive, loyal, and effective children and animals.[61]

Having set out a basis for a productive training relationship, the manuals elaborated a series of tasks that the well-prepared police dog should accomplish. The curriculum started with simple activities, such as recall, lying down, sitting, and standing on command, and then moved on to more complex ones, such as barking when hearing a noise and finding a lost object. The tasks up until this point were pertinent to more than just police work, since hunters required their dogs to find and carry dead game. But then they became more specific. Police dogs were expected to defend their master, jump through windows, pick out an individual from a crowd, and disable and guard a fugitive (fig. 4.2).[62]

At the heart of these training manuals lay a tension between nonviolent means and violent ends. We catch glimpses of dogs' violent potential within them. According to Lalloué, the police dog needed to bite anyone immedi-

FIGURE 4.2 Police dog exercises. Photograph by Agence Meurisse, 1914. Bibliothèque nationale de France.

ately upon their master's command, even if the dog knew the individual well and had previously enjoyed that person's company. Trainers portrayed the emotional connection between dog and police handler as the wellspring of canine ferocity. The properly trained dog would "rejoice" in attacking their master's enemy. Police dog training drew from nineteenth-century celebrations of canine loyalty, love, and obedience and harnessed these qualities to protect policemen through their dog's biting, snarling, and other forms of violent behavior.[63]

Considerations of intelligence and instinct also came into play. Some manuals drew a distinction between criminals and law-abiding citizens, and they claimed that dogs instinctively knew the difference between these types of humans. Pathfinder and Dalziel argued that dogs had "a marvelous instinct to distinguish between a friend and an enemy," and could differentiate between a "well-dressed person" and a "vagabond or criminal." They speculated that there was something "furtive in the manner and gait" of the latter that activated such instincts.[64] Unlike bloodhounds, who purportedly deciphered human difference through smell alone, the all-purpose police dog used instinct.

Other trainers, however, placed less faith in instinct. They maintained that training exercises should *teach* police dogs to identify criminal types, and they encouraged the policemen playing the role of criminals in these exercises to act and dress like Apaches or other criminals. On both sides of the Atlantic, trainers advised that dogs be handled and fed only by men in police uniform to help them realize the difference between criminals and enforcers of the law. The New York police dog trainers went one step further to cement the dogs' suspicion of nonpolicemen. An officer dressed in civilian clothes would disrupt the dogs' mealtimes and tease them: "needless to say, this procedure soon begat an irritation that quickly developed into a chronic suspicion that any one in plain clothes is an unpleasant sort of person, whose society should be shunned by every right-thinking dog," reported the *Brooklyn Daily Eagle*. Yet such attempts to foster criminal-hating habits did not convince everyone, and some journalists questioned the dogs' powers of discernment in the real world. After attending a police dog competition in Paris, the London *Daily Telegraph*'s correspondent for that city noted that "it was not explained how the dogs are to know the real Apache when they see him. Are all men wearing scarlet comforters to be nosed out and caught? And will the burglars oblige by arranging to always don the uniform?"[65]

Despite such doubts, police dog advocates treated the dogs' capacity for violence as a necessary social defense against supposedly pathological and incorrigible criminals. Training enabled police dogs to become socially useful animals at a time when criminal anthropologists likened criminals to dangerous beasts, even if there was no guarantee that police dog handlers had faithfully followed the advice laid out in the manuals. However, scrutiny of police dogs' capabilities intensified once they hit the streets of Paris and New York.

Police Dogs in Action

Newspapers in Paris and New York drew police dogs and their abilities into the cities' culture of spectacle, in which journalists dissected and critiqued urban life in often sensational tones. After much deliberation, the New York Police Department stationed its newly trained dogs at the Parkville police station in Flatbush, Brooklyn, which was a suburban area prone to burglaries. Lieutenant George R. Wakefield put his dogs to the test on the night of January 28, 1908, when his fellow dog trainer Officer Berrman pretended to burgle the house of John Cavanaugh, secretary of the Metropolitan Racing Association, who was out of town. Unaware that the trial was taking place and upon discovering the intruder, patrolman Michael Nicholson unmuzzled his dog Nogi and fired his gun at the presumed burglar. Nogi—described by the *Illustrated London News* as "one of the most promising members of the staff"—gave chase to Berrman down Ocean Parkway and eventually floored him. As his coat was being torn off, Berrman yelled out for Nicholson to pull Nogi off him. The experiment, attended by reporters, had worked despite the poor communication between the policemen. The *New York Times* reported that it had "convinced every one who witnessed it of the dog's efficiency as a thief-catcher."[66]

The New York press praised the success of the Parkville canine unit. These dogs patrolled Flatbush with their police companions, who would let them loose to patrol alleyways, roads, and properties. Having excelled in training, Jim had reportedly "got more criminals than most officers." "If there was a suspicious character lurking any where about, or a man climbing into a window, he was Jim's meat," marveled the *Brooklyn Daily Eagle.* Such were Jim's feats, and the effectiveness of his self-taught method of tripping up criminals until his handler arrived to arrest them, that the newspaper blamed his early death on criminal poisoning. With Jim "lying in state" at the Parkville police station, the newspaper concluded that "he wasn't a beautiful dog to look at, and he had no aristocratic pedigree. But he knew his business."[67] In stark contrast to dog breeders' pursuit of physical conformity to breed standards, when it came to police work the pedigree and appearance of the dogs were of less importance than their shrewdness, determination, and strength.

New York's police dogs also became participants in the policing of race in the Jim Crow era. A city judge praised Officer Smyth and his dog, April,

FIGURE 4.3 Police dogs in New York City. Photograph by Bain News Service, 1912. It is not clear where in New York this photograph was taken. Library of Congress, reproduction number LC-DIG-ggbain-00004.

for tracking down and arresting James M. Stokes, a Black man accused of "holding up countless lonely and unescorted women in Parkville." During his arrest, Stokes allegedly shot two policemen. When he told Stokes that "you are the type of human being that we are anxious to have caged up in Sing Sing [prison]," the judge gave the impression that police dogs defended white Americans by rounding up animalized criminals, paving the way for their imprisonment. At a time when many white Americans criminalized Blackness, April's role in arresting Stokes incorporated her into the policing and repression of Black men to soothe white fears. But unlike the bloodhounds who had tracked runaway slaves in the antebellum South, April and the other Flatbush dogs hunted Black men in the suburban north. Hence, police dogs became part of the history of white violence against Black New Yorkers.[68]

Newspaper reports suggested that the harnessing of canine intelligence, instincts, emotions, senses, and physical strength marked a new step toward the more effective policing of modern cities to protect the middle classes from animalized criminals (fig. 4.3). Deputy commissioner Arthur Woods declared that the police dogs had overseen a drastic reduction in crime in Flatbush, from twenty burglaries a month to only four, because they allowed policemen to cover terrain more capably. With some exaggeration, he claimed that "burglars are so rare in Flatbush now that we have to put fake burglars on the job to keep the dogs in practice." Burglars, he further claimed, were more afraid of the police dog than human cops: the canines were "the best guardians of the suburban districts that this city ever had." The dogs did indeed seem scary enough to terrorize burglars. One local returning home late at night encountered them firsthand as they ran up to inspect him when scouting out the streets for burglars: "they were muzzled, but to the pedestrian's wondering eyes," noted the *Brooklyn Daily Eagle,* "they appeared big enough and savage enough to handle a burglar easily."[69]

The newspapers in Paris also reported on how dogs aided the police. At times it was the animals' physical strength that made the difference. Whether fighting off raids on the Paris-Brest postal service, defending citizens and police officers from Apache attacks, or uncovering couples indulging in acts of public indecency, police dogs had their praises sung by the Parisian press. An article in the city newspaper *Le matin* singled out Stop, a dog belonging to Brigadier Mitry in Saint-Mandé, an eastern suburb. Stop's speed, strength, and "fearsome jaws" enabled Mitry to become the "terror of the 'terrors.'" The police dogs and their emboldened masters now seemed more than a match for France's hardened criminals. As the *Brooklyn Daily Eagle* reported, the Apache "finds himself sorely embarrassed when . . . he must dodge the deadly fangs of two alert dogs." Journalists noted that the police dogs' threat to Parisian criminals was such that Apache gangs began to mobilize their own dogs to fight those canines. Criminal gangs also allegedly trained their "Apache-dogs" (*chiens-apaches*) to bring down solitary pedestrians in Paris's suburbs and disable them until gang members arrived to relieve them of their possessions. In response, police authorities ordered their men to kill *chiens-apaches.*[70]

Like the training manuals, the press celebrated police dogs' multifaceted abilities. They possessed "remarkable intelligence" as well as physical strength, acute sensory awareness, and a calm demeanor. This was the case with Marcel, a police dog who spotted trouble brewing during a confrontation between a group of young men and two Apaches at Lilas. He managed to disable the gang members until a policeman arrived. Sometimes the canine sense of smell made the difference. During a police raid on a bar near Les Halles, two dogs used their "disconcerting" sense of smell to uncover hidden guns, daggers, rubber blackjacks, and razors. Alongside other new police techniques—two members of officer-researcher Alphonse Bertillon's anthropometric team were also in attendance at the raid—the dogs helped capture sixty-one suspected criminals, including renowned Apache chief Le Chopier.[71]

Yet within such reporting there lurked a tacit recognition and acceptance of both the dogs' capacity for violence and the limits of training. The police sometimes acknowledged that their dogs made mistakes because of poor training. In May 1912, a Parisian criminal gang sought refuge in Villa Bonheur. Monsieur Guichard, head of the Paris Police Criminal Investigation Department, admitted that the dogs unleashed during the police siege to "worry the bandits" were not trained to enter houses. Instead of attacking the criminals, they lunged at the policemen staking out the villa's grounds. The startled policemen "had to fight lustily to protect themselves from the animals' fierce onslaught."[72]

Police trainers themselves appeared to doubt whether training had entirely subdued their dogs to their command, so they resorted to muzzling. A bite by a police dog would be tolerated only if permitted by the handler, who had the job of releasing the muzzle, and only if directed toward a presumed criminal. The recourse to muzzling cast doubt on the dogs' trustworthiness and intelligence. They could not be relied on to *always* know the difference between a criminal and an innocent person, so they needed a device to constrain their bites. Police officials in New York and Paris also tried to neutralize fears about dog bites by arguing that the benefits of police dogs outweighed the risk to law-abiding citizens.[73] Even so, doubts began to emerge about the desirability of police dogs within dogopolis.

Doubting Police Dogs

Despite assurances by authority figures, more qualms about police dogs' savagery and deficiencies soon surfaced. Critics feared that training had not tamed the dogs' aggressive instincts, in particular their predilection for biting. Long-standing and continued concerns over rabies undoubtedly fueled these anxieties, as did reports of pets wounding and even killing their human companions.[74]

For some Parisian critics, potentially aggressive dogs should have no role in policing the modern city. In 1909 a municipal councilor wrote to Paris Police Prefect Lépine to protest the deployment of dogs against political demonstrators. Similarly, the lawyer of a protester arrested at a demonstration that year held in honor of Spanish anarchist Francisco Ferrer at Issy-les-Moulineaux complained about the "savage violence" of the police dogs there. Nineteenth-century public concerns about police violence in general lingered into the twentieth century and were extended to canines who might undermine public security rather than protect it.[75]

Apprehensions about the contingency and reversibility of the dogs' abilities and intelligence resonated with fears that base instincts, desires, and impulses could overwhelm human intelligence and morality. For French psychologist Théodule Ribot, "the nervous system is liable to cumulative functional disequilibrium due to the tendency of the more fixed and stable lower levels to overrun the higher, but more fragile and recently acquired, intellectual and moral capacities." Forebodings about the dogs' bestial urges also aligned them with the criminal anthropologists' vision of instinctive criminals. For Cesare Lombroso, "the facts clearly prove that the most horrendous and inhuman crimes have a biological, atavistic origin in those animalistic instincts that, although smoothed over by education, the family and fear of punishment, resurface instantly under given circumstances."[76] Frightening forces threatened to devour the fragile edifice of civilization that held back the harmful energies unleashed by mass culture and urbanization. Likewise, violent impulses could overrun the highly trained and controlled police dog, perhaps the epitome of the domesticated, skillful, loyal, and useful animal. The dogs' ability to think and their bond with their handlers had not tamed conclusively the "beast within." Nor had these traits guaranteed these canines' unconditional acceptance within dogopolis. Harnessed to alleviate fears of crime, police dogs stoked fears about violent and aggressive dogs.[77]

The crime-fighting abilities of the police department canine units and their capacity to act intelligently were viewed as provisional and brittle. This skepticism explains the muzzling and eventual demise of Parisian police dogs. By 1911, 145 dogs helped police Paris and the Seine *département*, but their number had dropped to forty in 1916, and the Paris police discontinued their use after World War I.[78]

A similar situation came to pass in New York. The "police dogs"—as German shepherds/Alsatians came to be increasingly known during the interwar period—became popular as pets and private guard dogs after proving their worth during World War I on the western front and at a time when many Americans believed they were living through a crime wave. Their fans praised their loyalty, intelligence, and emotional sensitivity. Members of this breed were reportedly very "responsive to the wishes and moods" of their owner, and one particularly bright dog named Fellow underwent testing in the psychology department at Columbia University, such were his linguistic and comprehension skills. But not everyone was convinced. In 1925 a Queens magistrate called for these "savage," wolflike, and biting dogs to be banned from the borough, which resulted in a controversial and somewhat ironic order for policemen to seize unmuzzled and unleashed hybrid pet-police dogs. Staten Island resident Dorothy V. Holden, meanwhile, signaled that she lived "in a semi-besieged state of terror" from the untrusty and vicious breed that possessed "only a thin veneer over the wolf." Here was a marked reluctance to welcome these dogs into dogopolis, even during the crime-ridden Prohibition era.[79]

Police officials were also skeptical. Despite owning a Belgian police dog called Thor (whom he lost on a trip to Paris in 1922), New York's police commissioner Richard E. Enright expressed misgivings about the use of dogs for police work. In 1920 he stated that "there is absolutely no record to prove that these dogs have been of any value whatever in the [police] department." By 1926 the canine unit was reduced to three dogs, who were kenneled at Sheepshead Bay in Brooklyn. The *New York Times* attributed this decline to both policemen's poor dog-handling skills and an insufficiently deep emotional bond between dog and trainer. Police dog numbers then rebounded and included Rex, a Belgian shepherd imported from Belgium who worked in Harlem with Sergeant Samuel Battle, the police department's first Black officer. The dogs enjoyed the odd moment of glory—in 1929 they were deployed in Staten Island against a deft pickpocket dubbed the "pants" burglar—but the buzz of the early twentieth century was gone. Not only did these dogs fail to catch the suspect, but the celebration of canine intelligence and emotional connection had withered. The dogs performed their police duty solely for food, declared the *Times*. In addition, they were increasingly usurped by technology in the form of burglar alarms.[80]

In interwar Britain, supporters of police dogs made some headway. "Police dog" displays of skill from exceptionally "clever" Alsatians were held at the Crystal Palace. In addition, some London police officers patrolled with their own dogs: in an echo of earlier narratives, one policeman who took Peeler, his Airedale, on patrol appreciated "the friendship on a lonely beat at night." Then in the late 1930s, the Metropolitan Police considered officially deploying dogs. One of the force's advisers recommended considering the "individuality" of each dog when assessing the animal for police work. The dogs' emotional character was important. Recruits should have "plenty of 'guts'" but not be "savage." The police force imported some bloodhounds from the United States to cross with otterhounds to create, it hoped, a robust dog adept at tracking. But in the end, a trial of two Labradors in South London in 1939 was not a resounding success. P. C. Allen reported that he could not release his dog "to search for a person, because I am certain he would attack the person and cause serious harm."[81] After these fears of canine aggression, the start of World War II nixed the experiment.

Conclusion

Police dogs emerged within a context of media-fueled anxieties about urban crime and security, the development of criminal anthropology, and new understandings of animal intelligence. In the wake of evolutionary theories, dogs appeared to be more intelligent creatures than previously thought and some humans less so. This assumption allowed trainers, handlers, and sympathetic commentators to position police dogs as intelligent and instinctual creatures who could make a difference in urban security through the harnessing of their emotions on the training ground. But the assumption that intelligence in canines could be overwhelmed by the reemergence of their violent instincts undermined optimistic claims that police dogs could make cities safer. Training and the affective attachment between trainer and dog had not tamed the dogs' atavistic biting instincts.

Police dogs' aggression was highly ambiguous. On the one hand, their violence protected the well-to-do and their property. But on the other hand, middle-class commentators worried that they might attack policemen and wealthy citizens, such as Flatbush residents returning home late at night. Newspapers ensured that their potential and actual violence became a matter for public discussion. For some commentators, it was simply beyond the pale that an animal might attack an innocent human whatever their race, political views, or social background: such savage violence had no place in urban societies that saw themselves as modern and civilized. Ultimately, police dogs were a failed experiment. Their entry into dogopolis was provisional. It was only in the postwar period that permanent police canine units were established in all three cities, and police dogs became enduring features of dogopolis.

The development of police dogs had been a transnational endeavor. But key differences were apparent. All-purpose police dogs were absent in London, and in New York dog bites exposed and reinforced the racial discrimination embedded in the criminal justice system. This aspect of police dog history has had a long and disturbing legacy. Having once celebrated Samuel Battle's detective dog and praised the qualities of German shepherds as pets, the *Baltimore Afro-American* went on to document the outrage caused by police dog attacks on Black people across the United States. From the deployment of police dogs against civil rights demonstrators in the 1960s to the police dog attacks on Black citizens in Ferguson, Missouri (as documented in a 2015 Department of Justice report following the killing of Michael Brown), the emotional charge and discriminatory dimensions of urban police dogs have intensified. For many Black Americans, police dog aggression—whether instinctive or forged in training—overshadows any considerations of their intelligence.[82]

CHAPTER 5

Defecating

The introduction of police dogs marked a novel development in urban human-canine relationships. A further transformation was under way in the early decades of the twentieth century, this time concerning attitudes about canine defecation. By the end of World War I, the contours of dogopolis were taking shape. In addition to the deployment of police dogs, stray dogs had been turned into outcasts, either (re)homed or killed "humanely" in increasing numbers in lethal chambers. Muzzling, Pasteurism, and heightened surveillance had quelled fears of biting. But canine excrement began to trouble physicians, councilors, and others and raised questions about the acceptability of pet dogs within dogopolis. These canines were bound to humans in knots of affection, but—as with the "poisoned kisses" of the rabid pet dog—their companionship brought potential dangers.

Dog mess once had medicinal uses. In the eighteenth and nineteenth centuries, physicians used it as an astringent in the form of album graecum (dried and whitened canine excrement). Noting physicians' additional use of album graecum as an antiseptic, the *Encyclopaedia Britannica* of 1797 described its potent powers. It was so "putrid" that it could "destroy almost every vegetable or animal substance." Some physicians even recommended it for sore throats. In 1899 physician W. T. Fernie quoted Richard Boyle's advice from 1696 that "a homely but experienced medicine for a sore throat [is] to take about one drachm of album graecum, or white dog's turd, burnt to perfect whiteness, and with about one ounce of honey of roses or clarify'd honey make thereof a Linctus to be very slowly let down the throat." But by the 1920s, dog mess had morphed from a marginal medicinal substance into a repulsive hazard to public health. It was "particularly disgusting and objectionable," according to a British Home Office civil servant. This chapter tracks these changing sensibilities concerning canine feces. As human defecation became increasingly private with the spread of lockable toilet and privy doors, and as roads and pavements became cleaner, physicians, public hygienists, journalists, councilors, and middle-class citizens identified canine "visiting cards" as a threat to public health and decency.[1]

While middle-class dog owners, egged on by dog care experts and dog food companies, paid ever more attention to what went into their dogs' stomachs, their indifference to where food waste was expelled from their pets' anuses sparked frustration and consternation. Disgust—and the anger and fear that accompanied it—at dogs' daily soiling of pavements and sidewalks led to campaigns to remove dog mess from London, New York, and Paris. Middle-class feelings of disgust informed these efforts, even though middle-class dog owners were often identified as the main culprits in allowing their dogs to foul.

Disgust is a complex and powerful emotion. Legal scholar William Ian Miller usefully defines it as conveying "a strong sense of aversion to something perceived as dangerous because of its powers to contaminate, infect, or pollute by proximity, contact or ingestion." Alongside this feeling might be "an accompanying nausea or queasiness," or perhaps "an urge to recoil and shudder from creepiness" and a "panic, of varying intensity, that attends the awareness of being defiled." Excrement provokes intense feelings of disgust. The anus, and the waste it expels, is "the essence of lowness, of untouchability, and so it must be hemmed in with prohibitions."[2] This sentiment came to be applied to dogs as well as humans.

Dog mess was deemed disgusting because it stank, polluted city streets, and contaminated bodies. It therefore required regulation. Once again, emotion led to action to alter human-dog relations in London, New York, and Paris. New knowledge about parasites coupled with feelings of disgust to propel public health officials, councilors, journalists, and voluntary groups to launch antifouling campaigns with varying degrees of success. But the continued fouling of streets provided stinking evidence that many dog owners met with indifference the feelings of disgust provoked by their pet's excrement. Yet behind this insouciant stance lay an unspoken sense of revulsion at canine feces that prevented owners from picking up their own dog's waste. Defecation raised questions about the smooth integration of pet dogs within dogopolis.

Disgust, Dirt, and Dogs

Disgust and excrement have a close relationship. On the one hand, some scientists claim that disgust at feces and revulsion at foul and diseased matter is innate. It is a transcultural, ahistorical, and biological emotion that served an evolutionary purpose in helping humans and other animals avoid infectious diseases. On the other hand, historians and anthropologists argue that human and animal shit is laden with historically and culturally specific meanings. History and culture, rather than biology, shape understandings of what is disgusting. Martha C. Nussbaum forges a middle way between these two approaches by suggesting that disgust is common to all humans and prevents us from contaminating our bodies with dangerous substances. Yet it is also profoundly shaped by historical contexts and diverse and changing cultural meanings. What is clear is that shifting attitudes toward shit have often revolved around questions of taboo and transgression. In particular, the handling of human excrement is infused with cultural significance, prohibitions, and fascination. Perhaps as a result of its noted similarities with human feces, dog excrement came to trigger strong feelings of disgust. It reminded humans of a shameful aspect of their own animality—the excretion of waste—that might contaminate their bodies, homes, and environments.[3]

Evolving responses to dog mess occurred within the wider realm of changing attitudes toward dirt in the modern West. Attitudes toward filth were transformed during the modern period. Increased intolerance of foul smells and waste matter crystallized from the eighteenth century onward, especially in elite circles. Revulsion to pungent smells and distancing from bodily functions marked someone as refined and civilized. Excrement became associated with animality and the lower classes, and hence with social disorder, poverty, and immorality. Slavery, racism, and colonialism also bound notions of cleanliness to whiteness. The miasma theory of disease causation, which held that putrid and rotting organic matter caused illness, underscored this cultural shift by making smelly waste material dangerous as well as disgusting.[4]

Heightened middle-class intolerance of dirt legitimized public hygienists' efforts to sanitize public spaces and private homes. Within the framework of modern urban public hygiene, individuals, the state, and private organizations all had a role in keeping bodies, homes, and cities healthy. In London, New York, and Paris, public health imperatives entered private homes and targeted individuals. Dampness, overcrowding, dust, dirt, rotting food, and poor ventilation were seen to make homes breeding sites of germs. Modern citizens, particularly women, were tasked with keeping homes clean and germ free. Individuals were also charged with keeping their bodies cleansed, exercised, and correctly fed. In wealthier homes, bathrooms and flush toilets underscored domestic hygiene and created more distance between the wealthy and their waste (these new conveniences also provided unintentional canine watering holes).[5]

Increasingly considered an intrinsic part of the modern urban household, pet dogs became entitled to clean and healthy living conditions. Veterinary surgeons and pet-keeping experts encouraged pet owners to manage their home with care, ensuring order and cleanliness to maximize the health of its human and canine inhabitants, just as the wealthy rural hunter was responsible for maintaining hygienic conditions in the kennels of hunting dogs.[6]

Hygiene became a central pillar of responsible modern dog ownership, and clean dogs were encouraged within dogopolis. Dog owners were charged with an ever-growing list of responsibilities. Outside the home, they had to distance their pet from filth. Pathfinder and Hugh Dalziel called on owners to stop their dogs from eating rubbish and rotting meat off the streets and rolling in dirt. These activities were bad for the dogs and distasteful for human bystanders. At home, owners had to observe their dogs closely for signs of disease and parasites (not least fleas, lice, and worms) and keep them clean. According to Alfred Barbou, "forgetfulness, negligence and inobservance" of hygienic "rules" on the dog owner's part would disturb the "balance" of a dog's "physiological functions," leading to disease. Ernest Leroy went so far as to claim that three-quarters of illnesses in dogs were caused by poor hygiene.[7]

Sound hygiene would not just benefit dogs: it would also prevent diseases from spreading to humans. For dogs could pose a threat to health within the home. An 1895 medical report on Paris's 14th arrondissement blamed diphtheria cases on the cohabitation of humans and dogs in residential buildings, and it called for "the elimination of all these useless animals." If the overcrowded households of the urban poor and the intimate cohabitation of animals and humans in rural households had frequently concerned hygienists, pet dogs in any home—including the middle-class ones targeted by pet-keeping manuals—also constituted a risk.[8] Owners had to make sure that their pets contributed to domestic cleanliness.

Germ theory may have slowly and unevenly undermined miasma theory by the end of the nineteenth century. But the scientific and popular linking of germs and dirt strengthened the resolve of public hygienists to manage substances and animals that they deemed dirty and diseased. Hence the housefly metamorphosed from a harmless household inhabitant into a dangerous and disease-carrying pest. By the early twentieth century, locating germs in animals and their excreta was a convenient way for public health officials to educate the public about where pathogens lived, and it provided them with visible targets for their campaigns. Animal pests and their waste became remnants of harmful and unwanted nature within modern and clean societies.[9] Herein lay one of the roots of the disgust provoked by dog mess.

As the digestive processes of domesticated dogs increasingly fell within the purview of dog care experts and the new dog food companies, advice was dished out on feeding and, less often, housebreaking as ways to civilize and sanitize these pets' natural functions.

Dogs, Digestion, and Defecation

Feeding was a major element of canine hygiene. An increasing amount of attention was paid to what went into pet dogs' stomachs. Feeding was another degree of separation between dogs in the home and those outside it within the emerging dogopolis. Ownerless and owned strays on the streets could feast on carrion and food waste, or they could endure pitiable rations in the pounds (fig. 5.1).

FIGURE 5.1 *The Pound: Preparing Soup for the Dogs and Cats.* Photograph by Agence Meurisse, 1919. Bibliothèque nationale de France.

What owners should put in their pet's food bowls caused much disagreement among dog care experts. While some experts suggested that dogs' teeth made them carnivores, others believed that domestication had transformed them into omnivores and so recommended vegetables, soups, and bread as suitable foods. Many saw no harm in dogs eating the same food as the human members of their household. Airedale expert William Haynes welcomed "table scraps," as they provided variety and nourishment. Stonehenge (J. H. Walsh) similarly suggested that a mixture of meat and vegetables from the table was enough to keep dogs healthy and avoid constipation. These shared foods cemented the pet dog as a family member. But variety was required. James R. Kinney, chief veterinarian of New York's Ellin Prince Speyer Hospital, and his collaborator Ann Honeycutt had heard tales of dogs in the Lower East Side surviving on a diet of spaghetti. After this not-so-subtle dig at Italian Americans, they recommended "meat, milk, toast or cereal, and a few vegetables" as healthier options.[10]

As was also the case with human health, a lack of dietary restraint was seen to undermine canine vigor. According to Eugène Gayot, France's overfed dogs were victims of their owners' "excess." Irresponsible dog owners passed on their own dietary recklessness to their pets and overfed them out of misguided sentimentality. Responsible owners should resist the temptation to overfeed their dog with unhealthy scraps from the family table. Most alarmingly in pre–germ theory days, an inappropriate diet combined with a lack of fresh air and exercise could lead to distemper and, for purebred dogs, the degeneration of breed characteristics, according to other French experts. A "candy diet" would similarly ruin American dogs, while British dogs were advised against drinking tea, a purported way of avoiding distemper, as it would cause digestive problems. In addition, to conform to Western assumptions that a lack of dietary restraint was uncivilized, dog owners needed to moderate their dogs' diets carefully. Male dog care experts parroted the myth of irresponsible and overly sentimental female dog owners whose apparent predilection for overfeeding and underexercising their dogs led to constipation and other digestive ailments, even if women were increasingly called on to provide care for dogs in domestic settings.[11]

Businesses sought to make money from responsible dog ownership by introducing biscuits that would purportedly meet the dogs' true nutritional needs. Spratt's Patent led the way. Sometime around 1860, American businessman James Spratt visited London and spotted stray dogs eating ship's biscuits on the docks, inspiring him to develop Spratt's Meat Dog Biscuits. By the beginning of the twentieth century, Spratt's London premises were the largest pet food factory in the world, and it sold its products across Europe and the United States, targeting urban and rural dog owners. Spratt's proudly presented itself as an international company. Its stand at the 1908 Franco-British Exhibition in London displayed the cities in which it had a presence: London, Paris, Berlin, Newark, and Montreal. Spratt's promoted its biscuits and other increasingly specialized products, such as Greyhound and Terrier Biscuits and Cod Liver Oil Biscuits ("Invaluable as a Pick-me-up for Dogs on return from a hard day's work"), as healthy, rational, and convenient ways to feed dogs. A key part of its sales pitch was that "injudicious feeding," especially letting dogs eat carrion and excessively rich food, was as injurious for dogs as it was for humans. It emphasized that "dietetic hygiene should rule feeding in dogs" and that the "scientific accuracy" with which it prepared its dog food would guarantee canine health. In this vein, Spratt's touted its Fibrine Dog Cakes, fortified with beetroot, as a way of keeping canine "bowels in perfect order." It also introduced its Charcoal Biscuits as a cure for canine digestive problems, from stomach gases to bad breath. As vivisectionists explored the science of gastric juices through experiments on dogs, Spratt's claimed that gnawing on Fibrine Dog Cakes would stimulate these vital fluids in canine stomachs. The company promoted its wares in newspaper advertisements and in its own and other dog care books, and it became a major presence at dog shows, helping expand the pet consumer industry. It portrayed the rational feeding of dogs with its biscuits as a key component in the making of the Western modern dog. It claimed that its "service" to dogs "has done more than anything else to raise the status of the poor dog from his level of pariah and scavenger in Oriental cities, to his proud position amongst the nobility of the animal world which he occupies to-day in humane England."[12]

In line with the rapid expansion of the processed food industry, other manufacturers joined the market, portraying themselves as beacons of scientific savoir-faire and middle-class propriety. Many were agricultural feed or human health food companies looking to expand their range. All boasted of their products' outstanding nutritional qualities. With scientists identifying ever-more vitamins (beginning with vitamin B1 in 1912) and social reformers increasingly concerned about nutritious diets, Spillers, a British company, reassured dog owners that its food aligned with the latest scientific knowledge on vitamins and other nutrients. Canned "wet" dog food followed in the early twentieth century as canning technology improved, and American stockyards looked for an outlet for meat deemed unfit for human consumption under the 1906 Pure Food and Drug Act. In the 1930s, dog food manufacturers even began to claim that their products would promote dogs' emotional as well as physical health. Spillers boasted that its food was the basis of a "good strong nervous system," from which is built a "dog's good disposition." But manufactured dog food was financially out of reach for poorer households, while many middle- and upper-class families preferred to continue feeding their dogs from the table or preparing their own dog stews and broths. Some dogs reportedly preferred a varied quasi-human diet to monotonous dog biscuits.[13]

While some dog care experts embraced Spratt's and other dog biscuits, others were more skeptical. Henry Clay Glover, veterinarian to New York's Westminster Kennel Club and a producer of digestive pills and other products, warned against dog biscuits in the starkest terms: a "direct change from home diet to dog biscuits has produced a very irritated and relaxed condition of the bowels, frequently resulting in inflammation and possibly death." Haynes advised owners not to offer biscuits for every meal: "you would not like to live on beefsteak three times a day, week in and week out."[14] But whatever owners chose to feed their dogs, responsible dog ownership now meant giving careful thought to their pet's digestive health.

Dog care books paid much attention to feeding but far less to its inevitable consequences. Such an attitude formed the bedrock of owners' indifference about canine excrement on the streets and raised questions about dogs' place within dogopolis. But canine care experts did discuss loose defecation or absent bowel movements as signs of illness. Paying attention to canine digestive ailments would offer clues for how to heal pet dogs and so keep the home healthy. French veterinarian Joanny Pertus stressed that "fecal matter" from sick dogs was often infected and needed speedy removal to prevent "emanations" threatening the air's "purity." Dog care experts also gave advice on how to treat diarrhea and constipation as well as colic and flatulence. Brandy was one preferred cure for smelly emissions, while Stonehenge offered detailed advice on treating colic (laudanum, ether, and castor oil would move the "offending matter") and constipation, for which he suggested a range of aperients of differing strengths designed to "wash" out the bowels. In Stonehenge's view, constipation could lead to agony and potentially fatal misunderstandings: "very often the dog suffers very severe pain from the obstruction afforded by pent-up faeces. . . . The dog thus affected is almost mad with pain; he runs to and fro, rushes into odd corners, and shakes his head in the most odd manner, and in this stage may very easily be mistaken for a 'mad dog'; but the suddenness of the attack, and the mass of hardened faeces easily felt in the flank mark the difference between two cases." Paying attention to canine digestive ailments would prevent a misdiagnosis of rabies and the dog's potential demise at the hands of a crowd or policeman. Kinney and Honeycutt in 1938 offered particularly detailed advice on treating these digestive conditions alongside others that affected the canine rectum and anus. Perhaps to ease owners' sense of revulsion at performing certain procedures, such as expressing a clogged anal gland or treating a prolapsed rectum, their tone was matter of fact and free from the language of disgust.[15]

Drug companies sought to replace the homemade cures suggested by Stonehenge and others, as well as dogs' own attempts to relieve their constipation by eating grass, with "definite, scientific diet and treatment." They would bring scientific expertise to bear within the middle-class home. The Brooklyn-based Delson Chemical Company sold medicines to treat gastrointestinal problems, comparing dogs to a "machine" of which digestion was the "power plant" in one of its dog care publications. Defecation expelled waste from digested food to allow more sustenance and energy to enter the body. Delson boasted that it had harnessed the modern science of chemistry to repair faults in the canine machine and keep it operating smoothly.[16] Treating dogs as easily fixable machines rather than animals with messy bodies offered a way to speak of defecation without provoking feelings of disgust.

Housebreaking

Many otherwise extensive dog-keeping manuals brushed past defecation, as if it were too abject a topic for their bourgeois readership. While some briefly discussed a dog's necessity to go outside to meet their "intimate needs," house-training tips likely were passed on by word of mouth instead.[17]

A handful of authors avoided coyness and euphemisms to offer practical advice for preventing defecation from soiling the domestic environment. Some counseled their readers to provide their dog with a plate or box of sand, earth, or wood chippings in the home alongside taking it for regular walks. Young dogs, in addition, required housebreaking. H. Ducret-Baumann emphasized that owners must teach puppies (who are "subject to needs as imperial as they are natural") that domestic carpets were not streets or grass. The house-trained adult dog was expected to relieve themself at set times during their walks. Those who failed to restrain themselves should be punished with a slap or whip on the hindquarters or side. Haynes agreed. Housebreaking was the "first lesson that has to be taught to the city dog." The young dog needed to be taken out at regular intervals, and "should he offend, he ought to be punished at the scene of his crime" with a "smart slap under the jaw, accompanied by a word-scolding in a severe tone and uncompromising manner." Theo Marples, editor of the weekly newspaper *Our Dogs*, recommended giving a "good skelping" to dogs caught "eas[ing] themselves" in the house. If the owner did not catch their pet in the act, they should rub the dog's nose in it, presumably to generate feelings of disgust in the animal.[18]

Other experts prescribed less harsh disciplinary methods. Housebreaking was a necessary—if at times emotionally fraught—"ordeal." But an owner's anger and frustration at a puddle or stool on the kitchen floor would dissolve in the face of the offending dog's sad eyes, according to James R. Kinney and Ann Honeycutt. They advised owners to carefully watch their dog and, should the animal begin to squat, quickly place their pet on a newspaper. This was harder to anticipate with puppies than with older dogs, who "sniff around and circle around and practically telegraph ahead for reservations." One dog they knew of reportedly was trained to press a buzzer under the dining room table, summoning a servant to take the animal out. Unlike William Haynes, Kinney and Honeycutt advised against punishment and the "disgusting and antiquated method of 'rubbing his nose in it.' A self-respecting dog would be well within his rights if he pulled a knife on a person who did that to him." They promised worried owners that one "holy day," their dog would go to the newspaper voluntarily, which was "one of the prettiest sights in the world."[19]

Responsible dog owners needed to pay strict attention to what went into their dog's mouth, but beyond making sure that their pet did not foul inside the home, little attention was paid to where the feces ended up outside domestic settings. Owners with yards and gardens had the easiest solution. Self-styled American dog psychologist Clarence E. Harbison counseled that dogs, especially bitches, could be easily house trained. Put them in the yard after meals or when it looked like they needed to defecate, he advised his readers. But for those owners without outdoor space, their dogs needed to relieve themselves off the premises. With experts underscoring the importance of walks to canine health, the street was framed as the main site of defecation for dogs. In this vein, Marples casually suggested that owners feed their dogs in the morning, then send them out onto the street to defecate in the afternoon.[20] Dog care experts like Marples presented streets as unproblematic places for canine defecation. But as streets became cleaner, this insouciant view was increasingly untenable.

Cleaner Streets

Filth characterized the rapidly expanding nineteenth-century metropolis. Effluent oozed from slaughterhouses and tanneries. Animal carcasses rotted. Cesspits overflowed and rivers stank, while piles of horse and livestock manure accumulated. Within the grubby urban landscape, dog mess formed but a small part of a city's "blood and guts" economy. Like other organic products in the urban economy, it was not yet treated as waste. Instead, some poor Parisians collected and sold it to *mégissiers*, tannery workers who turned sheepskin into leather. These workers used it to taw sheepskin: ten kilograms of dog feces could treat twelve thousand skins. The dog feces collectors formed a small grouping within the ranks of *chiffonniers* (ragpickers) who processed the waste on Paris's streets.[21]

Across the Channel, Henry Mayhew, the famous social investigator, wrote about pure finders in his book *London Labour and the London Poor* (1851). Pure was the name given to dog mess, because it was used to scour and purify goat- and calfskins in the Bermondsey tanyards. The excrement removed moisture from the skins, making the leather destined for book covers and other uses smell nicer. Women initially made up the bulk of pure finders, but men muscled in from the 1820s as the work became more lucrative. According to Mayhew, 240 pure finders worked London's streets, carrying covered baskets and leather gloves to pick up the feces, although some used their bare hands as they found it easier to wash their hands than keep the gloves clean. Those with connections visited kennels to gather pure. They then mixed it with street pure to make up the consistency favored by the Bermondsey tanners.[22]

Pure finders could expect to receive 8 to 10 pence per stable bucket of pure, allowing some to earn a decent living. Mayhew estimated the average weekly wage to be 5 shillings, while those who cleaned out kennels could make up to 15 shillings per week. Some tanners preferred their pure "dark" and "moist," while others wanted a dryer product. Pure finders would sometimes mix the excrement with mortar to create the kind of "dry, limey" product that the tanneries desired and so exact the best price. Alongside divulging this trick of the trade, Mayhew found the pure finders better educated than the bone grubbers: many were former tradespeople, mechanics, or semiskilled laborers who had fallen on hard times. One whom Mayhew encountered was a former Manchester cotton trader who had lost his money through "drink and neglect." Such pure finders were joined by destitute Irish immigrants who would sell pure to the more established pure finders.[23]

The occupation was far from appealing. In stark contrast to middle-class pet owners, who were encouraged to keep canine excrement out of their homes, pure finders would store it in their cramped lodgings in the "wretched locality" near the tanneries between the docks and Rosemary Lane. Mayhew spoke with a sixty-year-old pure finder whose father had been a well-off milkman. A series of unfortunate events had since reduced her to pure finding when her second husband became partially paralyzed. "At first I couldn't endure the business," she said. "I couldn't eat a morsel, and I was obliged to discontinue it for a long time." But she eventually overcame her disgust and helped her husband gather up the excrement. Despite the hardships of pure finding, it was better to work on the streets than live in a workhouse. She relayed how some pure finders had died on the streets next to their baskets: "I'd sooner die like them than be deprived of my liberty."[24] Based on this testimony, disgust at dog mess was not just a middle-class phenomenon. Economic necessity and a desire for independence had pushed this pure finder to conquer her revulsion. Wealthier dog owners, meanwhile, could adopt a far more distant relationship to their pet's waste.

The partial and contested sanitization of the urban environment turned dog mess from an economic resource into disgusting and dangerous matter. Public hygiene movements in metropolitan and colonial cities spread the notion, often in racialized and classed terms, that filth had no place in the modern city. Dirt undermined health, sapped morality, and thwarted progress. Engineers, physicians, and other public hygienists set about cleansing cities, encouraged by journalists and concerned citizens. In Paris, the "great stink" of 1880 led citizens to demand that the city's authorities combat filth, while the latter came to equate the fight against dirt with progress. Similarly, for Progressive Era campaigners in New York, cleaner streets would improve physical and emotional health, foster positive attitudes, and boost civic responsibility.[25]

The identification of dog mess as a public health threat sprung unintentionally from these efforts to create sanitary cities. First, cities became less smeared in excrement. For public hygienists, sewers offered a more effective and sanitary way of removing excrement from the city than the cesspits, which had to be emptied by hand, with their waste carted out of the city. But sewer systems were expensive, technologically challenging, and controversial. Supporters of sewers faced opposition from those who benefited financially from emptying cesspits as well as those who feared sewer gas leaching into their homes. But in all three cities, sewerage prevailed. The many cholera outbreaks in mid-nineteenth-century London pushed public hygienist Edwin Chadwick to envisage an expanded and centralized sewer system headed by the Metropolitan Commission of Sewers (which became the Metropolitan Board of Works in 1855). Inspired by French hygienists and supported by the 1848 Public Health Act, Chadwick and his supporters advocated the power of water to flush away filth rather than have it stagnating in stinking cesspits.[26]

Despite some dissenting views, flushing toilets and sewers represented hygienic progress. They now removed excrement from middle- and upper-class homes, unlike the situation in poorer dwellings, where "the state of . . . 'conveniences' with all their filth exposed above the ground level, may be more decently imagined than described."[27] Excrement now properly belonged underground, floating away in sewers, not at ground level, where it could be seen, smelled, or even touched.

The sewers that whisked away rain and surface water were a feted component of Georges-Eugène Haussmann's mid-nineteenth-century modernization of Paris. But these underground counterparts to the *grands boulevards* did not begin to carry human excrement and waste water out of the city until 1894, after a drawn-out debate. This development heralded the eventual end of leaving night soil out for collection, even if flushing toilets were far from universal.[28]

Across the Atlantic, residents of New York expelled vast quantities of night soil that night men lugged away in carts down to the docks. Piecemeal sewers arrived in the city along with an improved water supply in 1842 via the Croton aqueduct. City officials had taken charge of the sewers by 1850 and opened a citywide sewerage system in 1865. The sewers took human waste and dumped it in the nearby rivers, causing extensive and serious water pollution. By 1910 the city had pumped 600 million gallons of untreated sewage into its surrounding waters each day.[29] Human excrement now floated in the city's rivers rather than festering in its built environment. It had become a different type of pollution.

The demise of horse-drawn transportation removed another major source of excrement. Horses had kept nineteenth-century London, New York, and Paris moving, but they produced vast amounts of manure in the process. London alone had an estimated 200,000 horses at the beginning of the twentieth century. In New York, contractors carted horse manure off to surrounding fields via boats. But as the city expanded, the amount of manure outstripped the ability to remove it, so much so that horse feces lay splattered across the streets and amassed in stinking piles, much to the embarrassment and chagrin of New Yorkers. The *New York Times* complained of "a huge horse manure dump" on Manhattan's East River shoreline that "emit[ted] a stench which defies any attempt at description." Wind blew dust, odors, and germs from this dump far across the city, assaulting nostrils and spreading diseases.[30]

Changes to urban transportation slowly but surely removed these disgusting sights and smells. As overground and underground trains, trams, streetcars, bicycles, and motorized vehicles replaced horse-borne transport, the number of defecating horses declined in all three cities, particularly after World War I. Paris had 110,000 horses in 1902 and 22,000 in 1933, and while horses still worked on London's streets in the 1930s, the amount of horse-drawn traffic dropped by almost 66 percent from 1937 to 1938. Even though New York still had over 50,000 horses in 1924, this represented a substantial reduction from 108,036 in 1917.[31]

The motorization of urban transport created new forms of urban pollution, but the stench and flies caused by horse manure became far less bothersome. Furthermore, the arrival of the automobile also prevented dogs from defecating in the street. London's dogs had faced little danger from slow-moving hansom cabs, but the car was a different matter. Cars pushed them toward the pavement. Even so, dog mess may not have attracted flies like horse manure, nor did it waft so easily in the wind, but it was more likely to contaminate shoes and foul children's toys.[32]

Cleansing was the final change that transformed streets and pavements into a blank canvas for dog mess. Dirty streets offended public hygienist principles and undermined the assumption that London, Paris, and New York were the pinnacles of urban civilization. Gaining greater impetus during Haussmannization, regulations sought to cajole Parisians into creating less mess while municipal cleaners gradually took over from the *chiffioniers* who had previously removed rubbish from the streets. A prefectural order of September 1870 forbade the dumping onto the streets of household waste, which from 1884 had to be placed in communal bins for collection and timely removal from the city. Dusty and muddy streets, however, still marked the belle époque and created a headache for those charged with keeping Paris clean. Pavements were cleaner, but disgust at dirt and fears of germs fueled ongoing complaints about filthy streets.[33]

Similar processes were afoot in London and New York. Londoners increasingly expected their dustbins to be emptied efficiently. They wanted their roads to be kept clear of mud and snow in winter, and in summer they wanted them watered to combat dust. However, the mid-nineteenth-century system of parish vestries that paid private contractors to remove waste failed to meet public expectations or those of public hygienists and sanitary inspectors. Once the Metropolitan Board of Works, district boards of works, and vestries had merged into the London County Council and metropolitan borough councils by the beginning of the twentieth century, local authorities had greater powers to raise revenue to keep the streets clean, emboldened by the 1891 Public Health (London) Act. But efforts to improve and sanitize the collection of household and trade waste, and keep the streets free from mud, snow, sludge, and dust, were far from perfect, especially in poorer areas. Concerns over London's dirty streets continued. Nevertheless, some progress was made due to the introduction of more comprehensive waste management systems (agreed at a citywide public health conference in 1894), new street-cleaning technology, and the spread of asphalt surfaces.[34]

In New York and other American cities, the range and number of waste-cleaning occupations, mainly filled by African Americans and immigrants, exploded as the growth of consumerism generated more rubbish. New York City established a Department of Street Cleaning in 1881 to tackle the varied forms of garbage and excrement strewn across the streets. However, it was mired in political machinations and corruption. Then, in 1895, chemist and sanitary engineer George E. Waring Jr. took over and transformed the ineffectual department. Staffed disproportionately by Italian immigrants and African Americans, his White Wing sanitation workers (so called because of their white uniforms) swept the streets and removed garbage, which was sold, salvaged, taken to landfill, or dumped in the East River. The press celebrated Waring's achievements up until his departure in 1899. But despite his reforms, dirty streets continued to enrage New Yorkers. In 1902 W. D. wrote a letter to the *New York Times* lamenting over how the "Dago street cleaner" failed to water the streets before sweeping them, thereby spreading dangerous dust with his "infernal bacterial death dealer, the broom." As well as illuminating the exclusionary dynamics of dirt and cleanliness in the United States, W. D.'s letter shows how concerns about dirt mingled with germ theory.[35]

By the interwar period, dead animals, household waste, rags, blood, human excrement, ashes, horse manure, and rotting foodstuffs were less likely to blight streets and pavements. These post-sludge streets consequently provided a showcase for dog excrement, which gradually replaced horse manure as the main form of animal feces in the modern city. As *La presse médicale* stated in 1929, the disappearance of Paris's horses had exposed the "true horror" of dog excrement.[36]

Public hygienists had created cleaner streets and raised public expectations that modern and civilized cities *should* be clean. Dog mess undermined inhabitants' desires to wander the streets without stepping in foul matter or having their nostrils assailed by the smell of shit. The stage was set for the emergence of feelings of disgust about dog mess.

The Discovery of Dog Mess

It was hard for some observers to discuss the canine excrement that was now visible within the modern cityscape. In a letter to the *Times* of London, Bristol-based Dr. G. Knowles acknowledged the difficulty of discussing the foul matter: "I can only think that people have been comparatively silent regarding this disgusting nuisance out of a sense of delicacy." Euphemistic language, a common way to distance oneself from excrement in the modern West, came to the fore. In this vein, the chair of the Committee on Parks of the Women's Municipal League, a New York association dedicated to promoting personal and public hygiene, complained somewhat cryptically about dogs "loiter[ing]" on the sidewalk rather than being led to the street by their owner, whose inconsideration prevented the sidewalk from being kept in a "decent" state. Those who could bring themselves to mention the unmentionable struggled to describe the scale of the problem. New York's streets and stoops were "filthy beyond expression," wrote one *New York Times* reader.[37]

But a language of disgust did emerge to express revulsion at canine excrement. In New York, *defilement* became a key term to describe dogs' fouling of the pavement, one with strong moral overtones and connotations of corruption and desecration. It was not just paving slabs that were defiled but anything that happened to be on the streets. A *New York Times* reader noted how "one is often shocked and nauseated to see the defilement of ice, vegetables, flowers, &c. by dogs." Canine excrement corrupted objects of life and beauty that would otherwise brighten up New York's streets. It was "offensive" to see how dogs "defiled sidewalks, posts, steps, lamp posts &c," grumbled another reader of the paper. Dog mess sullied public and private property, and it insulted the sensibilities of all who saw themselves as defenders of "decency and cleanliness." The soiling of the street furniture intended to improve the cityscape and affirm New York's modernity weakened residents' faith in progress. The top of the lamp post may have radiated light and civilization, but its base remained mired in waste and backwardness.[38]

Parisians were the least coy when discussing dog mess. The term *souillure* (blemish) provided a way of speaking about canine excrement, suggesting it was a stain that needed to be wiped away. French physicians and public hygienists were struck by the diversity of dog feces. Dr. Marcel Clerc, a hygiene specialist at the Medical Faculty of Paris and member of the Society for Public, Industrial, and Social Hygiene, noted that it varied according to the particular dog's "intestinal situation" and "atmospheric conditions." Canine excrement ranged from the "dropping [*crotte*]" deposited by little dogs to the "human-sized faecal black pudding [*boudin*] of the police dog." Writing in *La presse médicale* and taking a dig at wealthy dog owners, "Un piéton" (whom Clerc identified as city councilor Jacques Romazzotti) similarly contrasted the "marble"-sized excrement of the "marquise's beloved little Pekingese" with the "enormous black-pudding created by the industrialist's wolfhound." But whatever its provenance and consistency, feces was a "disgusting spectacle" that made pavements "revolting" and turned them into "cesspits." For Harley Street physician and suffragette Agnes Savill, the streets of London had similarly become a "vast latrine for dogs." In all three cities, dog mess was an unwanted reminder of the city's dirtier recent past. Dogs had become regrettable features of the modern city's sensory landscape: "the presence of these animals is an offense to the senses of sight, smell, and hearing," noted one *New York Times* reader (who was also aggrieved by all the barking).[39]

Why did dog excrement seem so revolting? Clerc suggested that the similarities with human feces made it particularly "disgusting." Moreover, discreet defecation had become a marker of refinement and self-discipline. Like the shocking use of the word "merdre [*sic*]" in Alfred Jarry's play *Ubu Roi* (first performed in 1896), dog mess was an unwelcome and very public reminder of bodily functions. It became a filthy yet fascinating taboo in a culture "founded on the repudiation of bodily products."[40] For a growing band of concerned observers, dog mess was too disgusting for dogopolis.

That Which Lurks Within

With Louis Pasteur's vaccination reducing the threat of rabies, health-related anxieties fixated on parasite-infested dog feces. Tapeworms—whose eggs spread echinococcosis to humans—loomed large in this regard. Echinococcosis caused hydatid cysts containing these worms to develop, often in the lungs (alveolar) or liver (hepatic), leading to painful and life-threatening symptoms. With rabies largely tamed in Britain, the *Lancet* argued that "the danger of echinococcosis is probably the greatest that is run by man from dogs, as the symptoms in the infected animal are at most vague, and often absent; and there is no Pasteur treatment available." Physicians and other commentators now deemed dog mess disgusting and unhealthy: "it is generally known that the excreta of flesh-eating animals, such as dogs and cats, is not only more offensive but carries a greater menace to health than that of . . . herb-eating creatures," pointed out one *New York Times* reader. It was a question of "indecency" as well as health for another New Yorker.[41] Dog feces stank, but the real danger was what lurked within.

Hydatid cysts drew the most attention. Beginning with Hippocrates, physicians have long been aware of these cysts in livestock and humans. However, their parasitic origins became better understood in the seventeenth century, eventually being linked to tapeworms of the genus *Echinococcus*. Building on the pioneering work of Carl Rudolphi on intestinal worms, Carl von Siebold identified, in 1853 and 1854, the life cycle of the dog tapeworm *Echinococcus granulosus* that developed in intermediate hosts, such as cattle, horses, and occasionally humans. Shortly afterward, Rudolf Virchow outlined the clinical course of what is now known as alveolar echinococcosis (caused by the larval stage of the tapeworm *Echinococcus multilocularis*) in his groundbreaking research in 1855. This new scientific knowledge transformed tapeworms from a canine health problem, as discussed in many dog care books and to be treated with various medicines, into a human health problem.[42]

The dog's much-celebrated closeness with humans now represented a threat: the two species shared parasites and alarming illnesses. Columbia University–trained American surgeon James P. Warbasse warned that the "echinococcosis disease" "[gave] rise to cysts and abscesses of the liver" and was most common among those "who live in close social relation with the dog."[43]

Hydatid cysts caused alarm. They could grow to the size of a "child's head," reported the *Lancet*. In 1934 it provided X-ray images of one that had developed in the lung of an eight-year-old girl from Swansea who "fondled" her pet dog "a great deal." She had developed "lassitude, listlessness, anorexia and night sweats." She was admitted to the hospital after she began coughing up parts of the cyst walls. Becoming "gravely ill," the child was treated for cardiac and respiratory symptoms as well as an "urticarial rash" before eventually recovering and returning to school. The details of such cases spread from scientific journals to the mainstream press. In an echo of earlier warnings about rabies, intimacy with dogs was described as potentially deadly. In London, Ingleby Oddie, the Westminster coroner, warned readers of the *Times* against the "disgusting habit of kissing dogs" after a woman died at Charing Cross Hospital from a "hydatid cyst the size of a coconut," presumably contracted through her custom of kissing her pet terrier. In Paris, a cyst had killed a girl after she let her dog lick her face, reported *Le matin*. Dogs were now being regarded as disgusting spreaders of disease.[44]

The closeness of dogs and humans now threatened the most vulnerable family members. "Man's friend," warned F. M. Bogan in *Health*, "is allowed to go where he will, deposit his excreta indiscriminately, investigate the genitals and excreta of all the other dogs that he meets, and then our loyal friend returns to lick the hand of our baby girl or boy and perhaps infect them with a loathsome disease." Investigations, Bogan reported, had found that 5 percent of children in a Washington, DC, institution had tapeworm. Children needed to be protected from this risk. An image of a dog licking a baby accompanied a New York Department of Health leaflet warning high school students about how the parasites of dogs and other animals could transfer to humans.[45] This subverted the staple nineteenth-century image of children hugging, fondling, and kissing dogs. Imperceptible and insidious parasites, not just feelings of intimacy, now passed between the two species. Interspecies love had a disgusting—and potentially fatal—underbelly.

In a further reverberation of nineteenth-century rabies fears, dog mess generated anxiety without actually claiming the lives of many Parisians. Dr. Abel Lahille reported that hydatid cysts had killed seven citizens in 1937, six in 1938, and seven in 1939, but he was less clear about whether these deaths could be directly linked to canine feces. Nonetheless, the boundary-breaking character of dog excrement and its parasites fueled the public's fears. Clerc outlined how tapeworm eggs survived the eventual disintegration of fecal matter, at which time they would be "dispersed by the wind or water, or even introduced into our apartments on the soles of our shoes." Dangerous parasites could breach the supposedly private and secure space of the modern Parisian apartment.[46]

But the condemnation of dogs' threat to human health was not universal. Parisian cardiologist René Lutembacher warned against "abusing" the "specter" of harmful parasites. Dog feces caused very few health problems in humans, and pet dogs brought emotional comfort to lonely people. In Britain, a Wellcome Bureau of Scientific Research investigation, published in the *Lancet*, also downplayed the risk of dog mess to public health. The researchers' examination of dog stools around Bloomsbury's Gordon Square had found no evidence of hydatid disease, although they did find a new coccidium (a type of protozoan parasite) of the dog. After downplaying its impact on human health, the researchers concluded that dog mess might be cleaned up on "aesthetic grounds."[47]

Disgust versus Insouciance

Despite the Wellcome team's findings, dog mess raised troubling questions about dogs and public health. Owners who let their dogs lick their face chose to place themselves at risk. But owners who let their dogs defecate on the street exposed others to worrying health problems. Defecating dogs laid bare the tensions between the norms of responsible dog ownership and those of public hygiene. Dog owners who thoughtlessly turned out their pets each day to relieve themselves conformed to the aforementioned advice dished out by dog care experts. But in doing so, they transgressed public health principles and infuriated their fellow citizens, who increasingly demanded clean and healthy streets.

Revulsion clashed with nonchalance. Dog owners were accused of putting their own self-interest before that of their fellow citizens, who had a right to walk on clean sidewalks without feeling "uncomfortable" or "annoyed." Some owners even seemed to delight in letting their dog soil the streets in the most "annoying" place for other pedestrians, Romazzotti lamented.[48]

Critics attacked dog owners' character. They were "selfish" and did not think twice about inconveniencing others. One letter writer to the *New York Times* reported seeing "comparatively frail women engaged as janitresses, washing from the steps of apartment houses and sidewalks the disgusting 'evidence' of the 'dog lovers'' want of consideration." Dog owners' obsession with their pets had blinded them to the burden they placed on others. Other New Yorkers grumbled about the strain of keeping their stoops and newels clean: dog mess caused the "defilement" of their private property. The rights of dog owners clashed with those of property owners, triggering arguments in the streets and the *New York Times* letters pages. In London, Savill similarly complained about the impossibility of keeping doorsteps clean of excrement and urine even with "frequent doses of Lysol and sulphur."[49] Dog mess defied attempts to keep properties and cities clean.

The most inconsiderate dog owners were those who allowed their dogs to foul where children played. Perhaps most worryingly, Parisian babies made "sand pies" in the sandy spaces found in the middle of boulevards. Dog feces teeming with tapeworms dotted these play spaces. In London, K. A. Lumsden of Kensington Court wrote to the *Times* to express concern about the awful state of the pavements where dogs relieved themselves in the borough of Kensington. Most worryingly, the area known as the Nursery in Kensington Gardens was a "menace to the health" of the children who played in the grass where dogs relieved themselves. At a time when parks were said to allow children to realize their natural and healthy inclinations to play outdoors, canine fecal matter turned play areas into polluted places and exposed middle-class children to filth.[50]

Significantly, critics blamed wealthy dog owners for endangering the health of others. They pointed out that many defecating dogs were accompanied by servants. A letter writer to the *New York Times* observed that it was the "better sections" of the city near Central Park that were most affected. Similarly in London, Dr A. M. Ware of Queen's Gate Terrace blamed owners of expensive flats and mews in this area of Kensington for turning out their dogs for their morning and evening evacuations. These dog owners needed to learn "consideration for others." Clerc and Romazzotti also held well-heeled dog owners primarily responsible for the "fecalization" of Paris. Others observed that it was "maids" or "valets" who stood by while their owners' dogs "defile[d] walk or doorstep." Delegating the messiness of pet keeping to their servants was one way for wealthy urbanites to distance themselves from excrement. While public hygienists normally targeted the working classes, defecating dogs now brought their wealthy owners into the firing line.[51]

As with rabies, dog mess also became a gendered issue. Male observers complained how women's allegedly excessive fondness for dogs spread dirt and parasites. They identified the dog-loving bourgeois woman as the most incorrigible dog owner. One *New York Times* reader reported seeing women with "some education and apparently some reputation" allowing their dogs to foul while they assumed "an air of abstraction and unconsciousness." This lack of regard was infuriating: "how long is every one to submit to the impertinent selfishness and the vulgar ignorance of the boors who harbour these unmitigated and useless nuisances and parade them in public without the slightest regard for the feelings or rights or safety of others?" In Paris, female dog owners even brought the danger underground. J. Couturat was distressed that they took their dogs on the metro, thereby exposing their fellow passengers to parasites.[52]

Further echoing the debates around straying and biting, dog mess raised questions about the acceptability of dogs in the modern city. The branding of dogs as dirty defecators was a useful weapon in the arsenal of those who wanted to heavily restrict or remove dogs from urban areas. Defecating hogs and goats had been removed from New York, so why not dogs, went one argument. Dog mess even prompted self-confessed dog lovers to suggest that all dogs, or at the very least the largest ones, should be banned from cities. Their place was in the countryside. Dog mess called dogopolis into question. If the bestial excretions of even the cleanest dogs could not be hidden, could dogs ever be accepted within the Western metropolis?[53]

Other commentators defended dogs and directed their ire at the owners. A reader from Deptford in southeast London wrote the *Daily Mirror* to complain about defecating dogs, and he was told to "blame their owners," not the dogs. Martha L. Kobbe, a member of a New York humane society, echoed this refrain: it was not a dog's fault if their owner had not trained them to defecate in the gutter. Along with keeping the pet on a leash, taking them to the gutter to relieve themself should now be part of considerate dog ownership. Like other citizens, dog owners had a duty to help keep the streets clean. Allowing their dog to defecate in random places was a sign of lax discipline on the owners' part. Maybe owners should be wearing the collars instead of their dogs, quipped one *New York Times* reader. If, as Norbert Elias has argued, Western civilization partly rests on the "weeding out of the natural functions from public life," dog owners displayed an uncivilized and retrograde lack of self-restraint in allowing their dogs to foul the pavements.[54]

Canine excrement had become a disturbing and disgusting matter of public concern. Dr. Marcel Clerc insisted that dog feces on the streets was an attack on the freedom and rights of individual urban citizens. It threatened their ability to maintain their personal well-being and insulate themselves from foul matter: "the individual's liberty, particularly related to sanitary enforcement [*police sanitaire*], ends where others' begins." Given the seriousness of the problem, Clerc demanded that Paris's municipal council take the matter in hand.[55]

Combating Dog Mess

Despite Clerc's intervention, inaction marked the city authorities' response to dog mess in interwar Paris. When he pointed out the absurdity that the authorities had banned the dropping of litter but not the far more harmful depositing of canine excrement, he launched a much-repeated refrain that they were not doing enough to tackle the problem. He suggested raising the tax on dogs to reduce their number, as banning them completely would be impossible due to the emotional attachments between Parisians and their dogs. He also floated the possibility of owners cleaning up their dog's mess with a rake and shovel, though ultimately dismissing this form of proto–poop scooping because it would still leave traces of feces on the streets. Another option would be to require dogs to defecate in the gutter, while councilor

Jacques Romazzotti called for the creation of "canine vespasiennes," designated sandy areas that would be cleaned daily. These dog toilets *avant la lettre* would be the canine version of public street urinals, or *vespasiennes*, which derived their name from the Roman emperor Vespasian.[56]

But the municipal authorities did nothing. In response to their indifference, Romazzotti and other councilors argued, during a council assembly meeting in December 1935, that more must be done. They suggested mixing disciplinary and educational measures to persuade owners to take their dogs to the gutter. But despite recognizing that education was more effective than "fines or the brutality of repression," Romazzotti argued that the city's authorities should give dog owners the sense that they were under constant "surveillance." Leaving aside the question of whether such monitoring of citizens in democratic societies was even possible, city leadership remained reluctant to take responsibility for the resolution of this issue. At a meeting of the Paris municipal council in December 1937, the police prefect refused to introduce antifouling laws, declaring that all he could do was "appeal to the good sense of Parisians." He had no desire to address this "particularly delicate question" that would place the administration in the difficult position of arbitrating between dog owners and other pedestrians.[57] From the authorities' perspective, the health risks posed by inconsiderate canine defecation did not warrant the expense and potential confrontation entailed in trying to discipline or reform dog owners, let alone pay for more street cleaning.

Dog excrement therefore continued to provoke embarrassment. During the travails of the German occupation, Dr. Abel Lahille nonetheless found time to deplore the condition of the shoes of unobservant pedestrians, which bore "a disgusting reminder of [this] nauseating and hazardous matter." His observation that German occupying forces were "offended" by the sight of dog excrement articulated the oft-repeated notion that canine feces had sullied France's international reputation. The city police took a small step, however, during the early 1940s by ordering that dogs should defecate only in the gutter.[58]

New Yorkers seemed unaware that Parisians were bemoaning the canine excrement soiling their streets. They instead treated dog mess as contributing to the mass of litter strewn across Gotham's streets that threatened its status as a clean and civilized city in comparison to its European counterparts. Driving home the many deficiencies of New York's streets was a report on street cleaning in European cities by sanitation engineer George Soper for the New York Academy of Medicine's Committee of Twenty on Street and Outdoor Cleanliness. Soper had visited many Austrian, British,

French, German, and Italian cities and attended international congresses on street cleaning in Dresden, London, and Stuttgart. Amazed by the cleanliness of European cities—especially Munich—he was convinced that keeping cities clean was "a great cooperative undertaking in which everybody has a serious responsibility." The *New York Times* concurred. A sanitation department, however well run and technologically advanced, was not enough. The "people themselves who use the streets" had to act responsibly and hygienically. The Department of Sanitation recognized this challenge. In the words of its secretary, Matthew Napear, each day it had to undertake "THE EFFORT TO MAKE THE RESIDENTS OF THE CITY OF NEW YORK LITTER CONSCIOUS; and to force in the mind of all [New Yorkers] the desire to make the City the cleanest in the world, and in consequence, thereof, the healthiest."[59] The residents, of course, included insouciant dog owners.

In fact, disgust at dog mess had resulted in more action across the Atlantic than in Paris. Section 227 of the New York Sanitary Code (Amendment 74 [1918]) stated that "dogs [were] to be controlled so as not to commit nuisances." In somewhat euphemistic language, the code noted that owners must prevent their dog from committing "any nuisance upon any sidewalk of any public street, avenue, park, public square, or place in the City of New York; or upon the floor of any hall of any tenement house." The measure applied to fences, floors, walls, and stairways of all buildings, including factories, ferry ports, stations, hotels, and offices. It even covered the roof of tenement houses "used in common by the tenants thereof." Shared public spaces, in other words, were to be free of excrement. Unless the dog owner had a yard or garden—both rare commodities, especially in Manhattan—the only space available for canine waste was the gutter, where defecating dogs had to compete with cars and other traffic. But as the many letters of complaint to the *New York Times* suggested, many owners were either unaware of or unbothered by the code. It was a "dead letter," lamented one correspondent in 1935.[60]

To tackle owners' negligence, the Outdoor Cleanliness Association (OCA) of New York launched a campaign in 1936 to tackle the "dog nuisance." It was established by women who "felt that cleanliness should not be limited to the home," so it set about combating soot, litter, and grime in all its forms. The OCA continued the work of the women who had spearheaded the City Beautiful movements during the Progressive Era of reform between the 1890s and 1920s. These pioneers believed that cleanliness and beauty in the urban environment would uplift New Yorkers, and they were confident that their maternal instincts, educative expertise, and hygienic know-how perfectly placed them to cleanse and beautify cities and to educate urbanites out of unsanitary habits.[61]

Working with the Department of Sanitation in a bid to transform New Yorkers' attitudes toward dog mess, the OCA adopted a message for its campaign, then put up signs asking dog owners to "Please Keep Your Dog Near the Curb." It also arranged an educational radio broadcast, led a Midtown parade of dogs wearing placards inscribed with its campaign message, and sent out posters for display in shops, especially those on Madison and Lexington Avenues. Unlike other Progressive Era reform organizations led by women—such as the Women's Health Protective Association on the Lower East Side, which had sought to reform poor and immigrant neighborhoods—the OCA's focus on prestigious shopping districts targeted rich dog owners. In addition, the Department of Sanitation put up twenty-five Please Curb Your Dog signs in problem areas. In telling language, the *New York Times* suggested that the signs were to "train" dog owners whose behavior must change to conform to sanitary laws and norms. At the same time, Department of Sanitation inspectors fined more owners for contravening section 227, a measure supported by the OCA and its correspondents, who wrote in to request fines and arrests in their locality.[62] Discipline accompanied education in the attempt to prod owners out of their insouciance.

The OCA's campaign sought to convince dog owners that curbing their dog would counter those voices calling for dogs to be banned from the modern city. In 1939 member Helen Schwarz noted that "dog owners quickly realized that our interest was theirs. If we had not worked out a solution, dogs would very probably have been banished in time from the city." But the campaign struggled to deal with the sheer quantity of canine excrement produced by the estimated half a million dogs who lived in New York City in the late 1930s. The campaign also failed to address the problem of defecation in the gutter, where cars and other vehicles might hit dogs. One dog owner called on the city authorities to "furnish the required facilities" that would allow dogs to defecate in peace, and to stop putting the rights of car drivers before those of dog owners. Moreover, it was hard to catch dog owners contravening section 227. It took twenty inspectors to catch fourteen offenders in one day in Flatbush, Brooklyn, in 1936.[63] That was a lot of effort for little reward.

But there were signs that the OCA's campaign had begun to shift dog-keeping behaviors in New York. During the 1930s, dog care experts finally began to dispense advice about curb training. In their book, James R. Kinney and Ann Honeycutt stated that the owner's task was to get the dog off the pavement and into the gutter as soon as his pet gave signs that they needed to defecate. Luckily, the authors remarked, the dog would be drawn to the gutter by the smells left by other dogs. Scolding should be the owner's response to defecation on the pavement, and praise should not be spared when the dog used the gutter. Curbing dogs was seen to alter canine behavior. Trained dogs might display "idiosyncrasies," such as needing to go behind a car, over a manhole, or in familiar places.[64] Although many dog owners undoubtedly ignored Kinney and Honeycutt's advice, it was novel for a dog care book to advise owners to take their dog to the curb to spare fellow urbanites the sight and smell of dog mess.

In London, calls for something to be done about canine feces were made during World War I.[65] In 1918 Dr. Charles Porter, the medical officer of Marylebone Borough Council, answered these pleas. As public hygienists had done since the mid-nineteenth century, Porter set out to tackle the dangerous and disgusting "nuisance" of animal waste in the urban landscape. He persuaded Marylebone council to display a poster that declared,

> Nuisance and danger to health are caused by the excreta of dogs.
> You can train your dog to use the roadway.
> In the interests of the Public Health please try.[66]

The poster apparently helped reduce complaints about fouling in the short term. It also inspired Kensington Borough Council to introduce an experimental antifouling bylaw in 1922. The bylaw declared that "no person being in charge of a dog on a lead shall allow or permit such dog to deposit its excrement upon the public footway." Owners who contravened it were liable to pay a forty-shilling fine. However, as *Public Health* (the journal of the Society of Medical Officers of Health) pointed out, the measure did not apply to private property, such as doorsteps.[67] It was therefore nowhere near as comprehensive as the New York Sanitary Code.

Judging by the letters pages of the *Times* of London, the borough of Kensington was a fouling hotspot and a battleground between the disgusted and the insouciant emotional stances. James Fenton, Kensington's medical officer of health, noted that the number of flats and maisonettes without gardens contributed to the tensions there. *Public Health* reported that the Kensington bylaw succeeded in improving the state of the pavements and that the council had raised awareness of the issue among dog owners through posters, leaflets, and a printed slip on rate demand notices. Fenton was also pleased to receive many inquiries about the bylaw from other London borough Medical

Officers. But the number of convictions was low. The council issued just two warnings in 1922, two warnings and a summons in 1923, and four summonses and convictions in 1924.[68] Nonetheless, the bylaw may have been sufficient to shift attitudes and jolt some owners into taking their dogs to the gutter.

In 1936 the British Home Office intervened to remove the stipulation that only leashed dogs were subject to the measures. Henceforth, antifouling bylaws stipulated that the "owner of the dog shall be deemed to be in charge thereof." The prohibition now applied to *all* dogs, not only to owners choosing to keep their dogs leashed in line with the norms of responsible dog ownership. This change addressed a concern raised at a meeting between Kensington Borough Council officials and Home Office civil servants (including the appropriately named Mr. Crapper). The Kensington delegation complained about "deliberate evasion" of the bylaw by certain owners who kept their dog on the lead until they needed to defecate, then released their pet before putting the animal back on the lead after "evacuation." Despite confronting these owners, council officials were powerless to tackle this form of fouling.[69]

Yet while home secretary John Simon noted that the bylaw in Kensington had helped reduce fouling, he urged borough councils to act with caution and think carefully about whether such measures were needed. He was keen to avoid offending dog owners and the dog lobby. The National Canine Defence League had long treated antifouling bylaws as attacks on dog owners, and it worried that their full enforcement would make it "difficult to keep dogs in large towns." Less willing to take on dog owners than Walter Long, president of the Board of Agriculture, had done with muzzling several decades earlier, Simon was governed by caution. He declared that bylaws were to last initially for two years and could then be extended. Many London boroughs subsequently introduced versions of the 1936 bylaw, including Battersea, Bethnal Green, Deptford, Finsbury Park, Kensington, Wandsworth, and Westminster, as well as towns and cities beyond the metropolis, such as Bristol, Exeter, and Shrewsbury. These measures also attracted the attention of Marcel Clerc, who suggested them as a way of addressing dog mess in Paris. The police prefect dismissed this idea, incorrectly arguing that they were "recommendations" rather than orders.[70]

The bylaws represented a first step in trying to make dog owners feel responsible for where their pets defecated. Many pavements in London and all sidewalks and public spaces in New York were designated excrement-free spaces by the outbreak of World War II. However, it was still too much to expect dog owners to have to handle dog mess, and it was not until much later that councils required them to do so. The introduction of plastic pooper-scoopers and bags offered a hygienic and impermeable barrier between canine excrement and human hands, enabling the waste to be removed from pavements and placed in bins. New York's "poop scoop law" of 1978 led the way, with Paris following in 2002. A toxocariasis scare in Britain in the mid-1970s was not enough for its government to compel owners to pick up after their pets. That came in 1996 with the Dogs (Fouling of Land) Act. (*Toxocara canis* are roundworm parasites whose eggs can cause blindness in humans through contact with soil contaminated by dog feces.)[71]

Conclusion

Attitudes and actions concerning canine defecation underwent an enormous transformation in London, New York, and Paris. In the nineteenth century, dog mess was largely unseen and unmentionable, apart from limited discussions on housebreaking and canine digestion in dog care books as well as being a minor part of the urban fecal economy. This circumstance shifted in the interwar period. Changing sensibilities about foul matter and smells, new knowledge about parasites, and physical changes to city streets, particularly the disappearance of horse manure, provided the conditions for a new emotional stance to develop that was rooted in disgust, fear, and annoyance regarding canine excrement. Defecating dogs began to replace biting and straying ones as the most serious perceived canine threat to health. Like biting and straying, defecation exposed the provisional nature of dogopolis. Dogs were welcome in the metropolis as long as they were clean and did not threaten public health and middle-class sensibilities.

The sight and smell of canine deposits triggered disgust, fear, and anger in many Londoners, New Yorkers, and Parisians. They served as material reminders—replenished daily—that the cities were not as sanitary and civilized as many urbanites would have liked. With pet dogs being one of the most highly domesticated animals, their indiscreet defecation reflected badly on the modern urbanite, especially those who saw themselves as the most civilized: the middle classes. Furthermore, the presence of dog mess on the streets of the metropoles undermined British, French, and American assumptions that they were global innovators in sewerage and flushing toilets. They treated their sanitary know-how as confirmation of their supposed superiority over the peoples they had colonized and their geopolitical adversaries. In this vein, the medical officer of the 1924 British Empire Exhibition at Wembley had boasted of the extensive operation to remove excrement from the site, and he described the difficulty of keeping the latrines in the "native quarters" clean. Dog mess challenged the purported superiority of Western urban civilization, with its emphasis on controlled and sanitary excremental practices.[72]

The legacies of the disgusted stance taken on dog mess live on in current fears about the health impacts of canine feces, especially on children, and in how it still sparks mixed reactions of disgust and anxiety. Dog mess continues to give rise to questions about the place of dogs in the city, and it continues to embody a key tension in modern urban cultures torn between the desire for order and cleanliness and physical confrontations with the messiness and uncertainty of urban life.[73]

Coda

The ways in which dogs and humans lived together in London, New York, and Paris changed drastically from the beginning of the nineteenth century to the start of World War II. By 1939, hundreds of thousands of strays had been exterminated. Rabies had been partially tamed in New York and Paris, and it had been stamped out in London. Police dogs had begun patrolling the streets, canine suffering had been enveloped within humanitarian sentiments, and in addition to inducing disgust, canine excrement had become a public health issue. The period involved tightening human control over urban dogs, who were increasingly constrained by leashes, muzzles, and obedience training, while unwanted dogs were killed. Dogs became part of the management of urban street life, with these measures giving credence to Nicholas Kenny's view that "modern urbanism strove to evacuate the city of impracticality and fear, removing the obstacles impending its security and efficiency."[1]

What many in the Western world now take to be natural features of the human-canine bond was in fact rooted in the fraught emotional histories of urbanization in the modern West. The bond shifted within the broader classed, gendered, and racialized emotional contours of urban life, including fears of crime, vagabondage, and disease; disgust at dirt; and revulsion to suffering. Dogs were molded to fit middle-class values and norms, even if this process was always challenged and incomplete, and the middle classes often clashed over the most desirable ways of adapting dogs to modern city living. Nonetheless, dogopolis had arrived. Straying and biting dogs were contained, canine suffering was made tolerable through humane killing methods, and canine thinking was harnessed through the implementation of police dogs and the first steps taken to curb defecating.

Dogs' lives had changed. Some were elevated to quasi-human status, such as the four-legged crime investigators and pets. Others—strays and rabid dogs—became semisavage beasts on the streets and were treated as such. Only those who conformed most to middle-class norms of cleanliness, respectability, and domesticity were welcomed into dogopolis. But even their acceptance was provisional and challenged: pet dogs' feces sparked concerns, and worries lingered about bites from police dogs.

Overall, the similarities between London, New York, and Paris outweighed the differences. But there were important variations, most notably the early eradication of indigenous canine rabies in Britain. Of the three cities, New York and Paris were the most similar. Both tended to take their lead from developments in London, such as the founding of kennel clubs, dog shelters, and humane organizations. New York and Paris also introduced all-purpose police dogs and embraced Pasteurism more fully. The preexisting French influence on American medicine, the enthusiastic efforts of French physicians in New York, and the physical distance between rabies victims in the United States and the Pasteur treatment in Paris help explain Americans' enthusiastic if disputed acceptance of the pasteurization of rabies.

The evolution of the human-canine bond did not end in 1939. The outbreak of World War II in Britain immediately ushered in a dramatic development. Many London pet owners voluntarily had their pet cats and dogs humanely killed in anticipation of German bombing: four hundred thousand dogs and cats met their end in the capital's animal shelters at the start of September 1939. Other, less dramatic shifts in human-canine relations in London, New York, and Paris after the war include toxocariasis scares and the introduction of pooper-scooper laws in the 1970s; the creation of dog runs in New York; the growth of dog-sitting and dog-walking companies; the expansion of neutering as a way of controlling dog populations; and the heightened consumerization of pet keeping, including a short-lived *boulangerie* (bakery) for dogs in Paris. New emotional layers deepen the history of dogs and humans in London, New York, and Paris. Nowadays, antifouling campaigns often seek to *shame* owners into picking up after their pets. Shame as well as anger, fear, and disgust now stick to dog mess.[2]

The after-effects continue to be felt from the period covered in this book. They include continued anxieties about biting dogs, compassion for dogs in shelters and laboratories, celebrations and concerns regarding police dogs, regulations against straying, and encouragement given to owners to pick up their pet's mess. Some voices continue to celebrate canine intelligence and emotional sensitivity, while others play down these qualities and argue that dogs have no place in the modern city.[3] Kennel clubs, animal protectionists, the police, municipal authorities, and scientists continue to play leading roles in shaping human-canine relations. Dogopolis has changed, and it continues to be questioned. But for better or worse, Western urbanites are still living within it.

ACKNOWLEDGMENTS

I would like to thank many people and institutions for their help in bringing this book to fruition. First, I thank the University of Liverpool, the University of Warwick, the British Academy (Small Grant, award ID: SG110009), and the Wellcome Trust (Small Grant, award ID: 109404/Z/15/Z) for the funding that enabled me to conduct the archival research that is the book's foundation.

Thanks to Oxford University Press for permission to reprint excerpts from the following of my articles: "'Four-legged *Poilus*': French Army Dogs, Emotional Practices and the Creation of Militarized Human-Dog Bonds, 1871–1918," *Journal of Social History* 52, no. 3 (2019): 731–60; "Combating 'Canine Visiting Cards': Public Hygiene and the Management of Dog Mess in Paris since the 1920s," *Social History of Medicine* 32, no. 1 (2019): 143–65; and "Stray Dogs and the Making of Modern Paris," *Past and Present* 234 (2017): 137–72. Thanks to Cambridge University Press for permission to reprint excerpts from my article "Between Instinct and Intelligence: Harnessing Police Dog Agency in Early Twentieth Century Paris," *Comparative Studies in Society and History* 58, no. 2 (2016): 463–90.

A big thank you goes to the archivists and librarians in London, New York, and Paris who aided my research, especially Michael Cronin (New York City Police Museum); Dorothée Fabre, André Varlet, and Marie Ratiarson (Société centrale canine, Paris); Ciara Farrell (Kennel Club, London); Daniel Demellier, Johann Chevillard, and Elisabeth Liber (Institut Pasteur, Paris); Arlene Shaner and Danielle Aloia (New York Academy of Medicine); Lee R. Hiltzik and colleagues (Rockefeller Archive Center, Sleepy Hollow); and

Susan Wakefield (General Mills, Minneapolis). Alison Clarke provided some essential last-minute research assistance at the New York Public Library. For practical assistance, I am grateful to the Events, Finance, and Research teams in the School of Histories, Languages, and Cultures at the University of Liverpool. Special thanks also go to the app team at the University of Liverpool for producing the Sniffing the Past smartphone app (https://www.liverpool.ac.uk/csd/app-directory/sniffing-the-past/).

For advice and encouragement along the way, I thank former colleagues at Warwick (in particular, Roberta Bivins, Rebecca Earle, Anne Gerritsen, David Hardiman, Rainer Horn, David Lambert, Mia Lee, Penny Roberts, Rosa Salzburg, Claudia Stein, and Mathew Thompson) and former and current ones at Liverpool (especially Malcolm Bennett, Sam Caslin, Roland Clark, Marios Costambeys, Andy Davies, Celia Donert, Bonnie Effros, Georgina Endfield, Christienna Fryar, Marin Heale, Deana Heath, Jon Hogg, Richard Huzzey, Damien Kempf, Stephen Kenny, James Lowry, Graeme Milne, Andrew Redden, Mark Riley, Leon Rocha, Sally Sheard, Mark Towsey, Carri Westgarth, and Robin Whelan). Thanks also to Damien Baldin, Victoria Bates, Dorothee Brantz, Robert Bickers, Matt Black, Nickie Charles, Peter Coates, Tim Cole, Marianna Dudley, Kristen Greer, Cihangir Gundogdu, Susan Hamilton, Jane Hamlett, Clare Hickman, Philip Howell, Jane Hume, Julian Jackson, Colin Jones, David Joseph-Goteiner, Hilda Kean, Daniel Lee, Catherine McNeur, Chris Millington, David Moon, Eric Morgan, Elizabeth Murchison, Jan Oosthoek, Sara Owczarczak-Garstecka, Kevin Passmore, Harriet Ritvo, Jonathan Saha, Peter Sahlins, Vanessa Schwartz, Victoria Shea, the late Michael Sibalis, Krithika Srinivasan, Julie-Marie Strange, Sandra Swart, Jessica Wang, Tom Webb, Tamara Whited, Justyna Włodarczyk, Penny Woolcock, Michael Worboys, Chaz Yingling, and Dan and Nigel from the National Poo Museum, Sandown, Isle of Wight. A special shout-out goes to Neil Pemberton, who has provided endless support, advice, and insights along the way. Thanks, too, to all the contributors and readers of my blog *Sniffing the Past* (https://sniffingthepast.wordpress.com/).

For reading chapters, I am grateful to Brian Pearson, Anna Bocking-Welch, and Penny Summerfield, and for reading through the whole thing, Geoff and Moya Pearson.

Seminar audiences at Aberystwyth, Bristol, Chester, Durham, Liverpool, Manchester Metropolitan, Oxford, Swansea, and Warwick Universities helped me refine my ideas, as did those at the following conferences and workshops: American Society for Environmental History, Toronto (2013); "Brighton Nerd Nite" (2016); "Animals and Emotion," London (2017); Animal History Group, King's College London (2017); "Dogs in History and Culture" workshop, University of Manchester (2013), "Emotions and Work" workshop, London (2019); History and Theory, Wesleyan University (2013); "Remaking Zoopolis," New Delhi (2018); Royal Geographical Society–Institute of British Geographers, London (2015); "Pedigree Chums" workshop, University of Manchester (2015); and the Society for the Social History of Medicine, University of Kent (2016). For featuring my work, I am grateful to *BBC History Magazine*, CityLab/the *Atlantic*, and *Making History* (BBC Radio 4).

At the University of Chicago Press, I am indebted to Tim Mennel; Susannah Engstrom; Mary Corrado; the manuscript reviewers; the Animal Lives series editors, Jane C. Desmond, Kim Marra, and Barbara J. King; and the late Douglas Mitchell. My thanks and appreciation go to Sandra Hazel for her excellent copyediting skills. Many thanks to Tobiah Waldron for creating the index, and to Jess Farr-Cox as well as Geoff and Moya Pearson for their proofreading skills.

Thanks to all the friends who have helped along the way. Extra appreciation goes to those who let me stay with them during archival trips: Alex, Tom, Chris and Renee, Esme, and Maggie and Gareth. Extra thanks to Brian and Ronno for making my family and me feel so welcome in Chester and for general dog enthusiasm. Thanks to Mum, Dad, and the extended Cormack, Pearson, and Wilson families.

Thanks to all the dogs of friends and family who have walked with me throughout this book: Aengus, Tintin, Toby, and the incomparable Timmy.

This book is dedicated with love to Dulcie, Noak, and Jesse, who make it all worthwhile.

APPENDIX: REFLECTIONS ON ANIMALS, HISTORY, AND EMOTIONS

There is a widespread notion that a special relationship exists between humans and dogs. Often treated as a universal and natural phenomenon that has existed since the domestication of dogs approximately twelve thousand years ago, the human-canine relationship became a much-studied topic after Austrian zoologist Konrad Lorenz's postwar identification of that bond. Lorenz celebrated canine affection in these terms in 1949: "the whole charm of the dog lies in the depth of the friendship and the strength of the spiritual ties with which he has bound himself to man."[1] Since then, veterinarians, psychologists, archaeologists, and ethologists have examined the deep and multifaceted physiological, neurological, emotional, and cognitive entanglements between the two species. Their methodologies include observing dogs performing laboratory-based tasks, qualitative analysis of human-dog relations, and, more recently, neurological testing of dogs' emotional states. As illuminating as these studies sometimes are, they tend to frame the multiple emotional connections between humans and dogs as biological and ahistorical.[2] By placing far less emphasis on timeless biological factors, animal historians have shown the differing historical and geographical representations and manifestations of human-dog relatedness, demonstrating the shifting classed and gendered cultural dimensions of human-dog relations.[3] At the risk of oversimplifying the situation, we are confronted with, on the one hand, studies that stress the culturally malleable and contingent characteristics of human-dog attachments and, on the other, those that emphasize their innate and unchanging nature.

The concept of a special bond between humans and dogs that was forged through domestication and cemented by centuries of living and working together is not without merit, as it highlights the deep companionship and connections between the two species. But the history outlined in this book suggests that the notion of an ahistorical bond obscures more than it illuminates. Without denying the significance of long-standing affective ties between dogs and humans, it is important to recognize the fragmented, multifaceted, contested, and contingent qualities of human-dog relatedness. Rather than treat human-canine connections as ahistorical, I have argued that they were constructed, critiqued, and understood within the political, social, and cultural specificities of a particular historical context (urbanization in Europe and North America during the long nineteenth century), thereby aligning myself with historical approaches to human-dog connections, and emotions more generally. But a historical approach need not obscure the embodied dimensions of human-dog relations. In this vein, I have tried to show how human emotional reactions to actual dogs and canine actions (straying, biting, suffering, thinking, and defecating) led to action, transforming how humans and dogs live together in the Western world.

Emotion is emerging as a key area of inquiry within animal studies. Setting the transformation of the human-dog bond within the histories of urbanization in London, New York, and Paris thereby responds to a growing number of studies that explore the relationship between animals and emotions. Radhika Govindrajan's *Animal Intimacies* (2018) is an exemplary study that explores the webs of relatedness between rural humans and animals in the Indian Himalayan state of Uttarakhand. Emerging through living and working together, these relationships include care as well as violence. Focusing on cows, monkeys, goats, boars, and dogs, Govindrajan shows through her multispecies ethnography "how reflexive exchanges between particular humans and animals, facilitated through an embodied, touchy-feely, language of mutual recognition and response, were crucial to their coconstitution as subjects." Animals and humans shaped each other on affective levels, and in Govindrajan's analysis, animals are emotional creatures who "love, loathe, grieve, play, crave, and, indeed, relate."[4] Her anthropological methodology allows her to observe animal emotional states, but significantly, she does not attempt to write from an animal's viewpoint.

Historians' reliance on human-generated traces of past lives means that they are not so well placed as anthropologists to observe animal emotions in action. Nonetheless, some historians have sought to capture animal perspectives and emotional experiences. Most notably, Eric Baratay has offered a history of World War I from the perspective of animal combatants, and Philip

Howell and Hilda Kean have argued that British dogs and humans shared similar emotions during the Blitz.[5] I do not deny the existence of historical canine emotional states, and perhaps dogs drew Londoners, New Yorkers, and Parisians into their emotional worlds. But I treat canine emotional experiences as elusive and beyond my grasp. Instead, I have examined how human actors understood canine emotions, how dogs affect humans emotionally, and how human emotions have transformed the lives of urban dogs in the West.

My approach is informed by history of emotions scholarship that has emphasized the historical contingency of emotions. Although they do not claim direct access to individual feelings, historians of emotions have made emotion a key element of historical research. They have stressed the social, political, and cultural dimensions of emotional expression and its contestation, and how societies, groups, and individuals have sought to regulate and manage emotions. Alongside using emotion as the lens through which to explore subjectivity, identity formation, political change, and histories of class, race, gender, and sexuality, historians of emotions have traced shifting religious and secular conceptualizations of emotions and how emotions bring people together as well as divide them. Although often influenced by psychological theories, they have challenged the notion of ahistorical emotional expressions: what it meant to cry, say, was different in the fourteenth century than it was in the twentieth. As Barbara H. Rosenwein argues, "The history of emotions should take into account the latest scientific advances in our knowledge about emotions without adopting a presentist or universalist approach. Above all, it should be sensitive to the otherness, seriousness, and complexity of the past."[6] Within this burgeoning field, studies that highlight the emotional dimensions of city life, including such topics as the urbanite's search for love and emotional reactions to new urban technologies, have been particularly useful to this book's approach.[7]

Although historians of emotions tend to focus on the representation of emotions and to research emotional expressions through texts and images, new research stresses the material dimensions of emotions, such as Monique Scheer's model of "emotional practices."[8] Inspired by these arguments, and seeking to move the perspective from objects to animals, I have sought to show how emotional responses to canine straying, biting, suffering, thinking, and defecating materially transformed human-canine relations and the lives of dogs and humans. In doing so, I aim to build on the handful of studies that have sought to historicize the relationship between animals and emotions.

Within the history of emotions, studies on animals and emotions have shown how nineteenth-century animal protectionists and antivivisectionists promoted animals as sentient creatures, while comparative psychologists and physiologists debated the extent to which animals could feel and express emotions. Darwinian theories that stressed the emotional similarities between humans and the so-called higher animals fueled both approaches.[9] Within animal history, meanwhile, Joanna Bourke outlines the intense and controversial feelings of love and physical attraction that some humans have felt toward animals; Erica Fudge examines the affective ties that developed between agricultural workers and their cows in early modern Essex; Dolly Jørgensen uncovers the emotions (grief, sorrow, hope) that motivate attempts to reintroduce endangered animal species; Ryan Hediger analyzes the feelings of US soldiers about their dogs during the Vietnam War; Jonathan Saha argues that the colonizer-pet bond represented an emotional refuge and a marker of perceived civilization and superiority in colonial Burma ("felt encounters with animals—both real and imagined, as well as physical and affective—were a perennial aspect of British colonial culture in Burma"); and Andrea Gaynor, Susan Broomhall, and Andrew Flack explore the different ways that children and adults felt about frogs in twentieth-century Australia, unpacking the emotional dimensions of scientific knowledge.[10] For my own part, I have argued that French soldiers kept pet dogs as part of their "emotional practices" to survive trench warfare on the western front between 1914 and 1918, which army commanders sought to regulate and repress. Alongside Thomas Webb, Penny Summerfield, and Mark Riley, I have also explored the emotional communities of British muleteers in the Burmese jungles during World War II to show "how emotions stick to animals, and how feelings towards animals help bind humans together."[11]

Building on these studies, in *Dogopolis* I have tried to show how emotions, such as fear, disgust, and compassion, stuck to dogs and brought dog lovers and haters together as well as into conflict with each other. In addition to responding to the often-overlooked role of animals in the history of emotions, I have emphasized the emotional dimensions of urban human-animal histories. For all the insights contained within studies of the changing presence of animals in cities, they have tended to overlook this history of emotions.[12]

To sum up, I would like to offer some brief points on why it might matter to bring animals more fully into the history of emotions. First, it provides a historical perspective on human-animal relatedness, along with a way of exploring how this has changed over time and is rooted in broader emotional histories. Second, it underscores how humans have thought of animals as emotional beings, which helps makes the history of emotions less anthropocentric. Third, it demonstrates how humans both come together and divide themselves through their emotional responses to animals. And finally, we gain a better understanding of how animals have influenced human emotional states and how human emotions, such as fear, disgust, and compassion, have transformed animal lives, thereby highlighting the material as well as the representational dimensions of emotions.

CHRONOLOGY

1810s

Equation of stray dogs with the "dangerous" classes

"Law concerning Dogs," New York, June 1811: creates post of Dog Register and Collector

Attacks on dogcatchers, New York

Paris pound moves to 31 rue Guénégaud, 1813

Paris police ordinance of May 3, 1813: dogs must be "locked up, muzzled or kept on a lead"

1820s

Royal Society for the Prevention of Cruelty to Animals founded in London, 1824

1830s

"Era of canine madness," London: rabies panic; parliamentary commission; failed bill

Metropolitan Police Act of 1839, London: introduction of muzzling

1840s

Attempted poisoning of strays and bounties paid to police for their capture, Paris, 1842

Police ordinance of May 27, 1845, Paris: tightens measures against strays

Société protectrice des animaux (Animal Protection Society [SPA]) founded in Paris, 1845
"Great Dog War," New York, 1848: attacks on strays

1850s

Grammont Law, France, 1850: public cruelty to animals banned
Annual regular summer dog pound in New York beginning in 1850
Paris police force opens a new pound at 13 rue de Pontoise (5th arrondissement), 1851
Henry Mayhew writes about pure finders in *London Labour and the London Poor*, 1851
Carl von Siebold identifies the life cycle of the dog tapeworm *Echinococcus granulosus*, 1853–54
French dog tax, 1855

1860s

Temporary Home for Lost and Starving Dogs founded in Holloway, North London, 1860
American businessman James Spratt develops Spratt's Meat Dog Biscuits, 1860-ish
American Society for the Prevention of Cruelty to Animals (ASPCA) founded, New York, 1866
State of New York law of April 12, 1867: allows ASPCA to inspect and intervene in pounds
Metropolitan Streets Act, London, 1867: police can seize strays
Law bans unmuzzled dogs roaming the streets, New York, 1867

1870s

Police order of July 6, 1870: enables London police to take strays to the Temporary Home for Lost and Starving Dogs
The Temporary Home moves to Battersea and changes its name to Battersea Dogs' Home, 1871
Rabies is added to the British Contagious Diseases (Animals) Act, 1871
Publication of Charles Darwin's *The Expression of the Emotions in Man and Animals*, 1872
British Kennel Club created, 1873: rise of the dog breed
National American Kennel Club founded, 1876
Debate on whether rabies was primarily an emotional disease
Teeth blunting proposed to prevent rabies

Rabies deaths peak in Britain, 1877
New York pound personnel start exterminating dogs by drowning, 1877

1880s

Growing condemnation of vagabondage and fears of human and national degeneration
Central Society for the Improvement of Dog Breeds in France (Société centrale pour l'amélioration des races de chiens en France) founded, 1882
Battersea Dogs' Home installs its first lethal chamber, 1884
Louis Pasteur announces human rabies vaccine at the National Academy of Medicine in Paris on October 27, 1885
Newark, New Jersey, boys travel to Paris for the Pasteur treatment of their rabies, early 1886
The Motts open the American Pasteur Institute of New-York City, January 1886 (it closes in 1887)
Opening of the Pasteur Institute in Paris, 1888
Lethal chamber installed in New York pound, 1888
Metropolitan Police call in two bloodhounds to hunt Jack the Ripper, London, 1888

1890s

Paul Gibier opens the New York Pasteur Institute, February 1890
Continued debates over the causes of rabies (virus or emotions?)
ASPCA takes responsibility for managing New York's strays and enforcing muzzling regulations, 1894
Anna Wessels Williams, bacteriologist at the New York Department of Health's Research Laboratory, mass-produces rabies vaccine, 1898

1900s

James Gordon-Bennett, publisher of the *New York Herald*, creates a dog refuge at Gennevilliers, France, 1901
Assistance aux animaux donates a "cynoctone," lethal chamber, to the Paris pound, 1902
Last case of indigenous canine rabies reported in Britain, November 1902
Flora D'Auby Jenkins Kibbe sets up the Bide-A-Wee Home, New York, 1903
New York Herald donates a Richardson lethal chamber to the Paris pound, 1904
First police dogs used in France at Pont-à-Mousson (Meurthe-et-Moselle), 1905

Dogs deployed to "purge" the Bois de Boulogne, Paris, 1907
Long Island Railroad company deploys bloodhounds, New York, 1907
New York police force starts training police dogs imported from Belgium, 1907
Police, Game-Keeper, and Customs Dog Club founded in France, 1908
New York Board of Health ordinance, 1908: requires the leashing and muzzling of dogs from June to October
Paris creates an official police dog service, 1908
Dogs from Parkville police station patrol Flatbush, Brooklyn, 1908

1910s

Union of Guard and Police Dog Enthusiasts in France founded, 1910
Edwin H. Richardson starts training police dogs for use in British cities, 1910
Our Dumb Friends League founds North London Dogs' Home, 1912
Section 227 of the New York Sanitary Code (Amendment 74) states that dogs must "be controlled so as not to commit nuisances," 1918
Marylebone Borough Council puts up antifouling posters, 1918

1920s

Increasing concerns about dog mess
Kensington Borough Council introduces an experimental antifouling bylaw, 1922
Police dogs deployed on Staten Island, New York, 1929–30

1930s

Outdoor Cleanliness Association leads a campaign to tackle dog mess and the first "Curb Your Dog" signs appear, New York, 1936–37
Police prefect refuses to introduce antifouling measures, Paris, 1937
Unsuccessful bid to introduce police dogs, London, 1939

NOTES

Abbreviations

APP	Archives de la Préfecture de police, Paris
ASPCA	American Society for the Prevention of Cruelty to Animals, New York
BDE	*Brooklyn (New York) Daily Eagle*
BSPA	*Bulletin de la société protectrice des animaux*
LMA	London Metropolitan Archives
NA	National Archives, London
NYCMA	New York City Municipal Archives
NYT	*New York Times*
OAF	*Our Animal Friends*
OCA	Outdoor Cleanliness Association, New York

Introduction

Unless otherwise indicated, translations from French are my own.

1 George G. Vest, "Eulogy of the Dog," the Humane Society of New York, Eleventh Annual Report from January 1, 1914, to January 1, 1915; 16FA142, box 12, Rockefeller University Records, Special Events and Activities, Anti-Vivisection Activities, Rockefeller Archive Center; "Classic Senate Speeches: George Vest, Eulogy of the Dog," United States Senate, https://www.senate.gov/artandhistory/history/common/generic/Speeches_Vest_Dog.htm, accessed October 14, 2020.

2 Frances Power Cobbe, "The Consciousness of Dogs," *Quarterly Review* 133 (1872): 434; Baron de Vaux, "Notre ami le chien" [Our friend the dog], *L'ami des chiens*, n.d., clipping in Cimetière animalier d'Asnières: Dossier documentaire, Bibliothèque Marguerite Durand, Paris. Baron de Vaux was presumably Charles-

Maurice de Vaux, the author of *Notre ami le chien: Races françaises et étrangères . . .* [Our friend the dog: French and foreign breeds . . .] (Paris: J. Rothschild, 1897).

3 For more on the different approaches to human-dog bonds, please see the appendix.

4 "Dogopolis" represents a nod to Jennifer Wolch's concept of "Zoöpolis." I heed her call to consider "how and why city residents react to the presence of animals in their midst, why attitudes may shift with new forms of urbanization, and what this means for animals." Jennifer Wolch, "Zoöpolis," in *Historical Animal Geographies*, ed. Sharon Wilcox and Stephanie Rutherford (Abington: Routledge, 2018), 54. Lisa Warden has used the term *dogopolis* to refer to street dogs in India who have been "granted de facto denizenship." This may well hold true for contemporary India but was not the case in the cities and period under discussion in this book—when dogs' place in the city was much more provisional than that of dogs in urban India. Moreover, the language of rights was not deployed. Lisa Warden, "Street Dogs, Rights, and the Pursuit of Justice in India's Dogopolis," in *Dog's Best Friend?: Rethinking Canid-Human Relations*, ed. John Sorenson and Atsuko Matsuoka (Montreal: McGill-Queen's University Press, 2019), 176.

5 Jessica Wang, *Mad Dogs and Other New Yorkers: Rabies, Medicine, and Society in an American Metropolis, 1840–1920* (Baltimore: Johns Hopkins University Press, 2019), 22.

6 Peter Atkins, ed., *Animal Cities: Beastly Urban Histories* (Farnham: Ashgate, 2012); Dawn Biehler, *Pests in the City: Flies, Bedbugs, Cockroaches, and Rats* (Seattle: University of Washington Press, 2013); Olivier Faure, "Le bétail dans la ville au XIXe siècle: Exclusion ou enfermement?," *Cahiers d'histoire* 42, nos. 3–4 (1997): 555–73; Ann Norton Greene, *Horses at Work: Harnessing Power in Industrial America* (Cambridge, MA: Harvard University Press, 2008); Andrew A. Robichaud, *Animal City: The Domestication of America* (Cambridge, MA: Harvard University Press, 2019); Michael G. Vann and Liz Clarke, *The Great Hanoi Rat Hunt: Empire, Disease, and Modernity in French Colonial Vietnam* (New York: Oxford University Press, 2019). On animal protectionists' attempts to foster compassion for animals and their use of emotion as a trigger for action, see Eric Baratay, "S'émouvoir des animaux," in *Histoire des émotions*, ed. Jean-Jacques Courtine, gen. eds. Alain Corbin, Jean-Jacques Courtine, and Georges Vigarello, vol. 3, *De la fin du XIXe siècle à nous jours* (Paris: Seuil, 2017), 178–98.

7 For excellent introductions to exclusion in urban areas, see Carl H. Nightingale, *Segregation: A Global History of Divided Cities* (Chicago: University of Chicago Press, 2012); Dorceta E. Taylor, *The Environment and the People in American Cities, 1600s–1900s: Disorder, Inequality, and Social Change* (Durham, NC: Duke University Press, 2009). On animals and exclusion, see Radhika Govindrajan, *Animal Intimacies: Interspecies Relatedness in India's Central Himalayas* (Chicago: University of Chicago Press, 2018), 4, 10; Eva Hafia Giraud, *What Comes after Entanglement?: Activism, Anthropocentrism, and an Ethics of Exclusion* (Durham, NC: Duke University Press, 2019). Giraud insightfully argues that "it is important to more fully flesh out an ethics of exclusion, which pays attention to the entities, practices, and ways of being that are foreclosed when other entangled realities are materialized" (Giraud, 2). In this vein, *Dogopolis* shows how strays were pushed away while pet dogs were brought closer.

8 Frances Power Cobbe, "Zoophily," *Cornhill Magazine*, no. 45, January–June 1882, 279.

9 G. Paramaswaran Pillai, *London and Paris through Indian Spectacles* (Madras: Vaijavanti Press, 1897), 82.

10 Raymond Coppinger and Lorna Coppinger, *What Is a Dog?* (Chicago: University of Chicago Press, 2016), 20–21; Krithika Srinivasan, Tim Kurz, Pradeep Kuttava, and Chris Pearson, "Reorienting Rabies Research and Practice: Lessons from India," *Palgrave Communications* 5, no. 152 (2019): 4, https:/doi.org/10.1057/s41599-019-0358-y; Sarah Cheang, "Women, Pets, and Imperialism: The British Pekingese Dog and Nostalgia for Old China," *Journal of British Studies* 45, no. 2 (2006): 359–87. See also Sorenson and Matsuoka, *Dog's Best Friend?*; Dipesh Chakrabarty, *Provincializing Europe: Postcolonial Thought and Historical Difference* (Princeton, NJ: Princeton University Press, 2000). The Western model of human-canine relations was exported to other countries through direct and indirect colonialism and has been accepted to varying degrees. Alma Igra, "Mandate of Compassion: Prevention of Cruelty to Animals in Palestine, 1919–1939," *Journal of Imperial and Commonwealth History* 47, no. 4 (2019): 773–99; Shuk-Wah Poon, "Dogs and British Colonialism: The Contested Ban on Eating Dogs in Colonial Hong Kong," *Journal of Imperial and Commonwealth History* 42, no. 2 (2014): 308–28; Aaron Herald Skabelund, *Empire of Dogs: Canines, Japan, and the Making of the Modern Imperial World* (Ithaca, NY: Cornell University Press, 2011).

11 Philip Howell, *At Home and Astray: The Domestic Dog in Victorian Britain* (Charlottesville: University of Virginia Press, 2015), 2. On dog breeds, see Michael Worboys, Julie-Marie Strange, and Neil Pemberton, *The Invention of the Modern Dog: Breed and Blood in Victorian Britain* (Baltimore: Johns Hopkins University Press, 2018); Edmund Russell, *Greyhound Nation: A Coevolutionary History of England, 1200–1900* (Cambridge: Cambridge University Press, 2018). On middle-class formation and identities across London, New York, and Paris, see Sharon Marcus, *Apartment Stories: City and Home in Nineteenth Century Paris and London* (Berkeley: University of California Press, 1999); Rachel Rich, *Bourgeois Consumption: Food, Space and Identity in London and Paris, 1850–1914* (Manchester: Manchester University Press, 2011); Linda Young, *Middle-Class Culture in the Nineteenth Century: America, Australia and Britain* (Basingstoke: Palgrave Macmillan, 2003). Historians have mainly explored the relationship between the middle classes and dogs in terms of pet keeping and animal protection. Howell, *At Home and Astray*; Katherine C. Grier, *Pets in America: A History* (Chapel Hill: University of North Carolina Press, 2006); Kathleen Kete, *Beast in the Boudoir: Petkeeping in Nineteenth-Century Paris* (Berkeley: University of California Press, 1994); Scott Anthony Miltenberger, "Promiscuously Mixed Together: New Yorkers and Domestic Animals in the Nineteenth-Century" (PhD diss., University of California, Davis, 2006), ProQuest Dissertations Publishing, 3250836. *Dogopolis* broadens the scope by including police dogs, antifouling campaigns, and a more sustained focus on stray dogs and their slaughter, as well as considering the transnational and emotional elements of human-canine histories.

12 Nicolas Kenny, *The Feel of the City: Experiences of Urban Transformation* (Toronto: University of Toronto Press, 2014); Matteo Millan, "The Shadows of

Social Fear: Emotions, Mentalities and Practices of the Propertied Classes in Italy, Spain and France (1900–1914)," *Journal of Social History* 50, no. 2 (2016): 336–61; Adam Mack, *Sensing Chicago: Noisemakers, Strikebreakers, and Muckrakers* (Urbana: University of Illinois Press, 2015); Joseph Ben Prestel, *Emotional Cities: Debates on Urban Change in Berlin and Cairo* (Oxford: Oxford University Press, 2017); Hannah Rose Woods, "Anxiety and Urban Life in late Victorian and Edwardian Culture" (PhD diss., University of Cambridge, 2018), https://doi.org/10.17863/CAM.22085.

13 William M. Reddy, *The Navigation of Feeling: A Framework for the History of Emotions* (New York: Cambridge University Press, 2001); Barbara H. Rosenwein, *Emotional Communities in the Early Middle Ages* (Ithaca, NY: Cornell University Press, 2006); Peter N. Stearns and Carol Z. Stearns, "Emotionology: Clarifying the History of Emotions and Emotional Standards," *American Historical Review* 90, no. 4 (1985): 813–36; Peter N. Stearns, *American Cool: Constructing a Twentieth-Century Emotional Style* (New York: New York University Press, 1994).

14 Christopher E. Forth and Elinor Accampo, eds., *Confronting Modernity in Fin-de-Siècle France: Bodies, Minds, Gender* (Basingstoke: Palgrave Macmillan, 2010); Karen Halttunen, "Humanitarianism, and the Pornography of Pain in Anglo-American Culture," *American Historical Review* 100, no. 2 (1995): 303–34; Suellen Hoy, *Chasing Dirt: The American Pursuit of Cleanliness* (New York: Oxford University Press, 1995); David Huyssen, *Progressive Inequality: Rich and Poor in New York, 1890–1920* (Cambridge, MA: Harvard University Press, 2014); Melanie A. Kiechle, *Smell Detectives: An Olfactory History of Nineteenth-Century America* (Seattle: University of Washington Press, 2017); Stearns, *American Cool*, 42.

15 Eric Baratay, "Chacun jette son chien: De la fin d'une vie au XIXe siècle," *Romantisme* 153 (2011): 147; John K. Walton, "Mad Dogs and Englishmen: The Conflict over Rabies in Late Victorian England," *Journal of Social History* 13, no. 2 (1979): 221; John L. Rice, *Health for 7,500,000 People* (New York: Department of Health, 1939), 146. On the difficultly of obtaining accurate figures for the number of dogs, see Wang, *Mad Dogs and Other New Yorkers*, 24.

16 I do not claim unmediated access to middle-class emotions. As historians of emotions have highlighted, emotions are not the same as raw feelings. Instead, they are always social and occur between individuals within wider emotional conventions. Rosenwein, *Emotional Communities*, 27, 196; Reddy, *The Navigation of Feeling*, 128. On emotions "bind[ing] subjects together," see Sara Ahmed, "Affective Economies," *Social Text* 22 (2004): 119. On human-canine coshaping, see Donna Haraway, *When Species Meet* (Minneapolis: University of Minnesota Press, 2008).

17 Ahmed, "Affective Economies," 119. My approach is also informed by Monique Scheer's concept of emotional practices. Scheer defines these as "habits, rituals, and everyday pastimes that aid us in achieving a certain emotional state. This includes the striving for a desired feeling as well as the modifying of one that is not desirable." As Scheer clarifies, these practices—"the bodily act[s] of experience and expression"—are a form of emotional management, simultaneously embodied and cognitive. In other words, they are the things that individuals say and do to achieve certain emotional states. They are enacted in relationship with other "people, artifacts, aesthetic arrangements, and technologies." Animals should be added to Scheer's list, as dogs have become integrated into middle-

class emotional practices and emotional management. Monique Scheer, "Are Emotions a Kind of Practice (And Is That What Makes Them Have a History)? A Bourdieuian Approach to Understanding Emotion," *History and Theory* 51, no. 2 (2012): 209.

18 I adopt a comparative and transnational approach. As Nicolas Kenny and Rebecca Madgin argue, "To the extent that cities are the products as much of local imaginaries as of transnational flows, the portrait of their development, transformation and socio-cultural significance appears more fully when we question not just their similarities and differences, but also the impact of movement through and among different places." Nicolas Kenny and Rebecca Madgin, "'Every Time I Describe a City': Urban History as Comparative and Transnational Practice," in *Cities Beyond Borders: Comparative and Transnational Approaches to Urban History*, ed. Nicolas Kenny and Rebecca Madgin (Abington: Routledge, 2016), 6. Nicholas Daly, *The Demographic Imagination and the Nineteenth-Century City: Paris, London, New York* (Cambridge: Cambridge University Press, 2015), 7–12; Nicolas Kenny and Rebecca Madgin, eds, *Cities beyond Borders: Comparative and Transnational Approaches to Urban History* (Abington: Routledge, 2016); Daniel T. Rodgers, *Atlantic Crossings: Social Politics in a Progressive Age* (Cambridge, MA: Harvard University Press, 2000); Pierre-Yves Saunier and Shane Ewen, eds., *Another Global City: Historical Explorations into the Transnational Municipal Moment, 1850–2000* (New York: Palgrave Macmillan, 2008); Derek B. Scott, *Sounds of the Metropolis: The 19th Century Popular Music Revolution in London, New York, Paris and Vienna* (New York: Oxford University Press, 2008). Most animal histories focus on one country or city. For ones that adopt a transnational approach, oftentimes with a colonial lens, see Cornelia Knab, "Infectious Rats and Dangerous Cows: Transnational Perspectives on Animal Diseases in the First Half of the Twentieth Century," *Contemporary European History* 20, no. 3 (2011): 281–306; Projit Bihari Mukharji, "Cat and Mouse: Animal Technologies, Trans-imperial Networks and Public Health from Below," *Social History of Medicine* 31, no. 3 (2018): 510–32; James F. Stark, "Anthrax and Australia in a Global Context: The International Exchange of Theories and Practices with Britain and France, c. 1850–1920," *Health and History* 14, no. 2 (2012): 1–25.

19 Liautard became editor of the *American Veterinary Review*. Susan D. Jones, *Valuing Animals: Veterinarians and Their Patients in Modern America* (Baltimore: Johns Hopkins University Press, 2003), 28. On the broader French influence on American medicine, see John Harley Warner, *Against the Spirit of System: The French Impulse in Nineteenth-Century American Medicine* (Baltimore: Johns Hopkins University Press, 1998). De Vaux's *Notre ami le chien* was heavily based on the work of British dog expert Gordon Staples.

20 Frank Pearce, "Women and Foreign Dogs," *Daily Mail* (London), January 21, 1921; Baron de Lage de Chaillou, *Du chien de chasse (chiens d'arrêt)* (Paris: Auguste Goin, 1867). On British canine xenophobia, see also Philip Howell, "The Dog Fancy at War: Breeds, Breeding, and Britishness, 1914–1918," *Society and Animals* 21, no. 6 (2013): 546–67. France declared that rabies in nonflying mammals was officially eradicated in 2001. Canine rabies cases are still reported in the United States, but numbers are low in historic terms. "Is Rabies in Your State?," Centers for Disease Control and Prevention website, July 5, 2017, www.cdc.gov

/rabies/location/usa/surveillance/index.html. On obstacles to transnational mobility, see Nancy L. Green, *The Limits of Transnationalism* (Chicago: University of Chicago Press, 2019).

21 Thomas Bender, *The Unfinished City: New York and the Metropolitan Idea* (New York: New York University Press, 2007 [2002]); Nicholas Daly, *The Demographic Imagination and the Nineteenth-Century City: Paris, London, New York* (Cambridge: Cambridge University Press, 2015), 7; Patrice Higonnet, *Paris: Capitale du monde* (Paris: Tallindier, 2005); Marc Matera, *Black London: The Imperial Metropolis and Decolonization in the Twentieth Century* (Oakland: University of California Press, 2015). For innovation in other cities, see Liora Bigon, *French Colonial Dakar: The Morphogenesis of an African Regional Capital* (Manchester: Manchester University Press, 2016); Stephen Legg, *Spaces of Colonialism: Delhi's Urban Governmentalities* (Oxford: Blackwell, 2007); Harald L. Platt, *Shock Cities: The Environmental Transformation and Reform of Manchester and Chicago* (Chicago: University of Chicago Press, 2005); Carl Emil Schorske, *Fin-de-Siècle Vienna: Politics and Culture* (New York: Vintage Books, 1981).

22 The literature on Western cities and modernity is extensive. For useful interventions, see Marshall Berman, *All That Is Solid Melts into Air: The Experience of Modernity* (New York: Simon and Schuster, 1982); Christophe Charle, *Discordance des temps: Une brève histoire de la modernité* (Paris: Armand Colin, 2011); Richard Dennis, *Cities in Modernity: Representations and Productions of Metropolitan Space, 1840–1930* (Cambridge: Cambridge University Press, 2008); David Harvey, *Paris: Capital of Modernity* (London: Routledge, 2003); Max Page, *The Creative Destruction of Manhattan* (Chicago: University of Chicago Press, 1999). On ambivalence, see Woods, "Anxiety and Urban Life."

23 As Etienne Benson argues, "Animals have a 'solidity' or presence in written documents, scientific or otherwise, that goes beyond mere 'representation.'" "Animal Writes: Historiography, Disciplinarity, and the Animal Trace," in *Making Animal Meaning*, ed. Linda Kaloff and Georgina M. Montgomery (East Lansing: Michigan State University Press, 2011), 5. Wang accurately notes that newspaper reports on rabies offered "chilling entertainment." *Mad Dogs and Other New Yorkers*, 28. On newspapers and urban modernity more generally, see Julia Guarneri, *Newsprint Metropolis: City Papers and the Making of Modern Americans* (Chicago: University of Chicago Press, 2017), 5–10.

24 Williams Haynes, *The Airedale* (New York: Outing, 1911), 81; James R. Kinney with Ann Honeycutt, *How to Raise a Dog: In the City . . . in the Suburbs* (New York: Simon and Schuster, 1938), 259–60, 263. See also Claude Sisley, "Dogs in London," *Saturday Review*, December 4, 1926, 677. For a call to remove dogs from cities, see Nicolas Fétu, *Requête à mes concitoyens pour l'extinction de la race canine à Dijon* (Dijon: Imprimerie de Jobard, 1866).

Chapter One

1 Andrew Wells, "Antisocial Animals in the British Atlantic World: Liminality and Nuisance in Glasgow and New York City, 1660–1760," in *Animal History in the Modern City: Exploring Liminality*, ed. Clemens Wischermann, Aline Stein-

brecher, and Philip Howell (London: Bloomsbury Academic, 2019), 55–74; Mark S. R. Jenner, "The Great Dog Massacre," in *Fear in Early Modern Society*, ed. Bill Naphy and Penny Roberts (Manchester: Manchester University Press, 1997), 44–60; "Dogs Rampant: To the Rescue," *New York Daily Times*, July 11, 1856. In this chapter, I will mostly use the term *stray dog* rather than *street dog*, because *stray* (*chien errant* in French) was most commonly used by contemporaries. But I recognize that it is a loaded term implying that the dogs have strayed from their rightful place: the home. In India, in contrast, *street dog* denotes a sense that dogs legitimately belong outside homes. Krithika Srinivasan, "The Biopolitics of Animal Being and Welfare: Dog Control and Care in the UK and India," *Transactions of the Institute of British Geographers* 38, no. 1 (2012): 110.

2 George Fleming, *Rabies and Hydrophobia: Their History, Nature, Causes, Symptoms, and Prevention* (London: Chapman and Hall, 1872), 354. Studies have shown how elite fears and anxieties about urban life have produced crackdowns against strays. Kirsten McKenzie, "Dogs and the Public Sphere: The Ordering of Social Space in the Early Nineteenth-Century Cape Town," in *Canis africanis: A Dog History of Southern Africa*, ed. Sandra Swart and Lance van Sittert (Leiden: Brill, 2008) 91–110; Jesse S. Palsetia, "Mad Dogs and Parsis: The Bombay Dog Riots of 1832," *Journal of the Royal Asiatic Society of Great Britain and Ireland* 11 (2001): 13–30.

3 The literature on public health and nineteenth-century cities is vast. On Paris alone, see Ann La Berge, *Mission and Method: The Early Nineteenth-Century French Public Health Movement* (Cambridge: University of Cambridge Press, 1992); Sabine Barles, *La ville délétère: Médecins et ingénieurs dans l'espace urbain XVIIIe–XIXe siècle* (Seyssel: Champ Vallon, 1999); David S. Barnes, *The Making of a Social Disease: Tuberculosis in Nineteenth-Century France* (Berkeley: University of California Press, 1995); Fabienne Chevallier, *Le Paris moderne: Histoire des politiques d'hygiène (1855–1898)* (Rennes: Presses universitaires de Rennes, 2010). On blaming and combating "nuisance" animals, see Dawn Biehler, *Pests in the City: Flies, Bedbugs, Cockroaches, and Rats* (Seattle: University of Washington Press, 2013); Christos Lynteris, ed., *Framing Animals as Epidemic Villains: Histories of Non-Human Disease Vectors* (Cham, Switzerland: Palgrave Macmillan/Springer Nature, 2019).

4 Henry Bergh, "The Twentieth Year of the Official Existence of This Society Terminates Today!," in ASPCA, *Twentieth Annual Report for 1885* (1886), 6.

5 Alexandre Roger, *Les chiens, les chats, la vaccine et la canaille, philippique* (Paris: Germain Mathiot 1813), 7–9, 15–16, 19, 24. Roger foreshadowed H.-A. Frégier's *Des classes dangereuses de la population dans les grandes villes* (Paris: J.-B. Baillière, 1840). On *canaille*, see Centre national de ressources textuelles et lexicales, Ortolang website, www.cnrtl.fr/lexicographie/canaille, accessed October 15, 2020. The term *canaille* made it across the Atlantic when native-born New Yorkers used it to describe European immigrants. Lisa Keller, *Triumph of Order: Democracy and Public Space in New York and London* (New York: Columbia University Press, 2008), 154.

6 M.R., "Hydrophobia," *Times* (London), October 5, 1825; S.M., "Dogs," *Times* (London), July 13, 1825.

7 C.L.B., "Walks among the New-York Poor," *New York Daily Times*, April 19,1854.

See also Catherine McNeur, *Taming Manhattan: Environmental Battles in the Antebellum City* (Cambridge, MA: Harvard University Press, 2014), 8–12; Lisa Merrill, "Amalgamation, Moral Geography, and 'Slum Tourism': Irish and African Americans Sharing Space on the Streets and Stages of Antebellum New York," *Slavery and Abolition* 37, no. 3 (2016): 638–60; Scott Anthony Miltenberger, "Promiscuously Mixed Together: New Yorkers and Domestic Animals in the Nineteenth-Century" (PhD diss., University of California, Davis, 2006), 80–84; ProQuest Dissertations Publishing, 3250836. Given that German ragpickers used dogs to pull their carts, these dogs may have been working dogs. Andrew A. Robichaud, *Animal City: The Domestication of America* (Cambridge, MA: Harvard University Press, 2019), 167–68.

8 Susan McHugh, *Dog* (London: Reaktion, 2004), 133; Estelle Murail, "A Body Passes By: The Flâneur and the Senses in Nineteenth-Century London and Paris," *Senses and Society* 12, no. 2 (2017): 162–76; David Scobey, "Anatomy of the Promenade: The Politics of Bourgeois Sociability in Nineteenth-Century New York," *Social History* 17, no. 2 (1992): 203–27; Victoria E. Thompson, "Telling 'Spatial Stories': Urban Space and Bourgeois Identity in Early Nineteenth-Century Paris," *Journal of Modern History* 75, no. 3 (2003): 523–56.

9 McNeur, *Taming Manhattan*, 13.

10 Préfet de police, "Instruction concernant les chiens, instruction des boules dogues," August 19, 1840, DB 229, APP; Préfecture de police, "Ordonnance concernant les chiens et les chiens boule-dogues," May 27, 1845, DB 229, APP; Préfecture de police, "Rapport," May 17, 1845, DA 44, APP.

11 Quoted in Neil Pemberton and Michael Worboys, *Rabies in Britain: Dogs, Disease and Culture, 1830–2000* (Basingstoke: Palgrave Macmillan, 2013 [2007]), 9.

12 A Lady, "To the Editor of *The Times*," *Times* (London), June 3, 1830; "Police," *Times* (London), June 10, 1830; British Parliamentary Papers 1830 [519], "A Bill to Prevent the Spreading of Canine Madness," June 10, 1830; Pemberton and Worboys, *Rabies in Britain*, 34; Awake, "To the Editor of *The Times*," *Times* (London), September 7, 1853.

13 Ingrid H. Tague, "Eighteenth-Century English Debates on a Dog Tax," *Historical Journal* 51, no. 4 (2008): 901–20; William Youatt, *On Canine Madness* (London: Longman, 1830), 31; Awake, "To the Editor"; McNeur, *Taming Manhattan*, 13.

14 Bibliothèque municipale, *Code-formulaire du possesseur de chiens et d'animaux domestiques nuisibles ou incommodes* (Grenoble: Prudhomme 1855), 1; "Dogs of Luxury," *London Review*, September 20, 1862; Kathleen Kete, *Beast in the Boudoir: Petkeeping in Nineteenth-Century Paris* (Berkeley: University of California Press, 1994), 42–46.

15 Paul A. Gilje, *The Road to Mobocracy: Popular Disorder in New York City, 1763–1834* (Chapel Hill: University of North Carolina Press, 1987), 226–27.

16 McNeur, *Taming Manhattan*, 17–18.

17 "Common Council Proceedings," *Morning Herald* (New York), September 7, 1838.

18 Damien Baldin, *Histoire des animaux domestiques, XIXe–XXe siècle* (Paris: Seuil, 2014), 232; Préfecture de police, "Arrêté relatif à la mise en fourrière des animaux saisis ou abandonnés sur la voie publique," March 25, 1831, DB 226, APP.

19 Préfet de police to Commissaires de la police, April 30, 1841, DB 226, APP; Préfet

de police to Commissaires de la police, June 25, 1841, DB 229, APP; Préfet de police, "Circulaire," June 10, 1842, DB 229, APP.

20 Préfet de police, "Circulaire"; Préfet de police, "Salaire pour la conduite des chiens à la fourrière," October 31, 1842 DB 229, APP; Préfecture de police, "Exécution de l'ordre de police concernant les chiens et les boule-dogues," July 4, 1853, DB 226, APP.

21 I. N. Phelps Stokes, *The Iconography of Manhattan Island 1848–1909* (New York: Arno Press, 1967 [1922]), 4:110, 5:1490; Benjamin Brady, "The Politics of the Pound: Controlling Loose Dogs in Nineteenth-Century New York City," *Jefferson Journal of Science and Culture* 2 (2012): 11.

22 "In the New York Dog Pound," *Forest and Stream*, September 19, 1878. See also Robert M. Dowling, *Slumming in New York: From the Waterfront to Mythic Harlem* (Urbana: University of Illinois Press, 2007); Seth Koven, *Slumming: Sexual and Social Politics in Victorian London* (Princeton, NJ: Princeton University Press, 2004). Philip Howell dubs journalistic visits to the Battersea Dogs' Home "beastly slumming." "Between Wild and Domestic, Animal and Human, Life and Death: The Problem of the Stray in the Victorian City," in Wischermann, Steinbrecher, and Howell, *Animal History*, 150.

23 "The Dog Pound," *Harper's Weekly*, April 21, 1894.

24 "The Dog Pound," *NYT*, June 19, 1874; "The New York Dog-Pound," *Daily National Intelligencer* (Washington, DC), August 15, 1854; Susan J. Pearson, *The Rights of the Defenseless: Protecting Animals and Children in Gilded Age America* (Chicago: University of Chicago Press, 2011), 70.

25 "City Dogs," *New York Daily Times*, June 26, 1857; "Concerning Dogs," *BDE*, June 27, 1859; G. H. C., "Mr. Editor," *BDE*, July 28, 1857; "Dogs Rampant," *New York Daily Times*.

26 "Reforms and the Pound," *New York Daily Times*, June 30, 1854; "The Slaughter of the Dogs," *New York Daily Times*, August 2, 1854; "The Dog Pound, and the Fate of Its Inhabitants," *New York Daily Times*, September 9, 1857.

27 Quoted in Brady, "The Politics of the Pound," 12.

28 W.S., "The Dog Stealing Grievance," *New York Herald*, July 10, 1859. See also Miltenberger, "Promiscuously Mixed Together," 106; Gilfoyle, "Street Rats."

29 "The Dog Pound," *New York Daily Times*, June 2, 1855.

30 "The Dog Law," *New York Herald*, May 31, 1860; Jessica Wang, "Dogs and the Making of the American State: Voluntary Association, State Power, and the Politics of Animal Control in New York City, 1850–1920," *Journal of American History* 98, no. 4 (2012): 1006–7; Brady, "The Politics of the Pound"; Marriott's account given in "Scenes in the New York Dog Pound," *Inter Ocean* (Chicago), October 31, 1874, 7.

31 Mayor's Office, "Karl Meyer of 111 Ridge Street against Dog Catchers Driving Wagon no. 2156," May 24, 1887, Hewitt box 1339, 034–035, roll 3, NYCMA.

32 City Court of Brooklyn, "Margaretha Fuller against the City of Brooklyn," n.d. [October 1899?], 2013.015 box 6, folder 20, Case Files, Fuller, Margaretha—Dog Catchers Injury 1889–90, Corporation Counsel Records, ser. 1, Department of Law, Brooklyn Historical Society.

33 "Dog Pound," in *ASPCA Fourth Annual Report* (1870), 19; Diane L. Beers, *For*

the Prevention of Cruelty: The History and Legacy of Animal Rights Activism in the United States (Athens, OH: Swallow Press of Ohio University Press, 2006), 43–44, 58; "Laws of 1867," in *ASPCA First Annual Report* (1867), 63; "Act for the More Effectual Prevention of Cruelty to Animals," https://www.animallaw.info/statute/new-york-revised-statutes-1867-chapter-375-sections-1-10, accessed October 19, 2020.

34 "The Dog Pound," *NYT*, June 14, 1874; "Local Miscellany," *NYT*, June 24, 1874; "Dog-Catching," *Once a Week*, September 22, 1891.

35 "What a Wonderful Period of the World's History," *Times* (London), October 18, 1860; "Home for Lost Dogs," *Harper's Weekly*, January 20, 1872; Charles Dickens, "Two Dog-Shows," *All the Year Round*, August 2, 1862, 497. See also Philip Howell, *At Home and Astray: The Domestic Dog in Victorian Britain* (Charlottesville: University of Virginia Press, 2015), 25–49, 74–75.

36 *An Appeal for the Home for Lost and Starving Dogs by a Member of the Society* (London: W. H. Dalton, 1861), 10; "Lost and Starving Dogs," *London Reader*, December 16, 1876. See also Garry Jenkins, *A Home of Their Own: The Heart-Warming 150-Year History of Battersea Dogs and Cats Home* (London: Bantam Press, 2010), 20–81.

37 Quoted in William Kidd, "The Home for Lost Dogs," *Leisure Hour*, September 5, 1876, 566.

38 Harold King, "A Home for Homeless Dogs," *Once a Week*, November 4, 1865, 546.

39 "A Home for Lost Dogs in London," *Albion: A Journal of News, Politics and Literature*, April 25, 1874; "Home for Lost Dogs," *Harper's Weekly*; Hilda Kean, *Animal Rights: Political and Social Change in Britain since 1900* (London: Reaktion, 2000), 88–89; Julie-Marie Strange, "Tramp: Sentiment and the Homeless Man in the Late-Victorian and Edwardian City," *Journal of Victorian Culture* 16, no. 2 (2011): 249.

40 Kidd, "The Home for Lost Dogs," 565; "Lost and Starving Dogs," *London Reader*.

41 Howell, *At Home and Astray*, 91; J. Keri Cronin, *Art for Animals: Visual Culture and Animal Advocacy 1870–1914* (University Park: Pennsylvania State University Press, 2018), 185–87.

42 King, "A Home for Homeless Dogs," 545. Robert Southey and Samuel Taylor Coleridge envisaged the pantisocracy as an equal, democratic, anticolonial, and propertyless community that they hoped to establish by the Susquehanna River in Pennsylvania. Tim Fulford, *Romantic Indians: Native Americans, British Literature and Transatlantic Culture 1756–1830* (Oxford: Oxford University Press, 2006), 120–23.

43 Charles Dickens, "Pincher Astray," *All the Year Round*, January 30, 1864, 540; Kidd, "The Home for Lost Dogs," 566. On the tension between care and killing, see Eva Giraud and Gregory Hollin, "Care, Laboratory Beagles and Affective Utopia," *Theory, Culture and Society* 33, no. 4 (2016): 27–49.

44 O. S., "La fourrière de Paris," *Revue britannique* 5 (1873): 352; "The New York Dog-Pound," *Daily National Intelligencer*.

45 *An Act for Regulating the Traffic in the Metropolis, and for Making Provision for the Greater Security of Persons Passing through the Streets; and for Other Purposes* (House of Commons, March 27, 1867), 11; "Police Sale of Stray Dogs at Chelsea,"

Illustrated London News, November 14, 1868; *Report of the Commissioner of Police of the Metropolis* (London: HMSO, 1871), 38; Howell, *At Home and Astray*, 85–87.

46 Amable-Félix Couturier de Vienne, "La fourrière," *Bulletin de la Société protectrice des animaux* 9 (1863): 447.

47 Jules Maret-Leriche, *À bas la muselière: Pétition de messieurs les chiens et leurs maîtres, adressée à M. le Préfet de police* (Paris: Librairie théâtrale, 1861), 4. See also Catherine Pinguet, *Les chiens d'Istanbul: Des rapports entre l'homme et l'animal de l'antiquité à nos jours* (Saint-Pourçain-sur-Sioule: Bleu Autour, 2008); Ian Coller, "East of Enlightenment: Regulating Cosmopolitanism between Istanbul and Paris in the Eighteenth Century," *Journal of World History* 21, no. 3 (2010): 447–70.

48 Henry Blatin, *De la rage chez le chien et des mesures préservatrices* (Paris: E. Dentu, 1863), 27–29.

49 "The Dogs of London," *London Illustrated News*, January 2, 1886; J. Sully, "The Decay of Canine Fidelity," *Longman's Magazine*, December 1890, 148–49; Fleming, *Rabies and Hydrophobia*, 353; Vladimir Janković, *Confronting the Climate: British Airs and the Making of Environmental Medicine* (Basingstoke: Palgrave Macmillan, 2010), 2, 6–7; Jessica Wang, *Mad Dogs and Other New Yorkers: Rabies, Medicine, and Society in an American Metropolis, 1840–1920* (Baltimore: Johns Hopkins University Press, 2019), 46–47.

50 "London Dogs," *Leisure Hour*, August 23, 1860; Strange, "Tramp," 246–51. See also "Concerning Pedigrees," *Harper's Weekly*, June 29, 1895; Idstone, "Mongrels," *Gentleman's Magazine*, December 1870, 31–37. Idstone was the nom de plume of dog breeder Thomas Pearce.

51 Charles Henry Lane, *All about Dogs: A Book for Doggy People* (London: John Lane, 1900), vi. See also J. Maxtee, *Popular Dog-Keeping* (London: L. Upcott Gill, 1898), 85.

52 "Dog Days at the Garden," *NYT*, February 22, 1893; Margaret E. Derry, *Bred for Perfection: Shorthorn Cattle, Collies, and Arabian Horses since 1800* (Baltimore: Johns Hopkins University Press, 2003); Neil Pemberton, "The Bloodhound's Nose Knows? Dogs and Detection in Anglo-American Culture," *Endeavour* 37, no. 4 (2013): 196–208; Worboys, Strange, and Pemberton, *The Invention of the Modern Dog*; Miltenberger, "Promiscuously Mixed Together," 244, 250; "Dog Days at the Garden," *NYT*, February 22, 1893.

53 A.-C.-E. Bellier de Villiers, *Le chien au chenil* (Paris: Pairault, 1901); Martin Wallen, "Foxhounds, Curs, and the Dawn of Breeding: The Discourse of Modern Human-Canine Relations," *Cultural Critique* 79 (2011): 141; Katherine C. Grier, *Pets in America: A History* (Chapel Hill: University of North Carolina Press, 2006), 237–39.

54 Jonathan Hutchinson, "On Cruelty to Animals," *Fortnightly Review* 26 (1876): 310.

55 Clarence E. Harbison, *Our Dogs: What We Should Know about Them* (New York: Orange Judd, 1932), 2. See also Wallen, "Foxhounds, Curs, and the Dawn of Breeding"; Sujit Sivasundaram, "Imperial Transgressions: The Animal and Human in the Idea of Race," *Comparative Studies of South Asia, Africa and the Middle East* 35, no. 1 (2015): 156–72; James Warbasse, *The Conquest of Disease through Animal Experimentation* (New York: Appleton, 1910), 46–47.

56 Cynthia Huff, "Victorian Exhibitionism and Eugenics: The Case of Francis Galton and the 1899 Crystal Palace Dog Show," *Victorian Review* 28, no. 2 (2002): 15; Wang, *Mad Dogs and Other New Yorkers*, 45–46. Associations of race and breed continue into the present. See Meisha Rosenberg, "Golden Retrievers Are White, Pit Bulls Are Black, and Chihuahuas Are Hispanic: Representations of Breeds of Dog and Issues of Race in Popular Culture," in *Making Animal Meaning*, ed. Linda Kalof and Georgina M. Montgomery (East Lansing: Michigan State University Press, 2011), 113–25. Dog breeders were not alone in mixing animal breeding ideologies and practices with racial "science." See Brian Tyrrell, "Bred for the Race: Thoroughbred Breeding and Racial Science in the United States, 1900–1940," *Historical Studies in the Natural Sciences* 45, no. 4 (2015): 549–76.

57 George J. Romanes, *Animal Intelligence* (London: Kegan Paul, Trench, 1882), 439.

58 Michael Worboys, Julie-Marie Strange, and Neil Pemberton, *The Invention of the Modern Dog: Breed and Blood in Victorian Britain* (Baltimore: Johns Hopkins University Press, 2018), 50–52; Wallen, "Foxhounds, Curs, and the Dawn of Breeding," 147.

59 "The 'Dangerous Classes' of New York and Efforts to Improve Them: VI," *Appleton's Journal of Literature, Science and Art*, June 4, 1870, 631; Daniel Pick, *Faces of Degeneration: A European Disorder c. 1848–1918* (Cambridge: Cambridge University Press, 1989), 52–54; E. Ray Lankester, *Degeneration: A Chapter in Darwinism* (London: MacMillan, 1880); Bill Luckin, "Revisiting the Idea of Degeneration in Urban Britain, 1830–1900," *Urban History* 33, no. 2 (2006): 234–52; Emma J. Teng, "'A Problem for Which There Is No Solution': Eurasians and the Specter of Degeneration in New York's Chinatown," *Journal of Asian American Studies* 15, no. 3 (2012): 271–98.

60 Quoted in Diane B. Paul, "Darwin, Social Darwinism and Eugenics," in *The Cambridge Companion to Darwin*, ed. Jonathan Hodge and Gregory Radick (Cambridge: Cambridge University Press, 2009), 224. See also John Marriott, *The Other Empire: Metropolis, India and Progress in the Colonial Imagination* (Manchester: Manchester University Press, 2009), 166–68.

61 Lennie Orme, "Humanity to the Dogs," *Good Words*, December 1861, 486; "Vagrant Canines," *Inter Ocean* (Chicago), June 17, 1874.

62 "The New York Dog-Pound," *Daily National Intelligencer* (Washington City [DC]).

63 "In the New York Dog-Pound," *Forest and Stream*, September 19, 1878, 134.

64 A.-G. Beaumarié, *Le chien: Étude* (Paris: E. Dentu, 1874), 14–15; "Burmah," *Times* (London), November 24, 1890; "The Disaster in Manipur," *Times* (London), April 13, 1891; "Peculiarities of Peru," *NYT*, July 19, 1868; Vanja Hamzić, "The (Un)Conscious Pariah: Canine and Gender Outcasts of the British Raj," *Australian Feminist Law Journal* 40, no. 2 (2015): 185–98.

65 Our Special Correspondent, "The Dogs of Constantinople," *Times* (London), January 7, 1876.

66 Albert Bigelow Paine, "Some Phases of the Turk," *Harper's Weekly*, December 25, 1909.

67 *Hansard Parliamentary Debates*, 3rd ser., vol. 239 (1878), col. 1328; Paine, "Some Phases of the Turk"; Lucius A. Childress, "The Wrong of Dog License," *Forest and Stream*, October 14, 1899.

68 Marriott, *The Other Empire*, 160–66. On the importance of challenging Eurocentric visions of urban life and appreciating non-Western forms of urbanism innovation, see Jyoti Hosagrahar, *Indigenous Modernities: Negotiating Architecture and Urbanism* (Abingdon: Routledge, 2005); Joseph Ben Prestel, *Emotional Cities: Debates on Urban Change in Berlin and Cairo* (Oxford: Oxford University Press, 2017); Jennifer Robinson, *Ordinary Cities: Between Modernity and Development* (London: Routledge, 2006).

69 Christophe Traïni, *The Animal Rights Struggle: An Essay in Historical Sociology*, trans. Richard Jemmett (Amsterdam: Amsterdam University Press, 2016), 104; Ingrid H. Tague, *Animal Companions: Pets and Social Change in Eighteenth-Century Britain* (University Park: Pennsylvania State University Press, 2015), 184–228. On the varied emotional dimensions of pet keeping, see Erica Fudge, *Pets* (London: Routledge, 2014 [2008]).

70 Kete, *Beast in the Boudoir*; Sharon Marcus, *Apartment Stories: City and Home in Nineteenth Century Paris and London* (Berkeley: University of California Press, 1999); Millette Shamir, *Inexpressible Privacy: The Interior Life of Antebellum American Literature* (Philadelphia: University of Pennsylvania Press, 2008).

71 Stonehenge [J. H. Walsh], *The Dogs of the British Islands*, 4th ed. (London: Horace Cox, 1882), 187; See also Diana Donald, *Women against Cruelty: Protection of Animals in Nineteenth-Century Britain* (Manchester: Manchester University Press, 2020), 225–26.

72 Howell, *At Home and Astray*, 22–23; Grier, *Pets in America*; Kete, *Beast in the Boudoir*; H. Laligant, *De la rage chez le chien et de sa police sanitaire* (Dijon: Eugène Jobard, 1874), 30. See also Fleming, *Rabies and Hydrophobia*, 352; Jean Robert, *Le chien d'appartement et d'utilité* (Paris: Librairie Pairault, 1888), 29; Peter N. Stearns, *American Cool: Constructing a Twentieth-Century Emotional Style* (New York: New York University Press, 1994), 20–21.

73 Bellier de Villiers, *Le chien au chenil*, 42 (*flânerie* quotation); Yi-Fu Tuan, *Dominance and Affection: The Making of Pets* (New Haven, CT: Yale University Press, 1984), 102–13; Shamir, *Inexpressible Privacy*, 5.

74 "Un lecteur assidu," *Le petit journal* (Paris), March, 24 1870; Pick, *Faces of Degeneration*, 51–52; Susan D. Jones, *Valuing Animals: Veterinarians and Their Patients in Modern America* (Baltimore: Johns Hopkins University Press, 2003), 116; Alison Skipper, "The 'Dog Doctors' of Edwardian London: Elite Canine Veterinary Care in the Early Twentieth Century," *Social History of Medicine* (2019): 1–26, https://doi.org/10.1093/shm/hkz049; Sarah Amato, *Beastly Possessions: Animals in Victorian Consumer Culture* (Toronto: University of Toronto Press, 2015), 21–55; Eric Baratay, "Chacun jette son chien: De la fin d'une vie au XIXe siècle," *Romantisme* 153 (2011); Howell, *At Home and Astray*, 125–49; Hilda Kean, "Human and Animal Space in Historic "Pet" Cemeteries in London, New York, and Paris," in *Animal Death*, ed. Jay Johnston and Fiona Probyn-Rapsey (Sydney: Sydney University Press, 2013), 21–42; Kete, *Beast in the Boudoir*, 33–35.

75 *Q-W Dog Remedies and Supplies* (Bound Brook, NJ: Q-W Laboratories, 1922), 3, box 4, Trade Catalogs of Veterinary and Pet Supplies, American Kennel Club Library, New York.

76 Maurice Douville, *Traité pratique d'hygiène, d'élevage et des maladies du chien* (Paris: Librairie Garnier frères, 1922), 74–75; Anne McClintock, *Imperial Leather:*

Race, Gender and Sexuality in the Colonial Contest (New York: Routledge, 1995), 170, 211; Tom Quick, "Puppy Love: Domestic Science, 'Women's Work,' and Canine Care," *Journal of British Studies* 58, no. 2 (2019): 289–314.

77 Kinney with Honeycutt, *How to Raise a Dog*, 120–21, 128. See also Suellen Hoy, *Chasing Dirt: The American Pursuit of Cleanliness* (New York: Oxford University Press, 1995).

78 Howell, *At Home and Astray*, 158–60; Louis Lépine, "Loi du 21 juillet 1881 et Décret du 22 juin 1882: Mesures contre la rage," 1 July 1897, DB 229, APP; "Mesures contre la rage," *Revue municipale*, 1902, 3493–94, DB 229, APP.

79 John P. Haines, "Notice to the Owner of Dogs," *OAF*, June 1904.

80 Howell, *At Home and Astray*, 151–73.

81 Worboys, Strange, and Pemberton, *The Invention of the Modern Dog*, 184–96; Thomas Dolan, *The Nature and Treatment of Rabies or Hydrophobia Being the Report of the Special Commission Appointed by the Medical Press and Circular* (London: Baillière, Tindall and Cox, 1878), 201–2.

82 "Pet Dogs of Society Women," *NYT*, June 12, 1904; Miguel Zamacoïs, *Articles de Paris* (Paris: H. Simonis Empis, 1900), 64; "Dog Days at the Garden," *NYT*, February 22, 1893; Robert, *Le chien d'appartement et d'utilité*, 152; "Social Nuisances: The Lap-Dog," *New Monthly Magazine and Humorist*, April 1844, 511–13; André-Valdès [Mme Charles Boeswilwald], *Le chiens de luxe* (Paris: Librairie Nilsson, 1907), 25; Shamir, *Inexpressible Privacy*, 25–26; Stearns, *American Cool*, 35; David Vincent, *I Hope I Don't Intrude: Privacy and Its Dilemmas in Nineteenth-Century Britain* (Oxford: Oxford University Press, 2015); Amato, *Beastly Possessions*, 73–77.

83 Timothy B. Smith, "Assistance and Repression: Rural Exodus, Vagabondage and Social Crisis in France, 1880–1914," *Journal of Social History*, 32, no. 4 (1999): 821–46; Strange, "Tramp," 244; "New York Street Characters," *Ballou's Dollar Monthly Magazine*, June 1860, 505; Jacob A. Riis, *How the Other Half Lives: Studies among the Tenements of New York*, ed. Sam Bass Warner Jr. (New York: Charles Scribner's Sons, 1890), 55–57; Hidetaka Hirota, *Expelling the Poor: Atlantic Seaboard States and the Nineteenth-Century Origins of American Immigration Policy* (Oxford: Oxford University Press, 2017), 129–55; Eric H. Monkkonen, *Police in Urban America, 1860–1920* (Cambridge: Cambridge University Press, 1981), 88–89.

84 Edward Crapsey, "The Nether Side of New York: Outcast Children," *Galaxy*, September 1871.

85 "Canine Mendicancy," *NYT*, October 26, 1881; James Greenwood, *The Wilds of London* (London: Chatto and Windus, 1874), 178–79.

86 Beaumarié, *Le chien*, 14–15; Alfred Barbou, *Le chien: Son histoire, ses exploits, ses aventures* (Paris: Librairie Furne, 1883), 215–16, 256.

87 "Cities and Vagrant Dogs," *Forest and Stream*, August 1, 1896.

88 Adrienne Neyrat, "La fourièrre," *L'ami des bêtes*, December 1899, 115; Adrienne Neyrat, "Nouvelles et informations," *L'ami des bêtes*, September 1900, 98; Bellier de Villiers, *Le chien au chenil*, 41.

89 Tim Cresswell, *On the Move: Mobility in the Modern Western World* (New York: Routledge, 2006), 39–42; "The Dog Nuisance," *Turf, Field and Farm*, May 11, 1867; A Casual Visitor, "Vagabond Dogs," *Manchester Guardian*, April 24, 1902.

90 Miltenberger, "Promiscuously Mixed Together"; McNeur, *Taming Manhattan*,

6–44; Alan Mayne, "Representing the Slum," *Urban History Yearbook* 17 (1990): 72–74.

91 "Dogs Meet Sudden Deaths," *NYT*, June 22, 1896; "War on Dogs in the Park," *NYT*, December 22, 1899.

92 Préfet de police, "Circulaire no. 13: Transport en fourrière par voitures spéciales, des animaux vivants, des cadavres d'animaux et des objets matériels," n.d., DB 226, APP; Préfet de police, "Circulaire no. 16: Transport à la fourrière par voitures automobiles des chiens vivants, des objets et cadavres de chiens, chats et autres petits animaux," August 1, 1912, 187, 247, DB 226, APP; G. Cerbelaud, "La rage à Paris et dans le département de la Seine," *Le Monde illustré*, July 20, 1912, 54; "Les toutous," *La presse* (Paris), May 1, 1903; Préfet de police to Messieurs les Maires des Communes du Département de la Seine, "Circulaire no. 20," September 26, 1914, DB 229, APP. The Société protectrice des animaux struggled to keep up with the number of dogs entering its refuges and killed hundreds of abandoned dogs: "Procès-verbaux des réunions du conseil d'administration: Séance du 9 octobre 1914," *Bulletin de la Société protectrice des animaux* 10 (1914): 545–46.

Chapter Two

1 "A Child's Terrible Death," *NYT*, August 4, 1878.

2 For an excellent overview of rabies remedies, see Jessica Wang, *Mad Dogs and Other New Yorkers: Rabies, Medicine, and Society in an American Metropolis, 1840–1920* (Baltimore: Johns Hopkins University Press, 2019), 83–124.

3 "Hydrophobia," *Times* (London), July 23, 1830; "New York City," *New York Daily Times*, May 8, 1852; "Fifty Dog Catchers at Work This Week," *NYT*, May 25, 1908; John D. Blaisdell, "A Frightful, but Not Necessarily Fatal, Madness: Rabies in Eighteenth-Century England and English North America" (PhD diss., Iowa State University, 1995), https://core.ac.uk/download/pdf/38900778.pdf; Jolanta N. Komornicka, "Man as Rabid Beast: Criminals into Animals in Late Medieval France," *French History* 28, no. 2 (2014): 157–71; Bill Wasik and Monica Murphy, *Rabid: A Cultural History of the World's Most Diabolical Virus* (New York: Penguin, 2012); Hugh Dalziel, *Mad Dogs and Hydrophobia* (Dundee: James P. Mathew, 1886), 1–2; *Hydrophobia, or Fun Gone Mad: A Book for the Dog Days* (New York: s.n., 1877); "Hydrophobia," *Sixpenny Magazine*, February 1866. On fears of disease, see Amelia Bonea, Melissa Dickson, Sally Shuttleworth, and Jennifer Wallis, *Anxious Times: Medicine and Modernity in Nineteenth-Century Britain* (Pittsburgh: University of Pittsburgh Press, 2019); Daniel McCann and Claire McKechnie-Mason, eds., *Fear in the Medical and Literary Imagination, Medieval to Modern: Dreadful Passions* (London: Palgrave Macmillan, 2018).

4 F. J. Bachelet and C. Froussart, *Cause de la rage et moyen d'en preserver l'humanité* (Valenciennes: E. Prignet, 1857), iii. See also Horatio R. Bigelow, *Hydrophobia* (Philadelphia: D. G. Brinton, 1881), 91; Harriet Ritvo, *The Animal Estate: The English and Other Creatures in the Victorian Age* (London: Penguin, 1990 [1987]), 167–70.

5 George Fleming was heavily influenced by Henri Bouley, Camille Leblanc, and other French veterinarians. *Rabies and Hydrophobia: Their History, Nature,*

Causes, Symptoms, and Prevention (London: Chapman and Hall, 1872), 109–10, 128, 317. Charles P. Russel reproduced the text of London dog control orders in *Hydrophobia in Dogs and Other Animals, and the Sanitary Precautions against Its Transmission to the Human Race* (New York: Board of Health, 1875), 42–43.

6 For more on the nomenclature, see Wang, *Mad Dogs and Other New Yorkers*, 3–4.

7 Thomas Blatchford, *Hydrophobia: Its Origin and Development as Influenced by Climate, Season and Other Circumstances* (Philadelphia: T. K. and P. G. Collins, 1856), 9; William Youatt, *On Canine Madness* (London: Longman, 1830), 22, 34. It is important to note that the term *virus* here referred to a poison or toxin rather than a "biologically active, self-replicating virus." Wang, *Mad Dogs and Other New Yorkers*, 3.

8 Louis-François Trolliet, *Nouveau traité de la rage, observations cliniques, recherches d'anatomie pathologique et doctrine de cette maladie* (Paris: Méquignon-Marvis, 1820), 165; Damien Baldin, *Histoire des animaux domestiques, XIXe–XXe siècle* (Paris: Seuil, 2014), 205.

9 Youatt, *On Canine Madness*, 6; Henry Sully, *Observations on, and Plain Directions for, All Classes of People, to Prevent the Fatal Effects of the Bites of Animals Labouring under Hydrophobia* (Taunton: R. Hall, 1828), 11. On constructions of women's "potentially excessive emotionality," see Peter N. Stearns, *American Cool: Constructing a Twentieth-Century Emotional Style* (New York: New York University Press, 1994), 35.

10 Henri Bouley, *Hydrophobia: Means of Avoiding Its Perils and Preventing Its Spread as Discussed at One of the Scientific Soirees of the Sorbonne*, trans. Alexandre Liautard (New York: Harper and Brothers, 1874 [1870]), 10–11, 13; Thomas H. Gage, *A Case of Hydrophobia: With Remarks* (Worcester, MA: Worcester District Medical Society, 1865), 3; Wang, *Mad Dogs and Other New Yorkers*, 43; Kathleen Kete, *Beast in the Boudoir: Petkeeping in Nineteenth-Century Paris* (Berkeley: University of California Press, 1994), 97–114.

11 "Hydrophobia"; Trolliet, *Nouveau traité de la rage*, 17–23, 192–93; Blatchford, *Hydrophobia*, 77; David G. Schuster, *Neurasthenic Nation: America's Search for Health, Happiness, and Comfort, 1869–1920* (New Brunswick, NJ: Rutgers University Press, 2011), 86; Kete, *Beast in the Boudoir*, 98–102.

12 Bigelow, *Hydrophobia*, 80–81, 84; Griscom quoted in Blatchford, *Hydrophobia*, 82. See also Kete, *Beast in the Boudoir*, 100–101.

13 Trolliet, *Nouveau traité de la rage*, 16–17, 77, 346; M. E. Decroix, *De la rage: Curabilité-traitement* (Lille: Imprimerie de Lefebvre-Ducrocq, 1868) 27, 30; Fleming, *Rabies and Hydrophobia*, 342, 344. Fleming noted that "mental treatment is by no means to be neglected" (349).

14 Bouley, *Hydrophobia*, 50; Bigelow, *Hydrophobia*, 29, 121, 139; Gordon Stables, *Dogs in Their Relation to the Public: Social, Sanitary and Legal* (London: Cassell, Petter and Galpin, 1877), 29.

15 A Lady, "To the Editor of *The Times*," *Times* (London), June 3, 1830; "London Dogs," *Saturday Review*, September 26, 1868; Shu-Cauan Yan, "Emotions, Sensations, and Victorian Working-Class Readers," *Journal of Popular Culture* 50, no. 2 (2017): 317–40.

16 William Lauder Lindsay, *Mind in the Lower Animals in Health and Disease* (London: Kegan Paul, 1879), 2:176; Edouard-François-Marie Bosquillon, *Mémoire sur*

les causes de l'hydrophobie, vulgairement connue sous le nom de rage, et sur les moyens d'anéantir cette maladie (Paris: Gabon, 1802), 2, 22, 26; Vincent di Marco, *The Bearer of Crazed and Venomous Fangs: Popular Myths and Delusions regarding the Bite of the Mad Dog* (Bloomington, IN: iUniverse, 2014), 141–47; Neil Pemberton and Michael Worboys, *Rabies in Britain: Dogs, Disease and Culture, 1830–2000* (Basingstoke: Palgrave Macmillan, 2013 [2007]), 9; Daniel Hack Tuke, *Illustrations of the Influence of the Mind upon the Body in Health and Disease Designed to Elucidate the Action of the Imagination* (Philadelphia: Henry C. Lea, 1873), 198–99; Wang, *Mad Dogs and Other New Yorkers*, 151–52.

17 Tuke, *Illustrations of the Influence of the Mind*, 198–99, 207.

18 Ibid., 200–201; "London, Thursday April 11," *Daily Telegraph* (London), April 11, 1872; Peter Cryle, "'A Terrible Ordeal from Every Point of View': (Not) Managing Female Sexuality on the Wedding Night," *Journal of the History of Sexuality* 18, no. 1 (2009): 44–64.

19 Lindsay, *Mind in the Lower Animals*, 17; William Lauder Lindsay, "Madness in Animals," *Journal of Mental Science* 17, no. 78 (1871): 185; William Lauder Lindsay, "Spurious Hydrophobia in Man," *Journal of Mental Science* 23, no. 104 (January 1878): 551–53; Pemberton and Worboys, *Rabies in Britain*, 96–97; Liz Gray, "Body, Mind and Madness: Pain in Animals in the Nineteenth-Century Comparative Psychology," in *Pain and Emotion in Modern History*, ed. Rob Boddice (Basingstoke: Palgrave, 2014), 148–63; "Hydrophobia: The Subject Discussed by Medical Men," *NYT*, July 7, 1874; Wang, *Mad Dogs and Other New Yorkers*, 150–51; Bonea, Dickson, Shuttleworth, and Wallis, *Anxious Times*; Daniel Pick, *Faces of Degeneration: A European Disorder c. 1848–1918* (Cambridge: Cambridge University Press, 1989); Hannah Rose Woods, "Anxiety and Urban Life in late Victorian and Edwardian Culture" (PhD diss., University of Cambridge, 2018), https://www.repository.cam.ac.uk/handle/1810/274934; Andrew Scull, *Hysteria: The Disturbing History* (New York: Oxford University Press, 2009).

20 Edward Mayhew, *Dogs: Their Management Being a New Plan of Treating the Animal Based upon a Consideration of His Natural Temperament* (London: George Routledge and Sons, 1854), 5–6, 156, 160.

21 Blatchford, *Hydrophobia*, 10–11.

22 Sabine Arnaud, *On Hysteria: The Invention of a Medical Category between 1670 and 1820* (Chicago: University of Chicago Press, 2015), 245; Julien-Joseph Virey, *De la femme, sous ses rapports physiologique, moral et littéraire*, 2nd ed. (Paris: Crochard, 1825), 417; Bachelet and Froussart, *Cause de la rage*, 82–83, 85. See also Kete, *Beast in the Boudoir*, 102–3; Ritvo, *The Animal Estate*, 180–81.

23 "Rapport sur la rage," 1878, 6–7, 9, DA 45 [illegible], APP; Bachelet and Froussart, *Cause de la rage*, 143, 146; Thomas Dolan, *The Nature and Treatment of Rabies or Hydrophobia Being the Report of the Special Commission Appointed by the Medical Press and Circular* (London: Baillière, Tindall and Cox, 1878), 204, 245. See also J. Grandjean, "Du moyen préventif de la rage: Pétition à l'Assemblée nationale," May 1, 1878, DA 45, APP.

24 "Dogs," *Pall Mall Gazette* (London), December 31, 1871; Pemberton and Worboys, *Rabies in Britain*, 46. On the perceived emotional delicacy of dogs, see Edmund Ramsden and Duncan Wilson, "The Suicidal Animal: Science and the Nature of Self-Destruction," *Past and Present* 224 (2014): 205–17.

25 *Hydrophobia* (New York: M. B. Brown, 1874), Broadsides SY1874 no. 25, New-York Historical Society, capitals in the original; Trolliet, *Nouveau traité de la rage,* 274–75.

26 *Committee to Prevent the Spreading of Canine Madness, Report, Minutes of Evidence,* House of Commons, Parliamentary Papers 651, 1830, 3–4; Bouley, *Hydrophobia,* 28–29; "Hydrophobia," *Times* (London).

27 Stonehenge [J. H. Walsh], *The Dogs of the British Islands,* 4th ed. (London: Horace Cox, 1882), 24–25; Pemberton and Worboys, *Rabies in Britain,* 66; Comité consultatif d'hygiène publique de France, "Instructions relatives à la rage," n.d. [1878?], DB 229, APP.

28 Préfecture de police, "Instruction concernant les mesures à prendre à l'égard des chiens en execution de l'Ordonnance de police du 27 mai 1845," January 10, 1867, DA 44, APP.

29 M. J. Bourrel, *Traité complet de la rage chez le chien et chez le chat: Moyen de s'en preserver* (Paris: Chez l'auteur, G. Barbab, P. Asselin, 1874), 107, 117; M. J. Bourrel, *Réponse à quelques objections faites à la méthode de l'émoussement de la pointe des dents des chiens comme moyen préventif de l'inoculation du virus rabique* (Paris: Renou, Maulde et Cock, 1876), 26, 35–36.

30 Russel, *Hydrophobia in Dogs and Other Animals,* 47; "Hydrophobia: The Subject Discussed by Medical Men"; Fleming, *Rabies and Hydrophobia,* 306.

31 Leslie Topp, "Single Rooms, Seclusion and the Non-Restraint Movement in British Asylums, 1838–1844," *Social History of Medicine* 31, no. 4 (2018): 754–73.

32 Bibliothèque de l'École vétérinaire d'Alfort, Maisons-Alfort, Préfecture de police, "Ordonnance concernant les chiens errants," July 30, 1823; Préfecture de police, "Avis," August 29, 1828, DB 229, APP; [Doctor Delance?], letter to Préfet de police, 1878, DA 44, APP. See also Letter to Préfet de police, May 28, 1878, DA 44, APP; "Note," June 1878, DA 44, APP; [Doctor Malzer?] to Préfet de police, n.d., DA 44, APP.

33 "Common Council," *New York Herald,* July 4, 1848; "Proclamation," *New York Herald,* July 13, 1848; Benjamin Brady, "The Politics of the Pound: Controlling Loose Dogs in Nineteenth-Century New York City," *Jefferson Journal of Science and Culture* 2 (2012): 10–11; "Prospective War on Unmuzzled Dogs," *NYT,* May 28, 1874; "The Great Dog War of 1848," *New York Herald,* July 16, 1848; John Duffy, *A History of Public Health in New York City 1866–1966* (New York: Russell Sage Foundation, 1974), 33–34.

34 "An Act for Further Improving the Police in and near the Metropolis," August 17, 1839, www.legislation.gov.uk/ukpga/Vict/2-3/47, accessed October 20, 2020; "Police," *Times* (London), August 15, 1867; Pemberton and Worboys, *Rabies in Britain,* 54; "Police," *Times* (London), February 14, 1867.

35 *Report from the Select Committee of the House of Lords on the Traffic Regulation (Metropolis) Bill [H.L.] together with the Proceedings of the Committee, Minutes of Evidence and Index,* House of Commons, Parliamentary Papers 186, 1867, 26; "The New Law on Dogs," *Times* (London), October 4, 1867; Holmes Coote, "Hydrophobia: To the Editor of the Times," *Times* (London), September 21, 1868; Pemberton and Worboys, *Rabies in Britain,* 80.

36 Dolan, *The Nature and Treatment of Rabies,* 206, 219; Fleming, *Rabies and Hydrophobia,* 205–15, 374–76.

37 Stables, *Dogs in Their Relation to the Public*, 26; Snarleyow, "The New Dog Torture," *Daily Telegraph* (London), June 30, 1868. See also C.C.B., "The New Dog Torture," *Daily Telegraph* (London), July 2, 1868; "London Dogs," *Saturday Review*, September 26, 1868; Humanitas, "The New Dog Torture," *Daily Telegraph* (London), July 2, 1868; Pemberton and Worboys, *Rabies in Britain*, 82; *Report . . . on the Traffic Regulation (Metropolis) Bill*, 26; "He Don't Like Dogs," *NYT*, June 14 1886.

38 Bourrel, *Traité complet*, 100; Russel, *Hydrophobia in Dogs and Other Animals*, 43–44; Charles P. Russel, "Muzzling the Dogs," *NYT*, June 8, 1874; "Hydrophobia: The Subject Discussed by Medical Men"; Scull, *Hysteria*, 87.

39 Henry Blatin, *Nos cruautés envers les animaux au détriment de l'hygiène, de la fortune publique et de la morale* (Paris: Hachette, 1867), 99; M. L. Prangé, "De la muselière appliquée au chien," *Bulletin de la Société protectrice des animaux*, 8 (1862): 354; Eugène Meunier, *La liberté pour le chien: Plaidoyer historique, philosophique et physiologique dédié aux amis de la race canine* (Paris: F. Henry, 1863), 24. See also Dr. Belloli, "La muselière des chiens," *Bulletin de la Société protectrice des animaux* 8 (1862): 313–16; Bourrel, *Traité complet*, 98–99; Henry Blatin, "De la rage chez le chien et des mesures préservatrices," *Bulletin de la Société protectrice des animaux* 8 (1862): 158–68; "Encore la muselière," *Bulletin de la Société protectrice des animaux* 8 (1862): 420; Eugène Meunier, *Plaintes d'un muselé traduits par son maître* (Paris: Chez l'auteur, 1862).

40 "Local Intelligence: Hydrophobia," *NYT*, June 16, 1868; ASPCA, *Annual Report* (1868), 50; "Report," *The Proceedings at the Annual Meeting Held July 18th, 1868* (London: Royal Society for the Prevention of Cruelty to Animals, 1868), 42–43.

41 Préfecture de police, "Ordonnance concernant les chiens errants," June 7, 1830, DB 229, APP; Ann La Berge, *Mission and Method: The Early Nineteenth-Century French Public Health Movement* (Cambridge: Cambridge University Press, 1992), 120; Préfet de police, "Chiens," August 8, 1837, DB 229, APP; Préfet de police to [?], June 10, 1837, DB 229, APP; Conseil d'hygiène publique et de salubrité du département de la Seine, "Séance de la Commission de la Rage du 15 novembre 1862: Etude sur la prophylaxie administrative de la rage," 30–31, 54, 58, DA 44, APP; Bourrel, *Traité complet*, 100.

42 Préfet de police, "Ordonnance concernant les chiens," August 6, 1878, DB 229, APP; "Mesures preventatives contre la rage," August 24, 1878, DB 229, APP. The letters from concerned Parisians are collected in DA 44, APP.

43 "City Intelligence," *New York Herald*, May 25, 1848; Russel, *Hydrophobia in Dogs and Other Animals*, 43–44. See also "Dogs Rampant: To the Rescue," *New York Daily Times*, July 11, 1856; "An Hour at the Dog-Pound," *New York Daily Times*, August 5, 1856; "Dogs in Trouble," *NYT*, June 13, 1874; "The Dog-Days and the New Dog Law," *NYT*, June 2, 1867; "Hydrophobia," *NYT*, August 14, 1874.

44 Philip Howell, *At Home and Astray: The Domestic Dog in Victorian Britain* (Charlottesville: University of Virginia Press, 2015), 158–60.

45 William Lauder Lindsay, "The Pathology of Mind in the Lower Animals," *Journal of Mental Science* 21, no. 1 (April 1877): 18; Lindsay, *Mind in the Lower Animals*, 339.

46 Louis Pasteur, "Méthode pour prévenir la rage après morsure," *Bulletin de l'Academie nationale de médecine*, 49th year, 2nd ser., vol. 2 (Paris: G. Masson, 1885),

1432. See also Jean Théodoridès, "Pasteur and Rabies: The British Connection," *Journal of the Royal Society of Medicine* 82, no. 8 (1989): 488–89; Bert Hansen, "America's First Medical Breakthrough: How Popular Excitement about a French Rabies Cure in 1885 Raised New Expectations for Medical Progress," *American Historical Review* 103, no. 2 (1998): 393.

47 "Nos gravures," *L'illustration* (Paris), November 7, 1885. See also "Les travaux scientifiques de M. Pasteur," *Le journal illustré*, March 30, 1884.

48 Charles Talansier, "Les inoculations au laboratoire de M. Pasteur," *L'illustration* (Paris), April 10, 1886; Gilbert Martin, "L'ange de l'inoculation," *Le Don Quichotte*, March 13 1886; "Patients of M. Pasteur," *NYT*, January 18, 1886; "Hydrophobia," *Times* (London), October 28, 1885; "M. Pasteur," *Times* (London), October 31, 1885; George Fleming, "Rabies and Hydrophobia: To the Editor of *The Times*," *Times* (London), November 26, 1885; Dalziel, *Mad Dogs and Hydrophobia*, 51–52; Pemberton and Worboys, *Rabies in Britain*, 108–10.

49 "Travaux scientifiques," *La république illustrée* (Paris), November 7, 1885; "Pasteur and Mad Dogs," *NYT*, January 10, 1886.

50 "Une séance de vaccination antirabique à l'Institut Pasteur à Paris," *Lyon républicain: Supplément illustré*, April 24, 1898; Armand Ruffer, "Remarks on the Prevention of Hydrophobia by M. Pasteur's Treatment," *British Medical Journal* 2, no. 1499 (September 21, 1889): 643; Victor Horsley, "M. Pasteur's Prophylactic," *British Medical Journal* 2, no. 1342 (September 18, 1886): 573.

51 Pemberton and Worboys, *Rabies in Britain*, 112–15.

52 "The Mad Dog Scare," *NYT*, December 24, 1884; "Forty More Newark Dogs Poisoned," *NYT*, December 13 1885; "Newark Police in a Quandary," *NYT*, December 15, 1885; "Panic Caused by a Mad Dog," *NYT*, December 4, 1885.

53 "Pasteur and Mad Dogs"; "Patients of M. Pasteur," *NYT*, January 18, 1886; Hansen, "America's First Medical Breakthrough," 389–404, 409–10.

54 Valentine Mott, "Rabies, and How to Prevent It," *New York Medical Journal* 44, October 30, 1886, 491. See also "Using Pasteur's Method," *NYT*, July 7, 1886; "To Try Pasteur's Methods," *NYT*, January 3, 1886; "A Pasteur Institute Incorporated," *NYT*, January 5, 1886; Leonard J. Hoenig, Alan C. Jackson, and Gordon M. Dickinson, "The Early Use of Pasteur's Rabies Vaccine in the United States," *Vaccine* 36, no. 30 (2018): 4578–79. For an excellent and detailed overview of the American Pasteur Institute, see Wang, *Mad Dogs and Other New Yorkers*, 162–70.

55 "Pasteur Building Dedicated: Formal Opening of the New Home of the Institute," *NYT*, October 11, 1893; David Huyssen, *Progressive Inequality: Rich and Poor in New York, 1890–1920* (Cambridge, MA: Harvard University Press, 2014). For an extensive overview of the New York Pasteur Institute, see Wang, *Mad Dogs and Other New Yorkers*, 170–83.

56 "Editorial: Another Case of Madness versus Hydrophobia," *Bulletin of the Pasteur Institute* 5, no. 4 (December 1897), 84–86; "The First Decennial Work of the New York Pasteur Institute," *Bulletin of the Pasteur Institute* 8, no. 1 (March 1900): 1–4; "Dr. Gibier Killed in Runaway Accident," *NYT*, June 11, 1900; Anne Marie Moulin, "Les instituts Pasteur de la Méditerranée arabe: Une religion scientifique en pays d'Islam," in *Santé, médecine et société dans le monde arabe*, ed. Elisabeth Longuenesse (Paris: L'Harmattan, 1995), 130–64.

57 By January 1890, the fund had raised £2,839, a sum well short of the £5,000 target.

The money paid for thirty patients to travel to Paris, with the rest given to the Pasteur Institute. Pemberton and Worboys, *Rabies in Britain*, 122, 129–30.

58 Landon Carter Gray, "Hydrophobia: Its Clinical Aspect," *Transactions of the New York Academy of Medicine*, 2nd ser., 7 (1891): 336–40; Charles L. Dana, "The Reality of Rabies," *Transactions of the New York Academy of Medicine*, 2nd ser., 7 (1891): 345–50. See also John D. Blaisdell, "With Certain Reservations: The American Veterinary Community's Reception of Pasteur's Work on Rabies," *Agricultural History* 70, no. 3 (1996): 503–24; Wang, *Mad Dogs and Other New Yorkers*, 147–78.

59 "Pasteur Causes Trouble," *NYT*, June 12, 1890; Charles W. Dulles, *Pasteur's Method of Treating Hydrophobia* (New York: Trow's Printing and Bookbinding, 1886); Charles W. Dulles, "Report on Hydrophobia," *Medical Record*, June 26, 1897, 905–7; Irving C. Rosse, "Hydrophobia," *Washington Post*, November 26, 1895; J. C. Emory, "'Hydrophobia' Statistics," *NYT*, January 19, 1898; Arthur Westcott, "Hydrophobia Statistics," *NYT*, January 30, 1898; "Death from Fear vs. Hydrophobia," *Open Door*, December 1921; *Pasteurism: Its Commercialism and Its Dangers* (New York: New York Anti-Vivisection Society, n.d.), FA142, box 13, Rockefeller University Records, Special Events and Activities, Anti-Vivisection Activities, Rockefeller Archive Center.

60 Terrie M. Romano, "The Cattle Plague of 1865 and the Reception of 'The Germ Theory' in Mid-Victorian Britain," *Journal of the History of Medicine and Allied Sciences* 52, no. 1 (1997): 51–80; Thomas M. Dolan, "M. Pasteur's Prophylactic," *British Medical Journal* 2, no. 1340 (September 4, 1886): 475–76; Horsley, "M. Pasteur's Prophylactic"; Thomas M. Dolan, *Pasteur and Rabies* (London: George Bell and Sons, 1890); Ouida [Marie Louise de la Ramée], "Rabies: To the Editor," *Times* (London), November 7, 1885; "Kynophobia: A Fin-de-Siecle Nervous Disease," *Daily Mail* (London), April 17, 1897. See also Sally Shuttleworth, "Fear, Phobia and the Victorian Psyche," in McCann and McKechnie-Mason, *Fear in the Medical and Literary Imagination*, 177–99; David Trotter, "The Invention of Agoraphobia," *Victorian Literature and Culture* 32, no. 2 (2004): 463–74; Diana Donald, *Women against Cruelty: Protection of Animals in Nineteenth-Century Britain* (Manchester: Manchester University Press, 2020), 236–37.

61 Pemberton and Worboys, *Rabies in Britain*, 116–20. *Hydrophobia: Report of a Committee Appointed by the Local Government Board to Inquire into M. Pasteur's Treatment of Hydrophobia* (London: HMSO, 1887). The report's findings were summarized in "Report on Pasteur's Treatment of Hydrophobia," *Journal of the American Medical Association* 9, no. 4 (July 23, 1887): 119–21.

62 Auguste Lutaud, *M. Pasteur et la rage* (Paris: Publications du Journal de médecine de Paris, 1887), 8–9; Lizzy Lind Af Hageby and Leisa K. Schartau, *The Shambles of Science: Extracts from the Diary of Two Students of Physiology*, 5th ed. (London: Animal Defence and Anti-Vivisection Society, 1913), 143–44. See also Pemberton and Worboys, *Rabies in Britain*, 120; Baldin, *Histoire des animaux domestiques*, 169; Alceste, *Pasteur: Sa rage et sa vivisection* (Lyon: Association typographique, 1886); Auguste Lutaud, "M. Pasteur's Treatment of Hydrophobia," *British Medical Journal* 1, no. 1370 (April 2, 1887): 719–20.

63 C. A. Gordon, *Comments on the Report of the Committee on M. Pasteur's Treatment of Rabies and Hydrophobia* (London: Baillière, Tindal and Cox, 1888), 13, 15, 17;

Charles W. Dulles, *Pasteur's Method of Treating Hydrophobia* (London: Victoria Street Society for the Protection of Animals from Vivisection, 1886); Michael Worboys, *Spreading Germs: Disease Theories and Medical Practice in Britain, 1865–1900* (Cambridge: Cambridge University Press, 2000).

64 Quoted in "Patients of M. Pasteur," *NYT*, January 18, 1886.

65 Eugène Minette, *Notice sur la rage du chien* (Compiègne: Henry Lefebvre, 1890), 4; Ilana Löwy, "Cultures de bactériologie en France, 1880–1900: La paillasse et la politique," *Gesnerus* 67, no. 2 (2010): 190–91; David S. Barnes, *The Great Stink of Paris and the Nineteenth-Century Struggle against Filth and Germs* (Baltimore: Johns Hopkins University Press, 2006), 36–46.

66 Louis Moynier, *Lettres d'un chien errant sur la protection des animaux* (Paris: E. Dentu, 1888), 41, 47–48; Louis Lépine, "Loi du 21 juillet 1881 et Décret du 22 juin 1882: Mesures contre la rage," July 1, 1897, DB 229, APP; "Mesures contre la rage," *Revue municipale*, 1902, 3493–94; Joanny Pertus, *Le chien: Hygiène, maladies* (Paris: J.-B. Baillière et fils, 1905), 126–27; "L'actualité," *L'eclair*, October 3, 1897.

67 Conseil d'hygiène publique et de salubrité du département de la Seine, *Rapport sur les maladies contagieuses des animaux observées dans le département de la Seine pendant l'année 1893* (Paris: Imprimerie Chaix, 1893), DB 232, APP; Pertus, *Le chien*, 122; "Pour les chiens," *Le matin* (Paris), May 1, 1903; "Le massacre des chiens," *L'eclair*, June 13, 1892; Docteur Ox, "Chiens errants," *Le matin* (Paris), April 11, 1902.

68 Fleming, "Rabies and Hydrophobia."

69 Much of the preceding information came from Pemberton and Worboys, *Rabies in Britain*, 135–38; the Cobbe quotation is from p. 142. Howell argues that the creation of responsible and self-regulating dog-owner partnerships held together by leashes was more important than the muzzle. *At Home and Astray*, 150–73.

70 *Report from the Select Committee of the House of Lords on Rabies in Dogs; together with the Proceedings of the Committee, Minutes of Evidence and Appendix*, House of Commons, Parliamentary Papers 322, 1887, vii.

71 County of London, "Muzzling of Dogs Order of 1897," LCC-PC-ANI-01-03, LMA.

72 Pemberton and Worboys, *Rabies in Britain*, 137–57; quotation is from p. 155; A. J. Sewell and F. G. D., "The Muzzling Order," *Times* (London), April 15, 1897; Frank Kerslake, "Hydrophobia and Muzzling," *Times* (London), September 30, 1889; "Wire Muzzles—Mrs Henry Levy Writes," *Times* (London), April 10, 1897.

73 Pemberton and Worboys, *Rabies in Britain*, 161–62.

74 "Beware the Dog Catcher," *Forest and Stream*, May 31, 1888; "Stray Dogs and the A.K.C.," *Forest and Stream*, July 31, 1890; Shuttleworth, "Fear, Phobia and the Victorian Psyche." See also Charles W. Dulles, "Hydrophobia and the Pasteur Method: A Rejoinder," *Medical Record*, May 3, 1902; Follen Cabot, "Best Methods to Prevent Hydrophobia," *Medical News*, August 15, 1903; "The New York Academy of Medicine: Section on Medicine Stated Meeting, Held Tuesday April 17, 1900," *Medical News*, August 11, 1900; Tuke, *Illustrations of the Influence of the Mind*, 198–99; "Cynophobia," *NYT*, August 7, 1893; Gilroy box 1444, roll 6, New York City Municipal Archive.

75 As Wang notes, Pasteur's treatment had become established through trans-

atlantic exchanges and an "institutional environment of philanthropy, corporate enterprise and emerging public health." *Mad Dogs and Other New Yorkers*, 183–92; quotation is from p. 191. The three previous paragraphs are also based on the following: Wang, "Dogs," 1009–13; "Another Midsummer Madness: The Muzzle," *OAF*, July 1902; "Dogs Must Go Muzzled," *Medical News*, June 20, 1903; Elizabeth D. Schafer, "Williams, Anna Wessels," *American National Biography*, Oxford University Press, 1999, https://doi-org.liverpool.idm.oclc.org/10.1093/anb/9780198606697.article.1200984; "Recurrence of the 'Mad Dog Scare,'" *OAF*, July 1902; "News of the Week," *Medical Record*, April 18, 1903; Charles J. Bartlett, *Rabies with Report of a Case* (New Haven, CT: Van Dyck, 1907), 2; Anna Wessels Williams and Max Murray Lowden, "The Etiology and Diagnosis of Hydrophobia," *Annual Report of the Board of Health of the Department of Health of the City of New York for the Year Ending December 31, 1906* (New York: Martin M. Brown, 1907), 2:644–47; Duffy, *A History of Public Health*, 104–5.

76 "Muzzling Dogs Is the Only Way to Stamp Out Rabies, Says Pasteur Expert," *Washington Post*, June 28, 1908; George H. Hart, *Rabies and Its Increasing Prevalence* (Washington, DC: Government Printing Office, 1908), 23. Gibier was the nephew of the New York Pasteur Institute's founder, Paul Gibier.

77 A. D. Melvin, Chief of Bureau, E. C. Schroeder M.D.V., Superintendent of the Experiment Station, "Some Observations on Rabies," January 29, 1908, 2, 5, circular 120, Bureau of Animal Industry, U.S. Department of Agriculture.

78 "Scores of Mad Dogs Loose in City Island," *NYT*, January 5, 1907; Wang, "Dogs," 1013–15; "Cities and Vagrant Dogs," *Forest and Stream*, August 1, 1896. See also Dolan, *The Nature and Treatment of Rabies or Hydrophobia*, 190, 193; Everett Millais, "The New Muzzling Order," *Times* (London), April 20, 1897; "Another Midsummer Madness"; F. C. Walsh, "The Problem of Rabies," *Forum*, April 1911.

79 "Defends Ordinance to Muzzle Dogs," *NYT*, September 17, 1914.

80 "Maudlin Sentimentality Is Back of Protest against Ordinance for Muzzling City Dogs," *BDE*, October 4, 1914; "Find Good Dog Muzzle," *NYT*, October 16, 1915.

81 Wang, "Dogs," 1013–15.

82 *Information for Dog Owners: Why Dogs Must Be Muzzled When at Large* (New York: Department of Health, January 1919), 8; John L. Rice, *Health for 7,500,000 People* (New York: Department of Health, 1939), 146–47, 166, 263.

83 "Un nouvel arrêté du Préfet de police sur la circulation des chiens dans le département de la Seine," *Bulletin de Société protectrice des animaux*, October–December 1918, 212; *Protégeons les animaux, conseils pratiques, droits et devoirs: II Chiens et chats* (Paris: Société protectrice des animaux, 1927), 15. On Britain, see Frederick Hobday, "Observations on Some of the Diseases of Animals Communicable to Man," *Lancet* 197, no. 5092 (April 2, 1921): 727; Thomas W. M. Cameron, "The Dog as a Carrier of Disease to Man," *Lancet* 199, no. 5142 (March 18, 1922): 565.

84 Jean-Baptiste Fressoz, *L'apocalypse joyeuse: Une histoire du risque technologique* (Paris: Seuil, 2012); Peter Soppelsa, "The Fragility of Modernity: Infrastructure and Everyday Life in Paris, 1871–1914" (PhD diss., University of Michigan, 2009), https://deepblue.lib.umich.edu/handle/2027.42/62374.

85 Quoted in Jessica Wang, "Dogs and the Making of the American State: Voluntary Association, State Power, and the Politics of Animal Control in New York

City, 1850–1920," *Journal of American History* 98, no. 4 (2012): 1013. The figure of 150,000 comes from "Kill Off Stray Dogs to End Hydrophobia," *NYT*, May 23, 1908.

Chapter Three

1 Erica Fudge, *Brutal Reasoning: Animals, Rationality, and Humanity in Early Modern England* (Ithaca, NY: Cornell University Press, 2006); Peter Sahlins, *1688: The Year of the Animal in France* (New York: Zone Books, 2017).

2 Joanna Bourke, *The Story of Pain: From Prayer to Painkillers* (Oxford: Oxford University Press, 2014), 231–52; Karen Halttunen, "Humanitarianism, and the Pornography of Pain in Anglo-American Culture," *American Historical Review* 100, no. 2 (1995), 330; Christophe Traïni, *The Animal Rights Struggle: An Essay in Historical Sociology*, trans. Richard Jemmett (Amsterdam: Amsterdam University Press, 2016), 94–124.

3 Mona Caird, *A Sentimental View of Vivisection*, Bijou Library no. 3 (London: William Reeves, 1883), 19–20.

4 William Brown, *Our Lesser Brethren* (London: Headley Bros., 1920), 20–21.

5 "Mad Dog at Knightsbridge," *Times* (London), September 29, 1818; E. L. Richardson, "To the Editor," *Times* (London), September 22, 1818.

6 "Hydrophobia," *Times* (London), June 3, 1830; Beal quoted in Neil Pemberton and Michael Worboys, *Rabies in Britain: Dogs, Disease and Culture, 1830–2000* (Basingstoke: Palgrave Macmillan, 2013 [2007]), 42; Lisa Keller, *Triumph of Order: Democracy and Public Space in New York and London* (New York: Columbia University Press, 2008), 65–76.

7 "Another Mad Dog," *New-York Telescope*, August 21, 1830; "The Great Dog War of 1848," *New York Herald*, July 16, 1848; "Incidents Connected with the Great Dog War of 1848," *New York Herald*, July 29, 1848; "Police," *BDE*, August 16, 1842; Keller, *Triumph of Order*, 151–67; Timothy J. Gilfoyle, "Street Rats and Gutter-Snipes: Child Pickpockets and Street Culture in New York City, 1850–1900," *Journal of Social History* 37, no. 4 (2004): 853–82.

8 Préfecture de police, "Instructions concernant la destruction des chiens errans [*sic*]," December 5,1842, DB 226, APP; É. A. Duchesne, *Répertoire des plantes utiles et des plantes vénéneuses du globe* (Paris: Jules Renouard, 1836), 34; Préfecture de police, "Exécution de l'ordonnance de police concernant les chiens," July 29, 1838, DB 226, APP; Préfecture de police, "Envoi des ordonnance de police concernant les chiens et les boules-dogues: Instructions," July 7, 1849, DB 229, APP; Préfecture de police, "Rapport," June 22, 1843, DA 44, APP; Paul Glassacki to Ministère de l'Intérieur, May 4, 1853, DA 44, APP; George Fleming, *Rabies and Hydrophobia: Their History, Nature, Causes, Symptoms, and Prevention* (London: Chapman and Hall, 1872), 359; Yaron Finkelstein et al., "Colchicine Poisoning: The Dark Side of an Ancient Drug," *Clinical Toxicology* 48, no. 5 (2010): 407–11.

9 Mairie de Passy, 16e arrondissement, to Préfet de police, June 16, 1870, DA 44, APP; Richard S. Hopkins, "*Sauvons le Luxembourg*: Urban Greenspace as Private

Domain and Public Battleground, 1865–1867," *Journal of Urban History* 37, no. 1 (2011): 43–58.

10 *Plaidoyer prononcé par un chien de procureur en faveur des chiens de Paris, accusés d'avoir erré sans être muselés* (Paris: Chez les libraires du Palais-Royal, 1825), 7–8; *Lettre d'un chien de Paris à un de ses amis de province sur les massacres de la rue Guénégaud* (Paris: Chez les libraires du Palais-Royal, 1825); Richard D. E. Burton, *Blood in the City: Violence and Revelation in Paris, 1789–1945* (Ithaca, NY: Cornell University Press, 2001).

11 Peter Atkins, "The Urban Blood and Guts Economy," in *Animal Cities: Beastly Urban Histories*, ed. Peter Atkins (Farnham: Ashgate, 2012), 77–106; Alexandre-Jean-Baptiste Parent-Duchâtelet, *Hygiène publique, ou mémoire sur les questions les plus importantes de l'hygiène appliqués aux professions et aux travaux d'utilité publique* (Paris: J.-B. Baillière, 1836), 2:242, 347–48; Sabine Barles, "Undesirable Nature: Animals, Resources and Urban Nuisance," in Atkins, *Animal Cities*, 173–88; Sabine Barles, *L'invention des déchats urbains: France 1790–1970* (Seyssel: Champ Vallon, 2005). On public hygiene norms, see Jean-Baptiste Fressoz, *L'apocalypse joyeuse: Une histoire du risque technologique* (Paris: Seuil, 2012), 158–59.

12 "Chiens," n.d., DB 229, APP; Préfet de police, "Instruction concernant les chiens, instruction des boules dogues," August 19, 1840, DB 229, APP; Préfecture de police, "Exécution de l'ordre de police concernant les chiens et les boules-dogues," June 9, 1852, DB 229, APP; Jonathan Strauss, *Human Remains: Medicine, Death and Desire in Nineteenth-Century Paris* (New York: Fordham University Press, 2012); David Harvey, *Paris: Capital of Modernity* (London: Routledge, 2003).

13 Quotation is from "Chien poursuivi comme enragé," *BSPA* 9 (1863): 463; Éric Pierre, "La souffrance des animaux dans les discours des protecteurs français au XIXe siècle," *Études rurales* 147–48 (1998): 81–97; Damien Baldin, *Histoire des animaux domestiques, XIXe–XXe siècle* (Paris: Seuil, 2014), 232–37; "Rapport sur la fourrière," *BSPA* 10 (1864): 106.

14 Paul Friedland, *Seeing Justice Done: The Age of Spectacular Capital Punishment in France* (Oxford: Oxford University Press, 2012), 239–40; news article "La Société protectrice des animaux prend . . . ," *Le Figaro* (Paris), October 6, 1875, 2, newspaper clipping in DB 226, APP.

15 Préfecture de police, "Cahier des charges pour le service de l'abatage des chiens à la fourrière et l'enlèvement des dépouilles," March 31, 1877, DA 21, APP; "Paris: Une exécution à la fourrière de la préfrecture de police," n.d., carton 9, Serie iconographique, APP; Damien Baldin, "De l'horreur du sang à l'insoutenable souffrance animale: Élaboration sociale des régimes de sensibilité à la mise à mort des animaux, 19e–20e siècles," *Vingtième Siècle* 123 (2014): 59; A. Cartaz, "L'exécution des chiens," *La nature*, no. 625, May 25, 1885, 385–86.

16 "Dog Assassination: The New York Method," *Lowell (MA) Daily Citizen and News*, June 15, 1859; "An Hour at the Dog-Pound," *New York Daily Times*, August 5, 1856; Jason Urbanus, "New York City's Dirtiest Beach," *Archaeology* 71, no. 5 (2018): 56–63; "Drowning the Dogs," *NYT*, July 8, 1877.

17 "Destroying the Dogs," *NYT*, July 6, 1877; "Report of the Business of the Dog Pound for the Season Ending September 30th 1885," Grace box 1325, folder D18-02,

roll 2, New York City Municipal Archives; "The Dog Pound," *Harper's Weekly*, July 15, 1882; "A Dog-Pound," *Youth's Companion*, July 4, 1872; "The New York Dog-Pound," *(Cleveland) Ohio Farmer*, September 28, 1867.

18 "Cruelty to Stray Dogs," *NYT*, July 6, 1884; C. N., "Les chiens de New-York," *Revue britannique* 6 (1873): 228.

19 "Where the Dogs Go To," *Frank Leslie's Illustrated Newspaper*, August 14, 1858.

20 M. B. McMullan, "The Day the Dogs Died in London," *London Journal* 23, no. 1 (1998): 39; Isabel Burton, "The Dog Question: To the Editor," *Times* (London), October 29, 1886; "'A Dog's Life'—And Death," *Fun*, December 7, 1867.

21 Gwynfryn [pseud.], *Friends in Fur and Feathers* (London: Bell and Daldy, 1869), 73; Diana Donald, *Women against Cruelty: Protection of Animals in Nineteenth-Century Britain* (Manchester: Manchester University Press, 2020), 136–58; Frederick S. Milton, "Taking the Pledge: A Study of Children's Societies for the Prevention of Cruelty to Birds and Animals in Britain, c. 1870–1914" (PhD diss., Newcastle University, 2009), https://theses.ncl.ac.uk/jspui/handle/10443/1583.

22 Ward Richardson quoted in Basil Tozer, "The Dogs' Home, Battersea," *English Illustrated Magazine*, August 1895; "'A Dog's Life'"; B. J., "To the Editor," *Daily Telegraph* (London), October 9, 1868.

23 "Multiple News Items," *Standard* (London), September 21, 1868; "Mr. Charles Reade on Dogs' Homes," *NYT*, July 3, 1875.

24 William Youatt, *The Dog* (London: Charles Knight, 1845), 107–8. Youatt's book was published in the United States as *The Dogs* (Philadelphia: Blanchard and Lea, 1857). His ideas, along with those of other British dog experts, reached French readers in *Le chien: Déscription des races, croisement, élevage, dressage, maladies et leur traitement d'après Stonehenge, Youatt, Mayhew, Bouley, Hamilton, Smith etc*, 2nd ed. (Paris: J. Rothschild, 1884).

25 Henri Bouley, *Hydrophobia: Means of Avoiding Its Perils and Preventing Its Spread as Discussed at One of the Scientific Soirees of the Sorbonne*, trans. Alexandre Liautard (New York: Harper and Brothers, 1874 [1870]), 11, 13, 26; Fleming, *Rabies and Hydrophobia*, 196.

26 Charles Darwin, *On the Origin of Species by Means of Natural Selection*, ed. Joseph Carroll (Ontario: Broadview Press, 2003), 229–30; Charles Darwin, *The Works of Charles Darwin*, ed. Paul H. Barrett and R. B. Freeman, vol. 23, *The Expression of the Emotions in Man and Animals*, ed. Francis Darwin (New York: New York University Press, 1989), 41–42, 87–90; Emma Townshend, *Darwin's Dogs: How Darwin's Pets Helped Form a World-Changing Theory of Evolution* (London: Frances Lincoln, 2009). On the reception of *Expression*, see Thomas Dixon, *From Passions to Emotions: The Creation of a Secular Psychological Category* (Cambridge: Cambridge University Press, 2003), 165–68; Angelique Richardson, ed., *After Darwin: Animals, Emotions and the Mind* (Amsterdam: Rodopi, 2013).

27 Peter J. Bowler, *The Eclipse of Darwinism: Anti-Darwinian Evolution Theories in the Decades around 1900* (Baltimore: Johns Hopkins University Press, 1983); Rob Preece, *Brute Souls, Happy Beasts, and Evolution: The Historical Status of Animals* (Vancouver: University of British Columbia Press, 2005); 331–58; Philip Howell, *At Home and Astray: The Domestic Dog in Victorian Britain* (Charlottesville: University of Virginia Press, 2015), 102–24; Jed Meyer, "The Expression of the Emotions in Man and Laboratory Animals," *Victorian Studies* 50, no. 3 (2008):

399–417; Brown, *Our Lesser Brethren*, 52–56; Albert Larbalétrier, *Manuel pratique de l'amateur de chiens* (Paris: Garnier frères, 1907); Jennifer Mason, *Civilized Creatures: Urban Animals, Sentimental Culture, and American Literature* (Baltimore: Johns Hopkins University Press, 2005), 19; E. T. Brewster, "Studying the Animal Mind in Laboratories," *McClure's Magazine*, August 1909, 387.

28 "Our Object," *Animal World*, October 1, 1869. See also James Turner, *Reckoning with the Beast: Animals, Pain and Humanity in the Victorian Mind* (Baltimore: Johns Hopkins University Press, 1980); Janet M. Davis, *Gospel of Kindness: Animal Welfare and the Making of Modern America* (New York: Oxford University Press, 2016), 16; Frances Power Cobbe, "The Education of the Emotions," *Fortnightly Review* 43 (1888): 223–36.

29 Maria Deraismes, *Discours contre la vivisection* (Paris: Auguste Ghio/Ligue populaire contre l'abus de la vivisection, 1884), 24–25; *Protégeons les animaux, conseils pratiques, droits et devoirs: II Chiens et chats* (Paris: Société protectrice des animaux, 1927), 4.

30 Anna Kingsford, "The Uselessness of Vivisection," *Nineteenth Century* 11 (1882): 176–77; Richard D. French, *Antivivisection and Medical Science in Victorian Society* (Princeton, NJ: Princeton University Press 1975), 19, 38–48; Turner, *Reckoning with the Beast,* 92; J. Burdon Sanderson, ed., *Handbook for the Physiological Laboratory Containing an Exposition of the Fundamental Facts of the Science, with Explicit Directions for Their Demonstration* (Philadelphia: P. Blakiston, 1884 [1873]), 95, 331, 405, 476–77.

31 *Report of the Royal Commission on the Practice of Subjecting Live Animals to Experiments for Scientific Purposes, with Minutes of Evidence and Appendix* (London: HMSO, 1876).

32 Clare Midgley, Alison Twells, and Julie Carlier, eds., *Women in Transnational History: Connect the Local and the Global* (Abingdon: Routledge, 2016); J. Keri Cronin, *Art for Animals: Visual Culture and Animal Advocacy 1870–1914* (University Park: Pennsylvania State University Press, 2018); Leila J. Rupp, "Constructing Internationalism: The Case of Transnational Women's Organizations, 1888–1945," *American Historical Review* 99, no. 5 (1994): 1571–600; Frances Power Cobbe and Benjamin Bryan, *Vivisection in America* (London: Swan, Sonnenschein; Victoria Street Society, 1889), 23, 31–32; Diane L. Beers, *For the Prevention of Cruelty: The History and Legacy of Animal Rights Activism in the United States* (Athens, OH: Swallow Press of Ohio University Press, 2006), 123; Craig Buettinger, "Women and Antivivisection in Late Nineteenth-Century America," *Journal of Social History* 30, no. 4 (1997): 863.

33 Rob Boddice, "Vivisecting Major: A Victorian Gentleman Scientist Defends Animal Experimentation, 1876–1885," *Isis* 102, no. 2 (2011): 215–37; Frances Power Cobbe, "The Consciousness of Dogs," *Quarterly Review* 133 (1872): 429; Meyer, "The Expression of the Emotions," 400–401; George Hoggan, "Vivisection," *Fraser's Magazine* vol. 11, 1879, 522–23.

34 Caroline Earle White, "Is Vivisection Morally Justifiable?," n.d., FA142, box 2, Rockefeller University Records, Special Events and Activities, Anti-Vivisection Activities, Rockefeller Archive Center; Susan J. Pearson, *The Rights of the Defenseless: Protecting Animals and Children in Gilded Age America* (Chicago: University of Chicago Press, 2011); Halttunen, "Humanitarianism," 330; Susan Hamilton,

"Reading and the Popular Critique of Science in the Victorian Press: Frances Power Cobbe's Writing for the Victoria Street Society,' *Victorian Review* 36, no. 2 (2010): 72, 77–78.

35 "Vivisection and Anaesthetics," *British Medical Journal* 1, no. 753 (June 5, 1875): 749; Frédéric Borel, *Sur le vif: Considerations sur la vivisection* (Paris: Sandoz et Thuillier, 1883), 8; Philanthropos [Francis Heatherly?], *Physiological Cruelty, or Fact vs. Fancy: An Inquiry into the Vivisection Question* (New York: John Wiley and Sons, 1883), 19; Stephanie J. Snow, "Surgery and Anaesthesia: Revolutions in Practice," in *The Palgrave Handbook of the History of Surgery*, ed. Thomas Schlich (London: Palgrave Macmillan, 2018), 195–214; Rob Boddice, *The Science of Sympathy: Morality, Evolution and Victorian Civilization* (Urbana: University of Illinois Press, 2016).

36 "The Dog Ordinance," *BDE*, May 11, 1863; *Committee to Prevent the Spreading of Canine Madness, Report, Minutes of Evidence*, House of Commons, Parliamentary Papers 651, 1830, 10–11, 16, 21; Thomas Dolan, *The Nature and Treatment of Rabies or Hydrophobia Being the Report of the Special Commission Appointed by the Medical Press and Circular* (London: Baillière, Tindall and Cox, 1878), 202; Pemberton and Worboys, *Rabies in Britain*, 91, 94–95.

37 Camille Leblanc, *Statistique des maladies contagieuses observées dans le département de la Seine, pendant les années 1876, 1877, 1878 et 1879* (Paris: Vves Renou, Maulde et Cock, 1880) 9, 14; Camille Leblanc, *Statistique des maladies contagieuses observées dans le département de la Seine, pendant les années 1880 et 1881* (Paris: Vves Renou, Maulde et Cock, 1882), 6; *Journal officiel de la République française*, 11th year, no. 181 (July 4, 1879), 6091, https://gallica.bnf.fr/ark:/12148/bpt6k6386979g/f2.item#, 6091; Préfet de police, "Mesures préventives contre la rage," July 5, 1879, DB 229, APP.

38 Baldin, "De l'horreur du sang," 52–86; "The Gallows Torture," *Frank Leslie's Illustrated Newspaper*, April 30, 1870. The search for "humane" and "efficient" killing echoed developments in slaughterhouses. Paula Young Lee, ed., *Meat, Modernity, and the Rise of the Slaughterhouse* (Lebanon: University of New Hampshire Press, 2008).

39 Friedland, *Seeing Justice Done*, 240; Benjamin Ward Richardson, *On Local Anaesthesia or Ether Spray, as a Means for the Entire Extinction of Pain in Operations on the Inferior Animals* (London: Churchill, 1867); Tozer, "The Dogs' Home, Battersea"; Susan Hamilton, "Dogs' Homes and Lethal Chambers, or, What Was It Like to be a Battersea Dog?," in *Animals in Victorian Literature and Culture*, ed. L. W. Mazzeno and R. D. Morrison (Basingstoke: Palgrave, 2017), 83–105; Ouida [Marie Louise de la Ramée], "Cure for Rabies: Letters to the Editor," *Times* (London), November 4, 1886.

40 Colam quoted in "The Dogs' Home," *Sun* (New York), June 2, 1889; Onslow, "Dogs in Disgrace," *National Review* (London) 10, no. 57, November 1887.

41 "La fourrière," *La lanterne*, March 28, 1888, 2 ("less barbarous" and "terrible agony"); Cartaz, "L'exécution des chiens," 385–86 ("any suffering"); Emmanuel Taïeb, "La fabrique d'un intolérable: exécutions publiques et police des sensibilités," *Vingtième siècle* 123 (2014): 154.

42 Conseil d'hygiène publique et de salubrité du département de la Seine, *Rapport sur les maladies contagieuses des animaux observées en 1892 dans le département de*

la Seine (Paris: Imprimerie Chaix, 1893), 87, 90; Adrienne Neyrat, "À la fourrière," *L'ami des bêtes*, September 1899, 80.

43 Neyrat, "À la fourrière," 78–79; "Le Cynoctone," *L'assistance aux animaux*, March 1903, 2–6, 11 ("sleep from weariness"); "La fourrière," [1901?], newspaper clipping in DB 226, APP ("without pointless suffering"). See also Baldin, *Histoire des animaux domestiques*, 251–52; E. Nocard, "Modifications à apporter à la fourrière," Conseil d'hygiène publique, séance du 9 novembre 1900, 518–20, DB 226, APP.

44 Hébrard quoted in "À la fourrière," *Le matin* (Paris), July 18, 1903. According to Émile Massard, police agents wore gloves made from the skins of stray dogs. "Proposition relative à la répression des mauvais traitements infligés aux animaux et à la modification du règlement de la fourrière," May 6, 1910, 1215, DB 226, APP. From 1909, the pound collected the dog corpses from the streets and sold them to a renderer. "Rapport [illegible], budget de 1914," 18, 19, DB 226, APP.

45 "Lethal Chamber Presented by the 'Herald' Tried at the Fourrière Yesterday," *New York Herald* (European edition), December 18, 1904; Pierre, "La souffrance des animaux," 97; "Séance mensuelle du 15 juin 1916," *BSPA*, April–June 1916, 145.

46 G. Cerbelaud, "La rage à Paris et dans le département de la Seine," *Le Monde illustré*, July 20, 1912; Ernest Coyecque, "Les chiens devant le Conseil d'hygiène," *BSPA*, April–June 1916, 222; Pierre, "La souffrance des animaux," 93; Catherine Pinguet, *Les chiens d'Istanbul: Des rapports entre l'homme et l'animal de l'antiquité à nos jours* (Saint-Pourçain-sur-Sioule: Bleu Autour, 2008).

47 "The Persecuted Dogs," *NYT*, June 22, 1874; Benjamin Brady, "The Politics of the Pound: Controlling Loose Dogs in Nineteenth-Century New York City," *Jefferson Journal of Science and Culture* 2 (2012): 14; "A Disgusting Butchery," *NYT*, June 28, 1874; "Correspondence," *Yankton (SD) Press and Union and Dakotaian*, July 9, 1874.

48 Henry Bergh to Abram Hewitt, March 30, 1888, Hewitt box 1340, folder 036, New York City Municipal Archives; Bernard Unti, "The Quality of Mercy: Organized Animal Protection in the United States, 1866–1930" (PhD diss., American University, 2002), http://animalstudiesrepository.org/acwp_awap/40, 489; Jürgen Martschukat, "'The Art of Killing by Electricity': The Sublime and the Electric Chair," *Journal of American History* 89, no. 3 (2002): 900–921.

49 Chief Inspector Cyrus Edson to President James C. Bayles, Department of Health, December 13, 1888, Hewitt box 1340, folder 036, New York City Municipal Archives; "Killing Dogs Scientifically," *NYT*, December 25, 1888; "Where Dogs Are Doomed," *NYT*, July 25, 1889; Peter C. Baldwin, "In the Heart of Darkness: Blackouts and the Social Geography of Lighting in the Gaslight Era," *Journal of Urban History* 30, no. 5 (2004): 749–68; Jessica Wang, *Mad Dogs and Other New Yorkers: Rabies, Medicine, and Society in an American Metropolis, 1840–1920* (Baltimore: Johns Hopkins University Press, 2019), 77.

50 "The Dog Pound," *Harper's Weekly*, April 21, 1894.

51 Quotations are from Marie G., "Le bon refuge" and "Le refuge du boulevard Sérurier jugé par une dame sociétaire," both in *BSPA*, first semester 1915, 67–68. See also "Lethal Chamber Presented by the 'Herald'"; Baldin, *Histoire des animaux domestiques*, 161–62; Préfecture de police, "Ordonnance concernant les refuges de chiens et de chats dans le département de la Seine," July 26, 1913, DB 230, APP; Charles Chenivesse, "Le refuge pour chiens," *L'ami des chiens*, July

1899; "Une clinique de bêtes," *La patrie* (Paris), February 16, [1903?], press clipping in DB 232, APP; Traïni, *The Animal Rights Struggle*, 114–16.

52 "Séance mensuelle du 15 mars 1917," *BSPA*, January–March 1917, 37; Chris Pearson, "'Four-Legged *Poilus*': French Army Dogs, Emotional Practices and the Creation of Militarized Human-Dog Bonds, 1871–1918," *Journal of Social History* 52, no. 3 (2019): 731–60.

53 "History," *ASPCA: Fiftieth Annual Report* (1915), 58; "Pathos at Shelter," *OAF*, November 1934.

54 John P. Haines, "Address of the President," *ASPCA: Thirtieth Annual Report* (1896), 6–7; Scott Anthony Miltenberger, "Promiscuously Mixed Together: New Yorkers and Domestic Animals in the Nineteenth-Century" (PhD diss., University of California, Davis, 2006), 213, ProQuest Dissertations Publishing, 3250836.

55 Read quoted in H. W. L., "New York's Dog Shelter," *Forest and Stream*, July 14, 1894; "Fifty Dog Catchers at Work This Week," *NYT*, May 25, 1908. It is unclear whether these figures include the Brooklyn shelter, which between 1887 and 1896 killed 158,971 small animals. "Brooklyn Department," *ASPCA: Thirty-First Annual Report* (1897), 22.

56 Alfred Wagstaff, "Address of the President," in *ASPCA: Forty-Fifth Annual Report* (1910), 5–6; Freel quoted in "Fifty Dog Catchers."

57 *ASPCA: Fiftieth Annual Report* (1915), n.p.; "Report of the General Manager," *The ASPCA: Fifty-Eighth Report* (1923), 8.

58 "Dreadful News for the Animals," *NYT*, May 6, 1907; Davis, *Gospel of Kindness*, 95; Elizabeth Banks, "A Home Where the Despised Yellow Dog Is Welcome," *NYT*, March 18, 1906.

59 "Too Many Dogs," *NYT*, July 19, 1907; "Responsibility for Stray Dogs," *NYT*, July 21, 1907; "Editorial: The 'Bide-a-Wee Home' Experiment," *OAF*, August 1904, 535–37.

60 "Bide-a-Wee Dogs Ordered Turned Out," *NYT*, June 18, 1909; "Muzzles for Dog Owners," *NYT*, July 11, 1909.

61 "Stray Pets Doomed to Die," *People* (London), April 22, 1923, clipping in A A/FWA/C/D256/2, LMA; Arthur Goodiff to Captain S. Herbert M.P., "North London Dogs Home," December 5, 1933, 45/18462, NA. Our Dumb Friends League became the Blue Cross in 1958.

62 Note in 40/Dogs/4128, MEPO 2/4038, NA; Charles R. Johns, Secretary, National Canine Defence League, to Commissioner of Police, December 29, 1930, MEPO 2/4038, NA; F. T. G. Hobday to Commissioner of Police, October 16, 1930, MEPO 2/4038, NA; Captain Fairholme, Chief Secretary, Royal Society for the Prevention of Cruelty to Animals, to Norman Kendal, Metropolitan Police Office, September 25, 1930, MEPO 2/4038, NA.

63 National Canine Defence League, Annual Report, 1925, 14–16, A/FWA/C/D268/1, LMA; Veronica Bruce, "What to Do with the Submerged Tenth? The Social Question of Poverty in Late 19th Century England," *The Proceedings of the South Carolina Historical Association* (1996), 16–24.

64 "The Dogs' Home Battersea," *London Journal*, April 22, 1911, 602.

65 Kennedy quoted in "Problem of London's Stray Dogs," *Irish Times* (Dublin), January 5, 1928; *Humane and Inhumane Methods of Destroying Animals: Problems of Efficient Lethalisation* (London: Animal Defence Society, n.d.), 44. On the links

between care and coercion, see Eva Giraud and Gregory Hollin, "Care, Laboratory Beagles and Affective Utopia," *Theory, Culture and Society* 33, no. 4 (2016): 27–49.

66 *Humane and Inhumane Methods of Destroying Animals,* 10, 23.

67 *Humane and Inhumane Methods of Destroying Animals,* 24, 31; Hilda Kean, *The Great Cat and Dog Massacre: The Real Story of World War II's Unknown Tragedy* (Chicago: University of Chicago Press, 2017), 54.

68 *Humane and Inhumane Methods of Destroying Animals,* 24, 25; Rupp, "Constructing Internationalism."

69 "Contre l'élevage," *BSPA*, April–June 1916, 156; "Birth Control of Dogs Urged to Lessen London's Canines," *NYT*, January 29, 1928; National Canine Defence League, leaflet no. 434, "Mongrel Puppies," n.d., A/FWA/C/D268/1, LMA; National Canine Defence League, leaflet no. 417, "Destroying Dogs," n.d., A/FWA/C/D268/1, LMA.

70 "To Kill a Dog or Cat Humanely," in *ASPCA: Forty-Ninth Annual Report* (1914), 74. See also "To Policemen or Others," *Humane Society of New York: Eleventh Annual Report*, 1915, 30; Unti, "The Quality of Mercy," 486; Cornelius F. Cahalane, *Police Practice and Procedure* (New York: E. P. Dutton, 1914), 98.

71 H. E. G. Lewis, Secretary, Our Dumb Friends League, to S. W. Richards, New Scotland Yard, September 13, 1938, MEPO 2/4038, NA; note in 40/Dogs/4128, MEPO 2/4038, NA.

Chapter Four

1 "Max n'est pas psychologue," *Le matin* (Paris), December 30, 1907.

2 Chris Pearson, "Canines and Contraband: Dogs, Nonhuman Agency and the Making of the Franco-Belgian Border during the French Third Republic," *Journal of Historical Geography* 54 (October 2016): 50–62; Chris Pearson, "'Four-Legged *Poilus*': French Army Dogs, Emotional Practices and the Creation of Militarized Human-Dog Bonds, 1871–1918," *Journal of Social History* 52, no. 3 (2019): 731–60.

3 "Our Fun-Done Letter," *Fun*, August 15, 1868.

4 Neil Pemberton and Michael Worboys, *Rabies in Britain: Dogs, Disease and Culture, 1830–2000* (Basingstoke: Palgrave Macmillan, 2013 [2007]), 46; Andrew A. Robichaud, *Animal City: The Domestication of America* (Cambridge, MA: Harvard University Press, 2019), 166–70; Neil Pemberton, "Cocreating Guide Dog Partnerships: Dog Training and Interdependence in 1930s America," *Medical Humanities* 45, no. 1 (2019): 92–101; His-Huey Liang, *The Rise of the Modern Police and the European State System from Metternich to the Second World War* (Cambridge: Cambridge University Press, 2002 [1992]), 4.

5 Quentin Deluermoz, "Circulations et élaborations d'un mode d'action policier: La police en tenue à Paris, d'une police 'londonienne' au 'modèle parisien' (1850–1914)," *Revue d'histoire des sciences humaines* 19 (2008): 75–90; Eric H. Monkkonen, *Police in Urban America, 1860–1920* (Cambridge: Cambridge University Press, 1981), 37–42.

6 Thomas Almeroth-Williams, *City of Beasts: How Animals Shaped Georgian London* (Manchester: Manchester University Press, 2019), 187–211.

7 Alejandro Gordilla-García, "The Challenge of Instinctive Behaviour and Darwin's Theory of Evolution," *Endeavour* 40, no. 1 (2016): 49; René Descartes, *"Discourse on Method" and "The Meditations,"* trans. F. E. Sutcliffe (London: Penguin, 1968); Erica Fudge, *Brutal Reasoning: Animals, Rationality, and Humanity in Early Modern England* (Ithaca, NY: Cornell University Press, 2006); Paul White, "Becoming an Animal: Darwin and the Evolution of Sympathy," in *After Darwin: Animals, Emotions and Mind*, ed. Angelique Richardson (Amsterdam: Rodopi, 2013), 123.

8 Rob Boddice, "The Historical Animal Mind: 'Sagacity' in Nineteenth Century Britain," in *Experiencing Animal Minds: An Anthology of Animal-Human Encounters*, ed. Julie A. Smith and Robert W. Mitchell (New York: Columbia University Press, 2013), 65–78; Justyna Włodarczyk, *Genealogy of Obedience: Reading North American Pet Dog Training Literature, 1850s–2000s* (Leiden: Brill, 2018), 36–38.

9 Ernest Laut, "Le pays des apaches," *Le petit journal illustré* (Paris), September 22, 1907; Ernest Laut, "Police et criminalité," *Le petit journal illustré* (Paris), October 20, 1907; Dominique Kalifa, *Crime et culture au XIXe siècle* (Paris: Perrin, 2005), 47, 59, 63, 258; Robert A. Nye, *Crime, Madness and Politics in Modern France: The Medical Concept of National Decline* (Princeton, NJ: Princeton University Press, 1984), 199–200; Theodore A. Bingham, "Foreign Criminals in New York," *North American Review* 188, no. 634 (September 1908): 390.

10 Andrew August, "'A Horrible Looking Woman': Female Violence in Late-Victorian East London," *Journal of British Studies* 54, no. 4 (2015): 844–68; Lynda Nead, *Victorian Babylon: People, Streets and Images in Nineteenth-Century London* (New Haven, CT: Yale University Press, 2000), 71, 156–57; Chris Willis, "From Voyeurism to Feminism: Victorian and Edwardian London's Streetfighting Slum Viragoes," *Victorian Review* 29, no. 1 (2003): 70–86; Drew Gray, "Gang Crime and Media in Late Nineteenth-Century London: The Regent's Park Murder of 1888," *Cultural and Social History* 10, no. 4 (2013): 559–75; Heather Shore, *London's Criminal Underworlds, c.1720–c.1930: A Social and Cultural History* (Basingstoke: Palgrave MacMillan, 2015), 141–66.

11 Bingham, "Foreign Criminals," 384, 387; Gil Ribek, "'The Jew Usually Left Those Crimes to Esau': The Jewish Responses to Accusations about Jewish Criminality in New York 1908–1913," *AJS Review* 38, no. 1 (2014): 1–28. Out of a population of 1,515,301 in 1890, 43% of New Yorkers had been born abroad. Keith Gandel, *The Virtues of the Vicious: Jacob Riis, Stephen Crane, and the Spectacle of the Slum* (New York: Oxford University Press, 1997), 8–11. See also Paul Boyer, *Urban Masses and Moral Order in America 1820–1920* (Cambridge, MA: Harvard University Press, 1978), 123–31.

12 Gandel, *Virtues of the Vicious*, 8, 91–97; Jacob A. Riis, *How the Other Half Lives: Studies Among the Tenements of New York*, ed. Sam Bass Warner Jr. (New York: Charles Scribner's Sons, 1890), 264–66; Bonnie Yochelson and Daniel Czitrom, *Rediscovering Jacob Riis: Exposure Journalism and Photography in Turn-of-the-Century New York* (Chicago: University of Chicago Press, 2014 [2007]), 109–15.

13 John C. Waller, "Ideas of Heredity, Reproduction and Eugenics in Britain, 1800–1875," *Studies in History and Philosophy of Biological and Biomedical Sciences* 32, no. 3 (2001): 462–63; Jan Verplaetse, "Prosper Despine's *Psychologie naturelle* and the Discovery of the Remorseless Criminal in Nineteenth-Century France,"

History of Psychiatry 13, no. 2 (2002): 153–75; William Lauder Lindsay, *Mind in the Lower Animals in Health and Disease* (London: Kegan Paul, 1879), 2:176, 18, 150, 160; Emma J. Teng, "'A Problem for Which There Is No Solution': Eurasians and the Specter of Degeneration in New York's Chinatown," *Journal of Asian American Studies* 15, no. 3 (2012): 277.

14 Charles Darwin, *On the Origin of Species by Means of Natural Selection*, ed. Joseph Carroll (Ontario: Broadview Press, 2003), 225; Colin G. Beer, "Darwin, Instinct, and Ethology," *Journal of the History of Behavioral Sciences* 19, no. 1 (1983): 73; Gordilla-García, "The Challenge of Instinctive Behaviour," 50; Robert J. Richards, "Darwin on Mind, Morals and Emotions," in *The Cambridge Companion to Darwin*, ed. Jonathan Hodge and Gregory Radick, 2nd ed. (Cambridge: Cambridge University Press, 2009), 99; Charles Darwin, *The Descent of Man and Selection in Relation to Sex,* rev. ed. (New York: Merrill and Baker, 1874 [1871]), 64, 105, 111–12.

15 Cesare Lombroso, *Criminal Man*, trans. Mary Gibson and Nicole Hahn Rafter (Durham, NC: Duke University Press, 2006), 48, 63–65, 68; Greta Olson, *Criminals as Animals from Shakespeare to Lombroso* (Berlin: De Gruyter, 2013), 275–302; Piers Beirne, "The Use and Abuse of Animals in Criminology: A Brief History and Current Review," *Social Justice* 22, no. 1 (1995): 5–31.

16 Cesare Lombroso, *Criminal Man according to the Classification of Cesare Lombroso* (New York: G. P. Putman's Sons, 1911), 135, 136, 270.

17 Frances A. Kellor, "Criminal Sociology: The American vs. the Latin School," *Arena* 23, no. 3 (March 1900): 303; Martine Kaluszynski, "The International Congresses of Criminal Anthropology: Shaping the French and International Criminological Movement, 1886–1914," in *Criminals and Their Scientists: The History of Criminology in International Perspective*, ed. Peter Becker and Richard F. Wetzell (New York: Cambridge University Press, 2006), 301–16; Nicole Rafter, "Lombroso's Reception in the United States," in *The Eternal Recurrence of Crime and Control*, ed. David Downes, Dick Hobbs, and Tim Newburn (Oxford: Oxford University Press, 2010), 1–15; Peter D'Agostino, "Craniums, Criminals and the 'Cursed Race': Italian Anthropology in American Racial Thought, 1861–1924," *Comparative Studies in Society and History* 44, no. 2 (2002): 319–43.

18 Alexandre Lacassagne and Étienne Martin, "Anthropologie criminelle," *L'année psychologique* 11 (1904): 447; Marc Renneville, "La reception de Lombroso en France," in *Histoire de la criminologie française*, ed. Laurent Mucchielli (Paris: L'Harmattan, 1994), 107–35; Piers Beirne, *Inventing Criminology: Essays on the Rise of "Homo Criminalis"* (Albany: State University of New York Press, 1993), 147–64; Dominique Guillo, "Bertillon, l'anthropologie criminelle et l'histoire naturelle: Des résponses au brouillage des identités," *Crime, Histoire et Sociétés/ Crime, History and Societies* 12, no. 1 (2008): 97–117; Havelock Ellis, *The Criminal* (London: Walter Scott, 1890), 312.

19 Ellis, *The Criminal*, 91; Du Cane quoted in Neil Davie, "A 'Criminal Type' in All but Name: British Prison Medical Officers and the 'Anthropological' Approach to the Study of Crime (c. 1865–1895)," *Victorian Review* 29, no. 1 (2003): 8; T. S. Clouston, "The Developmental Aspects of Criminal Anthropology," *Journal of the Anthropological Institute of Great Britain and Ireland* 23 (1894): 215–25; Mathew Thomson, *Psychological Subjects: Identity, Culture and Health in Twentieth-Century Britain* (Oxford: Oxford University Press, 2006), 70; Gillian Swanson,

"Collectivity, Human Fulfilment and the 'Force of Life': Wilfred Trotter's Concept of the Herd Instinct in Early 20th-Century Britain," *History of Human Sciences* 27, no. 1 (2014): 21–50.

20 Robert J. Richards, *Darwin and the Emergence of Evolutionary Theories of Mind and Behavior* (Chicago: University of Chicago Press, 1987), 31, 105–10; Darwin, *The Descent of Man*, 64–65.

21 George J. Romanes, *Animal Intelligence* (London: Kegan Paul, Trench, 1882), 5, 11–17. See also Robert Boakes, *From Darwinism to Behaviourism: Psychology and the Minds of Animals* (Cambridge: Cambridge University Press, 1984), 24–27; Federico Morganti, "Intelligence as the Plasticity of Instinct: George J. Romanes and Darwin's Earthworms," *Theoretical Biology Forum* 104, no. 2 (2011): 30–31.

22 Idstone [Thomas Pearce], "Mongrels," *Gentleman's Magazine*, December 1870, 35–36; Harriet Anne de Salis, *Dogs: A Manual for Amateurs* (London: Longmans, Green, 1893), 1–2.

23 "Anecdotes of Dogs," *Harper's Weekly*, August 16, 1873. The anecdotes originally appeared in the *London Quarterly Review*.

24 Sofie Lachapelle and Jenna Healey, "On Hans, Zou and Others: Wonder Animals and the Question of Animal Intelligence in Early Twentieth-Century France," *Studies in History and Philosophy of Biological and Biomedical Sciences* 41, no. 1 (2010): 14, 16; *Notice historique sur la vie et les talens du savant chien Munito, par un ami des bêtes* (Paris: Cabinet d'illusions, n.d.); Charles Delattre, *Les animaux savants* (Limoges: E. Ardent, 1887); "Instinct ou intelligence," *Le matin* (Paris), March 23, 1903.

25 Pierre Hachet-Souplet, *De l'animal à l'enfant* (Paris: F. Alcan, 1913), 100–101; Pierre Hachet-Souplet, *Examen psychologique des animaux* (Paris: Schleicher frères, 1900), 78–87. On animal suicide, see Edmund Ramsden and Duncan Wilson, "The Suicidal Animal: Science and the Nature of Self-Destruction," *Past and Present* 224 (2014): 205–17; Włodarczyk, *Genealogy of Obedience*, 12.

26 Joseph Jastrow, "Fact and Fable in Animal Psychology," *Popular Science Monthly* 69, August 1906, 138–46; Burroughs quoted in Michael Pettit, "The Problem of Raccoon Intelligence in Behaviourist America," *British Journal for the History of Science* 43, no. 3 (2010): 406; Mason, *Civilized Creatures*, 166–67.

27 Georges Bohn, *La nouvelle psychologie animale* (Paris: Félix Alcan, 1911), 1. See also Henri Piéron, "Le problème des animaux pensants," *L'année psychologique* 20 (1913): 218–28; Marion Thomas, "Histoire de la psychologie animale: La question de l'intelligence animale en France et aux Etats-Unis au début du XXe siècle," *L'homme et la société* 167–69 (2009): 223–50.

28 Conwy Lloyd Morgan, *Animal Life and Intelligence* (London: Edward Arnold, 1890–91), 339–49, 365; Conwy Lloyd Morgan, *An Introduction to Comparative Psychology*, 2nd ed. (London: Walter Scott, 1903 [1894]), 53, 358 (the Canon quotation is from p. 53, italics in the original).

29 Edward E. Thorndike, *Animal Intelligence: An Experimental Study of the Associative Processes in Animals*, Psychological Review Series of Monograph Supplements, vol. 2, no. 4 (New York: Macmillan, 1956 [1898]), 44, 87, 98–100.

30 Petitt, "The Problem of Raccoon Intelligence."

31 "The Bloodhound: His Accuracy of Scent Tested in London," *BDE*, August 18, 1889; Neil Pemberton, "The Bloodhound's Nose Knows? Dogs and Detection

in Anglo-American Culture," *Endeavour* 37, no. 4 (2013): 201; Neil Pemberton, "Hounding Holmes: Arthur Conan Doyle, Bloodhounds and Sleuthing in the Late-Victorian Imagination," *Journal of Victorian Culture* 17, no. 4 (2012): 454–67; Emma Mason, "Dogs, Detectives and the Famous Sherlock Holmes," *International Journal of Cultural Studies* 11, no. 3 (2008): 289–300.

32 "Bitten by a Blood Hound," *Illustrated Police News,* December 16, 1876; "Savagely Attacked by a Bloodhound," *NYT*, April 11, 1884; "A Bloodhound on the Rampage," *NYT*, February 15, 1883; Gordon Stables, "Bloodhound as Detectives," *Manchester Times,* December 29, 1888.

33 Edwin Brough, "The Old English Bloodhound or Sleuthhound and His Capabilities as a Man-Hunter," *Times* (London), October 8, 1888; Tyler D. Parry and Charlton W. Yingling, "Slave Hounds and Abolition in the Americas," *Past and Present* 246, no. 1 (2020): 69–108.

34 Neil Pemberton, "Bloodhounds as Detectives: Dogs, Slum Stench and Late-Victorian Murder Investigation," *Cultural and Social History* 10, no. 1 (2013): 69–91; Knox quoted in "The Bloodhound as He Is: A Shattering of False Ideas about Him," *NYT*, July 1, 1906; Parry and Yingling, "Slave Hounds." On the American bourgeoisie's fascination with European aristocratic culture, see Sven Beckert, *The Monied Metropolis: New York City and the Consolidation of the American Bourgeoisie, 1850–1896* (Cambridge: Cambridge University Press, 1993), 258.

35 Leonhard Felix Fuld, "The Use of Police Dogs: A Summary," *Journal of the American Institute of Criminal Law and Criminology* 3 (1912): 124; Pemberton, "Hounding Holmes," 459. On smell and the production of social difference, see Mark M. Smith, *How Race Is Made: Slavery, Segregation, and the Senses* (Chapel Hill: University of North Carolina Press, 2006); William Tullett, "Grease and Sweat: Race and Smell in Eighteenth-Century English Culture," *Cultural and Social History* 13, no. 3 (2016): 307–22.

36 Nebraska lawyer quoted in Pemberton, "The Bloodhound's Nose Knows?," 208; Fuld, "The Use of Police Dogs," 126. But see also "Court Backs Bloodhounds," *NYT*, July 9, 1911.

37 "Police Bloodhounds to Track Criminals," *NYT*, August 31, 1907; Devery quoted in "What Dogs May Do as New York Detectives," *NYT*, September 8, 1907; "New York's Police Dogs and What They Can Do," *NYT*, January 19, 1908; "Detective Bloodhounds," *BDE*, July 23, 1911.

38 "Bloodhound Owns the Jail," *NYT*, June 27, 1908; *Los Angeles Times* quoted in Pemberton, "The Bloodhound's Nose Knows?," 207; "Mob Gets Negro on Vanderbilt Estate," *NYT*, August 20, 1907; Spencer D. C. Keralis, "Pet-Making and Mastery in the Slave's Friend," *American Periodicals* 22, no. 2 (2012): 121–38; Parry and Yingling, "Slave Hounds."

39 William G. Fitz-Gerald, "The Dog Police of European Cities," *Century*, October 1906, 824–25; Van Wesemael quoted in "What Dogs May Do as New York Detectives"; "Dogs as Policemen," *Daily Mail* (London), August 15, 1903. See also "Four-Footed Police," *Baltimore Afro-American*, February 3, 1906; J. E. Whitby, "Four-Footed Policemen," *Cosmopolitan Magazine* 38, September 1905, 515–18; J. W. G., "Use of Dogs for Police Purposes," *Journal of the American Institute of Criminal Law and Criminology* 2 (1911): 273–74.

40 "Emploi des chiens comme auxiliaires de la police à Pont-à-Mousson: Rapport

du commissaire de police," *Journal des commissaires de police*, April 1907, 116; Lalloué, *Méthode de dressage du chien de guerre, de police, de garde et de defense*, 4th ed. (Epinal: Chez l'auteur, 1918 [1907]), 9; Deluermoz, "Circulations et élaborations," 75–90; Kalifa, *Crime et culture*, 236.

41 Paul Villers, "Le chien, gardien de la société," in *Je sais tout: Encyclopédie mondiale illustrée*, vol. 2, July–December 1907, 362. See also "Mémoire sur la brigade canine: Projet de restructuration de la compagnie cynophile," September 1994, 2, 138 W 1, APP; "A l'hôtel de ville," *Le matin* (Paris), December 16, 1908.

42 René Simon, *Le chien de police, de défense, de secours* (Paris: A. Pedone, 1909), 3–11; Darwin, *The Descent of Man*, 558–59. See also Edwin H. Richardson, *War, Police and Watch Dogs* (Edinburgh: William Blackwood and Sons, 1910), 118–19.

43 Quotations are from *Carnet de juge avec nomenclature des penalisations spécifiées dans le programme des épreuves concours de dressage de chiens de défense et de police* (Paris: Imprimerie française/Maison J. Dangon, 1913), 4. See also Jean-Marc Berlière, *Le monde des polices en France* (Brussels: Éditions complexe, 1996), 74–87; *Status du club de chien de police, de garde-chasse et de douanier* (Sceaux: Imprimerie Charaire, 1908), 1–7; "Historique du club de chien de police," 2, 138 W 1, APP; "Réunion des amateurs du chien de défense et de police en France," in *Programme des épreuves des concours de dressage de chiens de défense et de police* (Paris: Imprimerie française, 1913); "Les chiens de police luttent devant M. Fallières," *Le matin* (Paris), May 10, 1909.

44 "Pour se débarrasser des apaches," *Echo de Paris*, January 7, 1907; "Organisation d'un service de chiens de police," September 23, 1908, 138 W 1, APP; Préfecture de police, "Minute: Chiens de police," December 29, 1910, 138 W 1, APP; Jean Marc Berlière, *Le préfet Lépine: Vers la naissance de la police moderne* (Paris: Denoël, 1993), 14; Dominique Kalifa, "Crime Scenes: Criminal Topography and Social Imaginary in Nineteenth-Century Paris," *French Historical Studies* 27, no. 1 (2004): 188–89.

45 Richardson, *War, Police and Watch Dogs*, 23; "Police Dogs on Trial," *Daily Mail* (London), August 15, 1907; "Dogs as Policemen: Remarkable Achievements," *Daily Mail* (London), August 17, 1907; "Dogs Aid Paris Police to Crush Desperadoes," *BDE*, April 28, 1907; "More Police Dogs for Paris," *NYT*, June 13, 1909.

46 "New York's Police Dogs and What They Can Do," *NYT*; "You May Not Raise Your Dog to Be a Soldier, but Send Him to College and He'll Be A Cop," *BDE*, November 21, 1915.

47 Richardson, *War, Police and Watch Dogs*, 26–28, 30; Edwin H. Richardson, "Police Dogs," *Manchester Guardian*, December 27, 1910; "Police Dogs a Success," *Observer*, (London), March 26, 1911; "Police Dogs: Views of Major Richardson," *Times of India* (Bombay [present-day Mumbai]), May 16, 1910. On provincial urban innovation, see Katy Layton-Jones, *Beyond the Metropolis: The Changing Image of Urban Britain, 1780–1880* (Manchester: Manchester University Press, 2016).

48 "Policemen's Dogs," *Daily Mail* (London), April 4, 1911; Binyamin Blum, "The Hounds of Empire: Forensic Dog Tracking in Britain and Its Colonies, 1888–1953," *Law and History Review* 35, no. 3 (2017): 621–65.

49 Damien Baldin, *Histoire des animaux domestiques, XIXe–XXe siècle* (Paris: Seuil, 2014), 115–17; John Carson, "The Science of Merit and the Merit of Science: Men-

tal Order and Social Order in Early Twentieth-Century France and America," in *States of Knowledge: The Co-Production of Science and Social Order*, ed. Shelia Jasanoff (London: Routledge, 2004), 185.

50 Niluar, "A propos de chiens de police," *Journal des commissaires de police*, May 1907, 144; Robert Gersbach, *Manuel de dressage des chiens de police*, trans. Daniel Elmer (Lyon: Fournier, 1911), 23, 152.

51 Richardson, *War, Police and Watch Dogs*, 31; Lalloué, *Méthode de dressage*, 15–19.

52 Hauri quoted in "You May Not Raise Your Dog"; Joseph Couplet, *Chien de garde de défense et de police: Manuel pratique et complet d'élevage et de dressage*, 2nd ed. (Brussels: J. Lebègue, 1909), 44–51, 78; Leonhard Felix Fuld, "Review," *Journal of American Institute of Criminal Law and Criminology* 2 (1911): 651–52; "Les chiens de police à Paris," *L'eleveur belge*, no. 30, July 25, 1909, 475.

53 Pierre Saint-Laurent, *Chiens de défense et chiens de garde: Races, éducation, dressage* (Bordeaux: Féret fils/L. Mulo, 1907), 10, 17, 23; "New York's Police Dogs and What They Can Do"; Simon, *Le chien de police*, 29–31.

54 "New York's Police Dogs and What They Can Do"; "Police Dogs Here; Kept from View," *NYT*, October 23, 1907.

55 "Jim, Veteran Police Dog, Dies Strangely on Post," *BDE*, April 8, 1911; "Police Dogs 'Make Good'; Are Feared by Thieves," *BDE*, July 17, 1910.

56 "Emploi des chiens comme auxiliaires de la police à Pont-à-Mousson," 116–17; "Les chiens de police à Paris," *L'Eleveur belge*, no. 30, 25 July 1909, 475.

57 "Championnat des chiens de police," *Le matin* (Paris), August 17, 1908; Christian Chevandier, *Policiers dans la ville* (Paris: Gallimard, 2012), 463; "Les expériences de Vittel," *La presse* (Paris), August 8, 1907.

58 Jean-Marc Berlière, "The Professionalisation of the Police under the Third Republic in France, 1875–1914," in *Policing Western Europe: Politics, Professionalism and Public Order, 1850–1940*, ed. Clive Emsley and Barbara Weinberger (Westport, CT: Greenwood Press, 1991), 44–47; Christopher P. Thale, "Civilizing New York City: Police Patrol, 1880–1935" (PhD diss., University of Chicago, 1995), 1:88, 480–82, Proquest ID 304250499; J. Maxtee, *Popular Dog-Keeping* (London: L. Upcott Gill, 1898), 56; Edward Mayhew, *Dogs: Their Management Being a New Plan of Treating the Animal Based upon a Consideration of His Natural Temperament* (London: George Routledge and Sons, 1854), 6; Włodarczyk, *Genealogy of Obedience*, 35, 40–46; Fuld, "Review," 652; Couplet, *Chien de garde*, vii; Pathfinder [pseud.] and Hugh Dalziel, *Dressage et élevage des chiens, de garde et d'agrément* (Paris: J. Dumoulin, 1906).

59 Morganti, "Intelligence as the Plasticity of Instinct."

60 Gaston de Wael, *Le chien auxiliaire de la police: Manuel de dressage applicable au chien de défense du particulier et au chien du garde-chasse* (Brussels: Imprimerie F. Van Buggenhoudt, 1907), 9–11, 14, 35, 57, 60–61. See also Romanes, *Animal Intelligence*, 437–70.

61 Lalloué, *Méthode de dressage*, 24, 34; Gersbach, *Manuel de dressage*, 24; Susan J. Pearson, *The Rights of the Defenseless: Protecting Animals and Children in Gilded Age America* (Chicago: University of Chicago Press, 2011), 46–55; Peter N. Stearns, *American Cool: Constructing a Twentieth-Century Emotional Style* (New York: New York University Press, 1994), 22.

62 Lalloué, *Méthode de dressage*, 27–34, 37–40; de Wael, *Le chien auxiliaire*, 43–44.

63 Lalloué, *Méthode de dressage*, 27; "Police Dog Trials for Van Cortlandt," *Sun* (New York), August 3, 1913.

64 Pathfinder and Dalziel, *Dressage et élevage*, 221, 224–25.

65 "New York's Police Dogs and What They Can Do," *NYT*; "Dogs Aid Paris Police to Crush Desperadoes," *BDE*; "Paris Police Dogs," *Daily Telegraph* (London), August 17, 1907.

66 Vanessa Schwartz, *Spectacular Realities: Early Mass Culture in Fin-de-Siècle France* (Berkeley: University of California Press, 1999); Lisa Duggan, *Sapphic Slashers: Sex, Violence and American Modernity* (Durham, NC: Duke University Press, 2000), 33–36; Gretchen Soderlund, *Sex Trafficking, Scandal, and the Transformation of Journalism, 1885–1917* (Chicago: University of Chicago Press, 2013); "Dogs as Detectives: Canine Auxiliaries to the New York Police," *Illustrated London News*, April 18, 1908; "Police Dog Test Made All Too Real," *NYT*, January 29, 1908.

67 "Jim, Veteran Police Dog," *BDE*.

68 "Negro Who Shot Police Confesses His Guilt," *BDE*, May 24, 1909. See also "Detectives Shot: Dogs Trail Shooter," *NYT* May 23, 1909; Lee Bernstein, "The Hudson River School of Incarceration: Sing Sing Prison in Antebellum New York," *American Nineteenth Century History* 14, no. 3 (2013): 261–82; James Campbell, "'You Needn't Be Afraid Here: You're in a Civilized Country': Region, Racial Violence and Law Enforcement in Early Twentieth Century New Jersey," *Social History* 35, no. 3 (2010): 253–67; Marcy S. Sacks, "'To Show Who Was in Charge': Police Repression of New York City's Black Population at the Turn of the Twentieth Century," *Journal of Urban History* 31, no. 6 (2005): 799–819; Khalil Gibran Muhammad, *The Condemnation of Blackness: Race, Crime and the Making of Urban America* (Cambridge, MA: Harvard University Press, 2011); Shannon King, "'Ready to Shoot and Do Shoot': Black Working-Class Self-Defense and Community Politics in Harlem, New York, during the 1920s," *Journal of Urban History* 37, no. 5 (2011): 757–74.

69 "Nothing Like a Canine Sherlock Holmes," *NYT*, September 6, 1908; "Police Dogs Trailing Good Flatbush Folks," *BDE*, September 7, 1908.

70 "La malle-poste défendue par les chiens de police," *Le matin* (Paris), October 25, 1908; "La sécurité à Paris," *La presse* (Paris), April 18, 1907; "Les débuts d'un chien policier," *Le matin* (Paris), November 19, 1907; "La malle-poste défendue par les chiens de police," *Le matin* (Paris), October 25, 1908; "La sécurité à Paris," *La presse* (Paris), April 18, 1907; "Stop, le chien du brigadier," *Le matin* (Paris), April 21, 1907; "Dogs Aid Paris Police to Crush Desperadoes," *BDE*; "Les chiens-apaches à Paris," *L'eleveur belge*, no. 46, November 14, 1911, 738; "Chiens policiers," *Journal des ouvrages de dames et des arts féminins*, 1908, 317; A.-H. Heym, "Les chiens de police (suite et fin)," *La "vraie police,"* March 15, 1902, 10, DB 41, APP; "Apache Dogs," *Daily Mail* (London), October 29, 1909.

71 "Les chiens de police de Neuilly-sur-Seine," *Le petit journal* (Paris), February 27, 1907; "Un chien policier arrête deux mystérieux malandrins," *Le matin* (Paris), December 16, 1913; "A travers Paris," *Le matin* (Paris), June 7, 1909.

72 Quoted in "Police Head's Story of Bandits' Siege," *NYT*, May 16, 1912. See also "Shots Fail to Stop Flatbush Robbers," *NYT*, July 19, 1913.

73 "Nothing Like a Canine Sherlock Holmes"; "Police Dogs Trailing Good Flatbush Folks"; Heym, "Le chiens de police."

74 "Killed in a Fight with a Bulldog," *NYT*, December 13, 1909.

75 "Les chiens de police," *Le matin* (Paris), October 24, 1909; "Tribunaux," *Le matin* (Paris), November 12, 1909; Deluermoz, "Circulations et élaborations," 84.

76 Ribot quoted in Ruth Harris, *Murders and Madness: Medicine, Law and Society in the Fin de Siècle* (Oxford: Clarendon Press, 1989), 41; Lombroso, *Criminal Man*, 91.

77 On the long history of the "beast within," see Joyce. E. Salisbury, *The Beast Within: Animals in the Middle Ages* (New York: Routledge, 1994).

78 Baldin, *Histoire des animaux domestiques*, 68; "Rapport," October 26, 1917, 138 W 1, APP.

79 David Brockwell, *The Police Dog* (New York: G. Howard Watt, ca. 1924); "Fellow Is a Dog that Grasp's [*sic*] Man's Language," *NYT*, November 11, 1928; Reginald M. Cleveland, "His Bark Is Heard above All Others," *NYT*, December 15, 1929; "Ban on Police Dogs in Queens Urged by Magistrate Conway," *NYT*, January 7, 1925; "Queens Police Ordered to War on Police Dogs," *BDE*, January 11, 1925; Dorothy V. Holden, "Police Dogs," *NYT*, July 20, 1924; Carolyn Strange, *Discretionary Justice: Pardon and Parole in New York from the Revolution to the Depression* (New York: New York University Press, 2016), 174–75.

80 Enright quoted in "Enright Calls Dogs Useless and Denies Robbery Increase," *BDE*, September 12, 1920; "Enright Loses his Dog," *NYT*, June 17, 1922; "Police Dog Aids Pass out of Use," *NYT*, October 31, 1926; "Police Dogs," *NYT*, December 5, 1936; Geo Taylor, "Police Dog Makes Good in New York," *Baltimore Afro-American*, April 7, 1928; "Our Police Dogs: Four in Number," *NYT*, September 22, 1929; "Staten Island Has a Crimeless Night," *NYT*, September 9, 1929; "10 Police Dogs Roam Richmond for 18 Months," *NYT*, November 17, 1930; "Radio Scores Point over Police Dogs," *NYT*, July 5, 1932.

81 "Clever Dogs," *Daily Mail* (London), November 22, 1928; "Dog Police," *Daily Mail* (London), February 16, 1920; J. E. M. Mellor, "Notes on Dogs for Police Work," n.d., MEPO 2/2910, NA; "Use of Dogs in Police Work," *Manchester Guardian*, March 1, 1938; P. C. Allen to District Chief Inspector, May 17, 1939, MEPO 2/6208, NA.

82 Bernard Wright, "Police Dogs," *Baltimore Afro-American*, July 2, 1932; "Citizens Hit Use of Dogs by Police," *Baltimore Afro-American*, September 23, 1967; "We Train Our Dogs to Bite Colored Only," *Baltimore Afro-American*, May 11, 1963; Larry H. Spruill, "Slave Patrols, 'Packs of Negro Dogs' and the Policing Black Communities," *Phylon* 53, no. 1 (2016): 42–66; Tyler Wall, "'For the Very Existence of Civilization': The Police Dog and Racial Terror," *American Quarterly* 68, no. 4 (2016): 861–82.

Chapter Five

1 "Canis," *Encyclopaedia Britannica* (Edinburgh: A. Bell and C. MacFarquhar, 1797), 4:102; "Canine Excrement," *Universal Magazine*, April 1812, 299; W. T.

Fernie, *Animal Simples: Approved for Modern Uses of Cure* (Bristol: John Wright, 1899), 122; note on "Byelaws RE Nuisance for Dogs Fouling Footways," November 5, 1933, HO 45/17553, NA; Conseil municipal de Paris, "Compte rendu de la séance du mardi 28 décembre 1937," *Supplément au Bulletin municipal officiel de la ville de Paris*, January 1, 1938, 16. Some observers raised concerns about dog mess before the 1920s, but they were minority voices. Docteur Ox, "Chiens errants," *Le matin* (Paris), April 11, 1902; I. T., "Dog Nuisances," *NYT*, December 24, 1900; George Soper, *Modern Methods of Street Cleaning* (New York: Engineering News, 1909), 8.

2 William Ian Miller, *The Anatomy of Disgust* (Cambridge, MA: Harvard University Press, 1997), 2, 100.

3 Valerie A. Curtis, "Dirt, Disgust and Disease: A Natural History of Hygiene," *Journal of Epidemiology and Community Health* 61, no. 8 (2007): 660–64; Martha C. Nussbaum, *Hiding from Humanity: Disgust, Shame and the Law* (Princeton, NJ: Princeton University Press, 2004), 98; William A. Cohen and Ryan Johnson, eds., *Filth: Dirt, Disgust and Modern Life* (Minneapolis: University of Minnesota Press, 2005); Dominique Laporte, *History of Shit*, trans. Rodolphe el-Khoury and Nadia Benabid (Cambridge, MA: MIT Press, 2000 [1978]); Peter Stallybrass and Allon White, *The Politics and Poetics of Transgression* (London: Methuen, 1986). For a detailed discussion of the relationship between disgust and animality, see Nussbaum, *Hiding from Humanity*, 72–99.

4 Dolly Jørgensen, "Modernity and Medieval Muck," *Nature and Culture* 9, no. 3 (2014): 225–37; Alain Corbin, *The Foul and the Fragrant: Odour and the Social Imagination* (Leamington Spa, England: Berg, 1986 [1982]); Virginia Smith, *Clean: A History of Personal Hygiene and Purity* (Oxford: Oxford University Press, 2007), 144–84; Carl A. Zimring, *Clean and White: A History of Environmental Racism in the United States* (New York: New York University Press, 2015).

5 John Duffy, *The Sanitarians: A History of American Public Health* (Urbana: University of Illinois Press, 1990), 139; David S. Barnes, *The Great Stink of Paris and the Nineteenth-Century Struggle against Filth and Germs* (Baltimore: Johns Hopkins University Press, 2006), 74–78; David Inglis, "Sewers and Sensibilities: The Bourgeois Faecal Experience in the Nineteenth-Century City," in *The City and the Senses: Urban Culture since 1500*, ed. Jill Steward and Alexander Cowan (Farnham: Ashgate, 2007), 105–30; Suellen Hoy, *Chasing Dirt: The American Pursuit of Cleanliness* (New York: Oxford University Press, 1995); Melanie A. Kiechle, *Smell Detectives: An Olfactory History of Nineteenth-Century America* (Seattle: University of Washington Press, 2017); Nancy Tomes, *The Gospel of Germs: Men, Women and the Microbe in American Life* (Cambridge, MA: Harvard University Press, 1998); James R. Kinney with Ann Honeycutt, *How to Raise a Dog: In the City . . . in the Suburbs* (New York: Simon and Schuster, 1938), 61.

6 Kathleen Kete, *Beast in the Boudoir: Petkeeping in Nineteenth-Century Paris* (Berkeley: University of California Press, 1994), 76–96; Pierre Mégnin, *Les chenils et leur hygiène* (Vincennes: Aux bureaux de "l'éleveur," 1905).

7 Pathfinder [pseud.] and Hugh Dalziel, *Dressage et élevage des chiens, de garde et d'agrément* (Paris: J. Dumoulin, 1906), 297; Georges Vigarello, *Concepts of Cleanliness: Changing Attitudes in France since the Middle Ages*, trans. Jean Birrell (Cambridge: Cambridge University Press, 1988), 167–214; Alfred Barbou, *Le chien: Son*

histoire, ses exploits, ses aventures (Paris: Librairie Furne, 1883), 99; Ernest Leroy, *L'enfance du chien* (Paris: Firmin-Didot, 1896), 140.

8 Barnes, *The Great Stink*, 74–78, 196–202; quotation is from p. 202.

9 Naomi Rogers, "Germs with Legs: Flies, Disease, and the New Public Health," *Bulletin of the History of Medicine* 63, no. 4 (1989): 559–617.

10 Paul Dechambre, *Le chien: Races, élevage, alimentation, hygiène, utilisation* (Paris: Librairie agricole de la Maison rustique, 1921), 216–17; David Brockwell, *The Alsatian* (London: Hutchinson, 1925), 90; William Haynes, *The Airedale* (New York: Outing, 1911), 41; Stonehenge [J. H. Walsh], *The Dogs of the British Islands*, 4th ed. (London: Horace Cox, 1882), 5; Kinney with Honeycutt, *How to Raise a Dog*, 53. On food and Italian identities, see Simone Cinotto, "Leonard Covello, the Covello Papers, and the History of Eating Habits among Italian Immigrants in New York," *Journal of American History* 91, no. 2 (2004): 497–521.

11 Eugène Gayot, *Le chien: Histoire naturelle, races d'utilité et d'agrément, reproduction, éducation, hygiène, maladies, législation* (Paris: Firmin-Didot frères, 1867), 458; A. Bénion, *Les races caninies* (Paris: Librairie agricole de la Maison rustique 1866), 93–94; Pierre Mégnin, *Le chien: Histoire, hygiène, médicine* (Paris: Émile Deyrolle, 1883), 143; Haynes, *The Airedale*, 35; *Our Friend the House-Dog* (London: Methuen, 1934), 22; Christopher E. Forth, "Fat, Desire and Disgust in the Colonial Imagination," *History Workshop Journal* 73, no. 1 (2012): 211–39; *Hints for Dog Owners: A Guide to the Treatment of Dogs in Health and Sickness* (London: A. F. Sherley, 1920), 78; Jean Robert, *Le chien d'appartement et d'utilité* (Paris: Librairie Pairault, 1888), 152; Tom Quick, "Puppy Love: Domestic Science, 'Women's Work,' and Canine Care," *Journal of British Studies* 58, no. 2 (2019): 289–314.

12 Spratt's Patent, *The Common Sense of Dog Doctoring* (London: Tucker, Johnson, [1884]), 114, 116, 121–22; Katherine C. Grier, *Pets in America: A History* (Chapel Hill: University of North Carolina Press, 2006), 281–88; Spratt's stand photograph, Franco-British Exhibition, 1908, box 4, Trade Catalogs of Veterinary and Pet Supplies, American Kennel Club Library, New York; *The Friend o' Man: A Book for Everybody Who Owns or Wishes to Own a Dog* (London: Spratt's Patent, n.d. [1922?]), 66.

13 *Everybody's Dog* (London: Spratt's Patent, 1934); Spratt's Patent, *The Common Sense of Dog Doctoring*, 116; Ian Gazeley and Andrew Newell, "Urban Working-Class Food Consumption and Nutrition in Britain in 1904," *Economic History Review* 68, no. 1 (2015): 103; Grier, *Pets in America*, 281–88; Ian Miller, "Necessary Torture? Vivisection, Suffragette Force-Feeding and Responses to Scientific Medicine in Britain, c. 1870–1829," *Journal of the History Medicine and Allied Sciences* 64, no. 3 (2009): 333–72; J. Maxtee, *Popular Dog-Keeping* (London: L. Upcott Gill, 1898), inside front cover; Brockwell, *The Alsatian*, 92; Spillers, *Feeding, Care and Training of Dogs* (New York: H. A. Robinson, 1930), 28, 32; Quick, "Puppy Love," 311.

14 H. Clay Glover, *Diseases of the Dog and How to Feed* (New York: H. Clay Glover, 1897), 5; Haynes, *The Airedale*, 41.

15 Joanny Pertus, *Le chien: Hygiène, maladies* (Paris: J.-B. Baillière, 1905), 122; Stonehenge, *Dogs of the British Isles*, 6, 9–10, 37; Haynes, *The Airedale*, 94; *Our Friend the House-Dog*, 34; *Hints for Dog Owners*, 90; Kinney with Honeycutt, *How*

to Raise a Dog, 228–29. On the importance of inspecting anal glands when buying a puppy, see *Hints for Dog Owners*, 24.

16 H. Clay Glover, *Diseases of the Dog and How to Feed* (New York: H. Clay Glover, n.d.), box 4, Trade Catalogs of Veterinary and Pet Supplies, American Kennel Club Library, New York; *Delcreo Kennel Manual* (Brooklyn: Delson Chemical, 1925), 3–5, box 4, Trade Catalogs of Veterinary and Pet Supplies, American Kennel Club Library, New York; Quick, "Puppy Love."

17 André-Valdès [Mme Charles Boeswilwald], *Le chiens de luxe* (Paris: Librairie Nilsson, 1907), 72; Grier, *Pets in America*, 76.

18 Paul de Grignon, *Nos chiens: Comment les élever, comment les soigner, comment les dresser* (Paris: France-Edition, 1923), 32; *Our Friend the House-Dog*, 26; H. Ducret-Baumann, *L'éducation et l'hygiène du chien: Ses maladies, ses misères, reproduction, élevage des chiots* (Paris: Louis Michaud, 1913), 1–2; Haynes, *The Airedale*, 82; Theo Marples, *Rational Dog-Keeping: Hints and Advice to Novices and Beginners* (Manchester: Our Dogs, 1915), 19–20.

19 Kinney with Honeycutt, *How to Raise a Dog*, 99–100.

20 Clarence E. Harbison, *Our Dogs: What We Should Know about Them* (New York: Orange Judd, 1932), 22; Paul Mégnin, *Nos chiens: Races, dressage, élevage, hygiène, maladies* (Paris: J-B Baillière, 1909), 312; Marples, *Rational Dog-Keeping*, 19.

21 Peter Atkins, "The Urban Blood and Guts Economy," in *Animal Cities: Beastly Urban Histories*, ed. Peter Atkins (Farnham: Ashgate, 2012), 77–106; Sabine Barles, *L'invention des déchets urbains: France 1790–1970* (Seyssel: Champ Vallon, 2005); Rodolphe Trouilleux, *Histoires insolites des animaux de Paris* (Paris: Bernard Giovanangeli, 2003), 121; Antoine Compagnon, *Les chiffonniers de Paris* (Paris: Gallimard, 2017). Dog excrement was also used in tanneries in parts of the Ottoman Empire. Thomas Smith, *The Wonders of Nature and Art* (London: J. Walker, 1803), 4:129. Marcel Clerc reported that New York tanneries imported eight hundred thousand kilograms of dog mess from Constantinople (present-day Istanbul) each year, but I have found no further evidence to support this claim. Marcel Clerc, "La souillure des villes par les excréments de chiens," *Archives médico-chirurgicales de Normandie* 65 (May 1929): 2294.

22 Henry Mayhew, *London Labour and the London Poor* (London: Griffin Bohn, 1861), 2:142. Tanners may also have mixed dog excrement with that of pigeons. "New Chemical for Tanners," *London Journal*, June 28, 1862, 412.

23 Mayhew, *London Labour and the London Poor*, 2:143–45.

24 Ibid., 2:144–45.

25 Michelle Allen, *Cleansing the City: Sanitary Geographies in Victorian London* (Athens: Ohio University Press, 2008), 11–15; Barnes, *The Great Stink*, 13; Warwick Anderson, "Excremental Colonialism: Public Health and the Poetics of Pollution," *Critical Inquiry* 21, no. 3 (1995): 640–69; Daniel Eli Burnstein, *Next to Godliness: Confronting Dirt and Despair in Progressive Era New York City* (Urbana: University of Illinois Press, 2006), 2–3, 39; Zimring, *Clean and White*.

26 Allen, *Cleansing the City*, 29–45; Michael Brown, "From Foetid Air to Filth: The Cultural Transformation of British Epidemiological Thought, ca. 1780–1848," *Bulletin of the History of Medicine* 82, no. 3 (2008): 515–44; Tom Crook, *Governing Systems: Modernity and the Making of Public Health in England, 1830–1910* (Oakland: University of California Press, 2016), 148–88; David L. Pike, "Sewage

Treatments: Vertical Space and Waste in Nineteenth-Century Paris and London," in Cohen and Johnson, *Filth*, 51–77.

27 R. Arthur Arnold, "Pure Air," *Once a Week*, August 11, 1866, 150; David Inglis, *A Sociological History of Excretory Experience: Defecatory Manners and Toiletry Technologies* (Lewiston, NY: Edwin Mellon, 2000), 267–73.

28 Sabine Barles, *La ville délétère: Médecins et ingénieurs dans l'espace urbain XVIIIe–XIXe siècle* (Seyssel: Champ Vallon, 1999), 238–48; Barles, *L'invention des déchets urbains*, 202; Matthew Gandy, "The Paris Sewers and the Rationalization of Urban Space," *Transactions of the Institute of British Geographers* 24, no. 1 (1999): 23–44; Donald Reid, *Paris Sewers and Sewermen: Realities and Representations* (Cambridge, MA: Harvard University Press, 1991).

29 John Waldman, *Heartbeats in the Muck: The History, Sea Life, and Environment of New York Harbor* (New York: Empire State Editions, 2013 [1999]), 54–56; Ted Steinberg, *Gotham Unbound: The Ecological History of Greater New York* (New York: Simon and Schuster, 2014), 115–22.

30 Ralph Turvey, "Horse Traction in Victorian London," *Journal of Transport History* 26, no. 2 (2005): 57; "Contagion in the Air," *NYT*, May 11, 1884. See also Clay McShane and Joel A. Tarr, *The Horse in the City: Living Machines in the Nineteenth Century* (Baltimore: Johns Hopkins University Press, 2007), 169.

31 Sabine Barles, "Undesirable Nature: Animals, Resources and Urban Nuisance in Nineteenth-Century Paris," in Atkins, *Animal Cities*, 186; Ghislaine Bouchet, *Le cheval à Paris de 1850 à 1914* (Geneva: Libraire Droz, 1993), 3; Hannah Velton, *Beastly London: A History of Animals in the City* (London: Reaktion, 2013), 74–75; "Superintendent's Report," *The American Society for the Prevention of Cruelty to Animals, Sixty-First Annual Report* (1927–28), 33. See also Ann Norton Greene, *Horses at Work: Harnessing Power in Industrial America* (Cambridge, MA: Harvard University Press, 2008), 244–74; Steinberg, *Gotham Unbound*, 112–13.

32 H. C. Brown, G. E. F. Stammers, and Andrew Balfour, "Observations on Canine Faeces on London Pavements: Bacteriological, Helminthological, and Protozoological," *Lancet* 200, no. 5179 (December 2, 1922): 1165.

33 Fabienne Chevallier, *Le Paris moderne: Histoire des politiques d'hygiène (1855–1898)* (Rennes: Presses universitaires de Rennes, 2010), 228–49; Jeanne-Hélène Jugie, *Poubelle-Paris (1883–1896): La collecte des ordures ménagères à la fin du XIX*[e] *siècle* (Paris: Larousse, 1993); Barles, *La ville délétère*, 231–49; Barnes, *The Great Stink*.

34 Lee Jackson, *Dirty Old London: The Victorian Fight against Filth* (New Haven, CT: Yale University Press, 2014); Andrea Tanner, "Dust-O!: Rubbish in Victorian London, 1860–1900," *London Journal* 31, no. 2 (2006): 157–78; Ralph Turvey, "Street Mud, Dust and Noise," *London Journal* 21, no. 2 (1996): 131–48; "Keeping London Clean," *Daily Telegraph* (London), July 5, 1930.

35 W. D., "The 'White Wing's' Deadly Broom," *NYT*, October 12, 1902; Burnstein, *Next to Godliness*, 32–48; Hoy, *Chasing Dirt*, 78–80; Martin V. Melosi, "'Out of Sight, Out of Mind': The Environment and Disposal of Municipal Refuse, 1860–1920," *Historian* 35, no. 4 (1973): 626–30; Zimring, *Clean and White*, 109–18.

36 Un piéton, "Chiens et trottoirs: Lettre ouverte à messieurs les conseillers nouvellement élu," *La presse médicale* 54, July 6, 1929, 889.

37 Dr. G. Knowles, "Points from Letters: Dogs in Towns," *Times* (London), Decem-

ber 16, 1927; David Inglis, "Dirt and Denigration: The Faecal Imagery and Rhetorics of Abuse," *Postcolonial Studies* 5, no. 2 (2002): 213; L. P., "Dogs and Cats and Little Back Yards," *NYT*, October 11, 1903; Vincent, "The Dog Question," *NYT*, October 4, 1903.

38 W. G., "Defilement by Dogs," *NYT*, March 24, 1915; J. S. M., "Dogs in Public Places," *NYT*, April 29, 1900; Richard Dennis, *Cities in Modernity: Representations and Productions of Metropolitan Space, 1840–1930* (Cambridge: Cambridge University Press, 2008), 113–43.

39 J. Couturat, "Les inconvénients et le danger des chiens surtout dans les villes," *Presse médicale* 23, June 19, 1943, 334; Clerc, "La souillure des villes par les excréments de chiens," 2294; Marcel Clerc, "La souillure des villes par les chiens," *Aristote* 30, June 1929, 81; Un piéton, "Chiens et trottoirs"; Conseil municipal de Paris, "Compte rendu de la séance du 30 décembre 1935," *Bulletin municipal officiel de la ville de Paris*, January 10, 1936, 300; Animal Lover, "Dogs in London," *Saturday Review*, December 11, 1926, 725; Agnes Savill, "Fouling of Footways by Dogs," *British Medical Journal* 1, no. 3723 (May 14, 1932): 911; J. S. M., "Dogs in Public Places."

40 Marcel Clerc, "La souillure des villes par les chiens," *Annales d'Hygiène publique, industrielle et sociale*, May 16, 1938, 203; Neil Blackadder, "*Merdre!* Performing Filth in the Bourgeois Public Sphere," in Cohen and Johnson, *Filth*, 198. See also Crook, *Governing Systems*, 177.

41 Thomas W. M. Cameron, "The Dog as a Carrier of Disease to Man," *Lancet* 199, no. 5142 (March 18, 1922): 565; W. G., "Defilement by Dogs"; I. T., "Dog Nuisances." See also Mary Douglas to OCA, October 23, 1936, box 3, 002, OCA Records, New York Public Library.

42 John Farley, "Parasites and the Germ Theory of Disease," in *Framing Disease: Studies in Cultural History*, ed. Charles E. Rosenberg and Janet Golden (New Brunswick, NJ: Rutgers University Press, 1997 [1992]), 33–49; P. L. Moro and P. M. Schantz, "Echinococcosis: Historical Landmarks and Progress in Research and Control," *Annals of Tropical Medicine and Parasitology* 100, no. 8 (2006): 703–14; Dennis Tappe and Matthias Frosch, "Rudolf Virchow and the Recognition of Alveolar Echinococcosis, 1850s," *Emerging Infectious Diseases* 13, no. 5 (2007): 732–34; Glover, *Diseases of the Dog*, 22; Stonehenge, *Dogs of the British Isles*, 41; Alfred W. Meyer, *Dogs: Their Care and Training, Breeds and Selection* (New York: McGraw-Hill, 1936), 14; *Hints for Dog Owners*, 53; Maurice C. Hall, "The Use of Drugs in the Treatment of Diseases Caused by Worms," *Journal of Comparative Pathology and Therapeutics* 43 (1930): 99–108.

43 James Warbasse, *The Conquest of Disease through Animal Experimentation* (New York: Appleton, 1910), 142. See also Rea Smith, "Multiple Hydatic Cyst of Liver," *American Journal of Surgery* 7, no. 6 (December 1929): 847–49.

44 Cameron, "The Dog as a Carrier"; R. G. Prosser Evans, "Hydatid Disease of the Lung with a Case Report," *Lancet* 223, no. 5781 (June 16, 1934): 1281–83; "Danger of Kissing Dogs," *Times* (London), August 26, 1931; Docteur Ox, "Toutous et loulous," *Le matin* (Paris), January 1, 1904, clipping in DB 230, APP.

45 F. M. Bogan, "Are Pets Dangerous?," *Health*, October 1911, 222; "Public Health Leaflet no. 9: Some Important Animal Parasites of Man," Bureau of Public Health Education of the Department of Health, New York City Hall Library.

46 Abel Lahille, "Les inconvenients et le danger des chiens surtout dans les villes," *Annales d'Hygiène publique, industrielle et sociale*, 1941, 30; Clerc, "La souillure des villes par les chiens" (1929), 81; Sharon Marcus, "Haussmannization as Anti-Modernity: The Apartment House in Parisian Urban Discourse, 1850–1880," *Journal of Urban History* 27, no. 6 (2001): 723–45.

47 René Lutembacher, "L'hygiène et le chien," *La presse médicale* 97, December 4, 1929, 1585; Brown, Stammers, and Balfour, "Observations on Canine Faeces," 1166; "Fouling of Footways by Dogs," *Lancet* 206, no. 5327 (October 3, 1925): 714–15.

48 Human Rights, "Dogs as Germ Distributors," *NYT*, November 23, 1902; E. L. M., "Sidewalk Annoyances," *NYT*, April 4, 1936; Un piéton, "Chiens et trottoirs."

49 W. G., "Defilement by Dogs"; Hoy, *Chasing Dirt*; Savill, "Fouling of Footways by Dogs"; S. E. F., "To the Editor," *NYT*, April 3, 1915; Richard Deeves, "To the Editor," *NYT*, March 27, 1915; A Disgusted Citizen, "Not a Lover of Dogs," *NYT*, April 26, 1900; J. Charles Totten, "Inconsiderate Dog Owners," *NYT*, February 2, 1934.

50 Un piéton, "Chiens et trottoirs"; K. A. Lumsden, "Points from Letters: Fouled Pavements," *Times* (London), October 7, 1937; Ruth Colton, "From Gutters to Greensward: Constructing Heathy Childhood in the Late-Victorian and Edwardian Public Park" (PhD diss., University of Manchester, 2016), www.research.manchester.ac.uk/portal/en/theses/from-gutters-to-greensward-constructing-healthy-childhood-in-the-latevictorian-and-edwardian-public-park(34fd4ec1-30ae-4cd4-b231-632083475eae).html. For a call to keep dogs out of New York's parks, see W. G., "Defilement by Dogs."

51 E. W. Estes, "Dogs in the City," *NYT*, January 26, 1931; Dr A. M. Ware, "Points from Letters: Dogs in Towns," *Times* (London), December 12, 1927; Un médecin parisien, "A propos de la fécalisation des trottoirs," *La presse médicale* 58, July 20, 1929, 955; I. T., "Dog Nuisances"; J. S. M., "Dogs in Public Places," *NYT*; Disgusted, "Dogs in the City," *NYT*, November 13, 1933.

52 Médecin parisien, "Fécalisation des trottoirs," 955; J. S. M., "Dogs in Public Places"; Reader, "The Dirty Sidewalks," *NYT*, December 30, 1900; Couturat, "Les inconvénients et le danger des chiens."

53 Citizen, "The Peripatetic Pup," *NYT*, December 30, 1900; Lumsden, "Fouled Pavements"; Knowles, "Dogs in Towns," *Times* (London); J. S. M., "Dogs in Public Places"; I. T., "Dog Nuisances"; "Notes of the Week," *Saturday Review*, November 27, 1926, 635.

54 "Our Live-Letter Box: Woof! Woof!," *Daily Mirror* (London), September 16, 1936; Martha L. Kobbe, "Addressed to Dog Owners," *NYT*, March 29, 1935; "Anti-Litter Rules Set Forth in Leaflet," *NYT*, May 5, 1931; D. W., "Dogs Not to Blame," *NYT*, November 9, 1935; Norbert Elias, *The Civilizing Process: Sociogenetic and Psychogenetic Investigations*, trans. Edmund Jephcott (Oxford: Blackwell, 2000 [1939]), 118.

55 Clerc, "La souillure des villes par les chiens" (1938), 203.

56 Clerc, "La souillure des villes par les excréments de chiens," 2294, 2297; Clerc, "La souillure des villes par les chiens" (1938), 209; Un piéton, "Chiens et trottoirs." The city council finally experimented with dog toilets in the mid-1970s before introducing them more extensively in the 1980s. Chris Pearson, "Combat-

ing 'Canine Visiting Cards': Public Hygiene and the Management of Dog Mess in Paris since the 1920s," *Social History of Medicine* 32, no. 1 (2019): 156–57.

57 Conseil municipal de Paris, "Compte rendu de la séance du 30 décembre 1935," 300; Conseil municipal de Paris, "Compte rendu de la séance du mardi 28 décembre 1937," 31. For a thoughtful discussion on the limits of surveillance in democratic societies, see Chris Otter, *The Victorian Eye: A Political History of Light and Vision in Britain, 1800–1910* (Chicago: University of Chicago Press, 2008), 3–5.

58 Lahille, "Les inconvenients et le danger des chiens," 31; Couturat, "Les inconvénients et le danger des chiens."

59 George A. Soper, *Street Cleaning and Refuse Collection and Disposal in European Cities with Suggestions Applicable to New York 1929: Report to the Committee of Twenty on Street and Outdoor Cleanliness Appointed by the New York Academy of Medicine*, October 1929 (New York: Press of C. C. Morchand, 1929), 4; "A New Broom Needed," *NYT*, November 4, 1933; Matthew Napear, Department of Sanitation, "Public Education as a Function in Street Sanitation," paper presented at the 1938 Public Works Congress, October 3–5, 1938, 3; box 3, 002, OCA Records, New York Public Library, capitals in the original. On the transnational dimensions of public health, see Paul Weindling, ed., *International Health Organisations and Movements, 1918–1939* (Cambridge: Cambridge University Press, 1995).

60 *Information for Dog Owners: Why Dogs Must Be Muzzled When at Large* (New York: Department of Health, January 1919), 5; T. G. H., "Laws Governing Dogs," *NYT*, March 25, 1935.

61 Mrs. Henry Martyn Alexander, "The Outdoor Cleanliness Association," n.d. [1940/1941?], box 3, 004, OCA Records, New York Public Library; Burnstein, *Next to Godliness*, 109–10; Hoy, *Chasing Dirt*, 100–112.

62 "Cleanliness Drive Is On," *NYT*, May 21, 1936; Burnstein, *Next to Godliness*, 130–32; "'Traffic' Sign for Dogs," *NYT*, November 12, 1937; Corresponding Secretary, OCA, to A. Gordon, June 19, 1936, box 3, 002, OCA Records, New York Public Library; Douglas to OCA.

63 Schwarz quoted in Elizabeth La Hines, "Drive Is Begun for a Tidy City during the Fair," *NYT*, April 9, 1939; John L. Rice, *Health for 7,500,000 People* (New York: Department of Health, 1939), 146; Indignant, "A Dog Owner's Viewpoint," *NYT*, November 14, 1935; "Dog Nuisance Drive Spreads to Flatbush," *NYT*, July 29, 1936.

64 Kinney with Honeycutt, *How to Raise a Dog*, 101–3. On how *curbing* became a verb, see Robert L. Chapman, "Semantic Generalization: 'Curb Your Dog,'" *American Speech* 43, no. 4 (1968): 314.

65 Mongrels Second, "The Dog Nuisance," *Times* (London), February 22, 1917.

66 Quoted in "The Two Voices," *Public Health* 35 (May 1922): 224. See also Peter Atkins, "Animal Wastes and Nuisances in Nineteenth-Century London," in Atkins, *Animal Cities*, 28–29; Christopher Hamlin, "Public Sphere to Public Health: The Transformation of 'Nuisance,'" in *Medicine, Health and the Public Sphere in Britain, 1600–2000*, ed. Steve Sturdy (Abington: Routledge, 2002), 194–95.

67 "The Two Voices," 224.

68 "Fouling of Footways by Dogs," *Public Health* 37 (October 1923): 13–14. "Dog Nuisance Bye-Law Made Permanent," *Public Health* 37 (November 1923): 41; James Fenton, "Fouling of Footways by Dogs," *Public Health* 39 (October 1925): 24.

69 "Good Rule and Government Byelaws: Dog Fouling Footways," February 1936, HO 45/17553, NA.

70 "Good Rule"; "Byelaws RE Nuisance from Dogs Fouling Footways," National Canine Defence League, Annual Report, 1925, 28, A/FWA/C/D268/1, LMA; "Memo on Working of the New Form of Model Byelaw," August 1938, HO 45/17553, NA. Copies of the London borough bylaws can be found in the National Archives and London Metropolitan Archives. Clerc, "La souillure des villes par les chiens" (1938), 210–11, 215.

71 Michael Brandow, *New York's Poop Scoop Law: Dogs, the Dirt, and Due Process* (West Lafayette, IN: Purdue University Press, 2008); "Dogs (Fouling of Land) Act 1996," www.legislation.gov.uk/ukpga/1996/20/contents/enacted, accessed October 27, 2020; Neil Pemberton, "The Burnley Dog War: The Politics of Dog-Walking and the Battle over Public Parks in Post-Industrial Britain," *Twentieth Century British History* 28, no. 2 (2017): 239–67; Pearson, "Combating 'Canine Visiting Cards,'" 161. From 2004 onward, Parisian owners also had to scoop the poop from the gutter as well as the pavements.

72 "Sanitation at the British Empire Exhibition, 1924," *Public Health* 38, issue C (1924): 61. See also Anderson, "Excremental Colonialism"; Susan L. Carruthers, "Latrines as the Measure of Men: American Soldiers and the Politics of Disgust in Occupied Europe and Asia," *Diplomatic History* 42, no. 1 (2018): 112; Jean-Pierre Goubert, "La ville, miroir et enjeu de la santé: Paris, Montréal et Alger au XIXe siècle," *Histoire, économie, et société* 20, no. 3 (2001): 355–70.

73 Pearson, "Combating 'Canine Visiting Cards'"; Nicolas Kenny, *The Feel of the City: Experiences of Urban Transformation* (Toronto: University of Toronto Press, 2014), 8–9.

Coda

1 Nicolas Kenny, "City Glow: Streetlights, Emotions, and Nocturnal Life, 1880s-1910s," *Journal of Urban History* 43, no. 1 (2017): 108.

2 Hilda Kean, *The Great Cat and Dog Massacre: The Real Story of World War II's Unknown Tragedy* (Chicago: University of Chicago Press, 2017), 47–68; Michael Brandow, *New York's Poop Scoop Law: Dogs, the Dirt, and Due Process* (West Lafayette, IN: Purdue University Press, 2008); Stephanie Fellenstein, "New York City Veterinarian Takes on Pet Overpopulation," *DVM Magazine*, July 2011, 43–44; Pemberton, "The Burnley Dog War"; Harry Porter, "A Home from Home for a Best Friend," *Daily Telegraph* (London), March 4, 2017; Sylvie Tissot, "Of Dogs and Men: The Making of Spatial Boundaries in a Gentrifying Neighbourhood," *City and Community* 10, no. 3 (2011): 265–84; Chris Pearson, "Combating 'Canine Visiting Cards': Public Hygiene and the Management of Dog Mess in Paris since the 1920s," *Social History of Medicine* 32, no. 1 (2019): 160. On the complex relationship between shame and law, see Martha C. Nussbaum, *Hiding from Humanity: Disgust, Shame and the Law* (Princeton, NJ: Princeton University Press, 2004), 222–79.

3 Jerome Starkey, "Drop Dangerous Dog Ban, says RSPCA," *Times* (London), May 15, 2018; Georgina Mills, "Dangerous Dogs: Culprits or Victims?," *Veterinary*

Record 175, no. 22 (December 6, 2014): 554; "La loi sur les chiens dangereux est adoptee," *Liberation*, https://www.liberation.fr/societe/2008/06/12/la-loi-sur-les-chiens-dangereux-est-adoptee_21575, accessed October 27, 2020; Andrei S. Markovits and Katerine N. Crosby, *American Dog Rescue and the Discourse of Compassion* (Ann Arbor: University of Michigan Press, 2014); Nathalie Leblanc, "La place de l'animal dans les politiques urbaines," *Communications* 74 (2003): 159–75; "C'est 'Rex,' chien policier, qui a fait arrêter ces 3 cambrioleurs de Neuilly," December 29, 1967, press clipping in DB 41, APP; "Tragic French Police Dog Diesel to Receive Supreme Honour for Gallantry," People's Dispensary for Sick Animals website, December 27, 2015, https://www.pdsa.org.uk/press-office/latest-news/tragic-french-police-dog-diesel-to-receive-supreme-honour-for-gallantry, accessed October 27, 2020; Tyler Wall, "'For the Very Existence of Civilization': The Police Dog and Racial Terror," *American Quarterly* 68, no. 4 (2016): 861–82; Jean-Pierre Adine, Stéphane Bugat, and Olivia Liger, "Villes: Le temps des chiens," *Le point*, no. 502, May 3–9, 1982, 87–94; Colette Arpaillange, *Un chien heureux en ville* (Paris: Éditions Rustica, 2010), 10, 40; Hervé Perton, *Police municipale et animaux errants* (Voiron: Territorial Editions, 2006); Harlan Weaver, "Pit Bull Promises: Inhuman Intimacies and Queer Kinships in an Animal Shelter," *GLQ: A Journal of Lesbian and Gay Studies* 21, nos. 2–3 (2015): 343–63.

Appendix

1 Konrad Lorenz, *Man Meets Dog* (Abington: Routledge, 2002 [1949]), ix.

2 Lorenz Gygax et al., "Dog Behavior but Not Frontal Brain Reaction Changes in Repeated Positive Interactions with a Human: A Non-invasive Pilot Study Using Functional Near-Infrared Spectroscopy (fNIRS)," *Behavioural Brain Research* 281 (2015): 172–76; Linda M. Hines, "Historical Perspectives on the Human-Animal Bond," *American Behavioral Scientist* 47, no. 1 (2003): 7–15; Ádam Miklósi, *Dog Behaviour, Evolution and Cognition* (Oxford: Oxford University Press, 2007); Darcey F. Morey, *Dogs: Domestication and the Development of a Social Bond* (New York: Cambridge University Press, 2010); and many articles in such journals as *Journal of Veterinary Behavior: Clinical Applications and Research.*

3 On Britain alone, see Philip Howell, *At Home and Astray: The Domestic Dog in Victorian Britain* (Charlottesville: University of Virginia Press, 2015); Hilda Kean, *The Great Cat and Dog Massacre: The Real Story of World War II's Unknown Tragedy* (Chicago: University of Chicago Press, 2017); Neil Pemberton and Michael Worboys, *Rabies in Britain: Dogs, Disease and Culture, 1830–2000* (Basingstoke: Palgrave Macmillan, 2013 [2007]); Harriet Ritvo, *The Animal Estate: The English and Other Creatures in the Victorian Age* (London: Penguin, 1990 [1987]).

4 Radhika Govindrajan, *Animal Intimacies: Interspecies Relatedness in India's Central Himalayas* (Chicago: University of Chicago Press, 2018), 4, 10, 20.

5 Eric Baratay, *Bêtes des tranchées: Des vécus oubliés* (Paris: CNRS, 2013); Philip Howell and Hilda Kean, "The Dogs That Didn't Bark in the Blitz: Transspecies and Transpersonal Emotional Geographies on the British Home Front," *Journal of Historical Geography* 61 (2018): 44–52. See also Eric Baratay, *Le point de vue ani-*

mal: Une autre version de l'histoire (Paris: Seuil, 2012); Gervase Philips, "Writing Horses into American Civil War History," *War in History* 20, no. 2 (2013): 160–81.

6 Jan Plamper, "The History of Emotions: An Interview with William Reddy, Barbara Rosenwein, and Peter Sterns," *History and Theory* 49, no. 2 (2010): 261; Thomas Dixon, *Weeping Britannia: Portrait of a Nation in Tears* (Oxford: Oxford University Press, 2015). For an excellent introduction to the field, see Rob Boddice, *The History of Emotions* (Manchester: Manchester University Press, 2018).

7 Joseph Ben Prestel, *Emotional Cities: Debates on Urban Change in Berlin and Cairo* (Oxford: Oxford University Press, 2017); Nicolas Kenny, *The Feel of the City: Experiences of Urban Transformation* (Toronto: University of Toronto Press, 2014).

8 Rebecca Wright, "Mass Observation and the Emotional Energy Consumer," *Canadian Journal of History* 53, no. 3 (2018): 423–49; Monique Scheer, "Are Emotions a Kind of Practice (And Is That What Makes Them Have a History)? A Bourdieuian Approach to Understanding Emotion," *History and Theory* 51, no. 2 (2012): 193–220. See also Sarah Randles, "The Material World," in *Sources for the History of Emotions: A Guide*, ed. Katie Barclay, Sharon Crozier-De Rosa, and Peter N. Stearns (Abington: Routledge, 2021), 159–71; Stephanie Downes, Sally Hollyway, and Sarah Randles, eds., *Feeling Things: Objects and Emotions through History* (Oxford: Oxford University Press, 2018).

9 Otniel E. Dror, "The Affect of Experiment: The Turn to Emotions in Anglo-American Physiology, 1900–1940," *Isis* 90, no. 2 (1999): 205–37; Liz Gray, "Body, Mind and Madness: Pain in Animals in Nineteenth-Century Comparative Psychology," in *Pain and Emotion in Modern History*, ed. Rob Boddice (Basingstoke: Palgrave, 2014), 148–63; Jed Meyer, "The Expression of the Emotions in Man and Laboratory Animals," *Victorian Studies* 50, no. 3 (2008): 399–417; Edmund Ramsden and Duncan Wilson, "The Suicidal Animal: Science and the Nature of Self-Destruction," *Past and Present* 224 (2014): 205–17; Paul S. White, "The Experimental Animal in Victorian Britain," in *Thinking with Animals: New Perspectives on Anthropomorphism*, ed. Lorraine Daston and Gregg Mitman (New York: Columbia University Press, 2005), 60–81.

10 Joanna Bourke, *Loving Animals: On Bestiality, Zoophilia, and Post-Human Love* (London: Reaktion, 2020); Erica Fudge, *Quick Cattle and Dying Wishes: People and the Animals in Early Modern England* (Ithaca, NY: Cornell University Press, 2018); Dolly Jørgensen, *Recovering Lost Species in the Modern Age: Histories of Longing and Belonging* (Cambridge, MA: MIT Press, 2019); Ryan Hediger, "Dogs of War: The Biopolitics of Loving and Leaving the US Canine Forces in Vietnam," *Animal Studies Journal* 2, no. 1 (2013): 55–73; Jonathan Saha, "Among the Beasts of Burma: Animals and the Politics of Colonial Sensibilities, c. 1840–1940," *Journal of Social History* 48, no. 4 (2015): 921; Andrea Gaynor, Susan Broomhall, and Andrew Flack, "Frogs and Feeling Communities: A Study in History of Emotions and Environmental History," *Environment and History* (2020), https://doi.org/10.3197/096734019X15740974883861.

11 Chris Pearson, "'Four-Legged *Poilus*': French Army Dogs, Emotional Practices and the Creation of Militarized Human-Dog Bonds, 1871–1918," *Journal of Social History* 52, no. 3 (2019): 731–60; Tom Webb, Chris Pearson, Penny Summerfield, and Mark Riley, "More-Than-Human Emotional Communities: British Soldiers

and Mules in Second World War Burma," *Cultural and Social History* 17, no. 2 (2020): 245–62.

12 For excellent introductions to the growing field of urban animal history, see Peter Atkins, ed., *Animal Cities: Beastly Urban Histories* (Farnham: Ashgate, 2012); Dawn Biehler, *Pests in the City: Flies, Bedbugs, Cockroaches, and Rats* (Seattle: University of Washington Press, 2013); Thomas Almeroth-Williams, *City of Beasts: How Animals Shaped Georgian London* (Manchester: Manchester University Press, 2019); Frederick A. Brown, *The City Is More Than Human: An Animal History of Seattle* (Seattle: University of Washington Press, 2016); Joanna Dean, Darcy Ingram, and Christabelle Sethna, eds., *Animal Metropolis: Histories of Human-Animal Relations in Urban Canada* (Calgary: University of Calgary Press, 2017); Andrew A. Robichaud, *Animal City: The Domestication of America* (Cambridge, MA: Harvard University Press, 2019).

INDEX

Page numbers in italics refer to figures.

Lightning Source UK Ltd.
Milton Keynes UK
UKHW021150090921
390255UK00002B/165